A Theory
of
Everything
Else

A Theory of Everything Else

of

Essays

Laura Pedersen

SWP

She Writes Press, a BookSparks imprint
A Division of SparkPointStudio, LLC.

Published 2020

Printed in the United States of America

ISBN: 978-1-63152-737-1 pbk
ISBN: 978-1-63152-738-8 ebk
Library of Congress Control Number: 2020905903

For information, address:
She Writes Press
1569 Solano Ave #546
Berkeley, CA 94707

She Writes Press is a division of SparkPoint Studio, LLC.

Contents

ESTROGEN-AMERICANS

HUMAN KIND

Time is a great teacher,
but unfortunately it kills all its pupils.

–Hector Berlioz (1803-1869)

Introduction

That elusive Holy Grail of modern physics, A Theory of Everything (ToE), would explain the universe in a single set of equations. Albert Einstein and Stephen Hawking avidly confronted the problem during their lifetimes, and scientists on *The Big Bang Theory* continue the quest to this day, at least in reruns.

Leaving string theory, galaxy clusters, and supersymmetry to the safety goggle, quantum computer, and Hadron Collider crowd, I've now taken up the rest; that is, A Theory of Everything Else (ToEE), based on my own groundbreaking experiences as a dog walker, camp counselor, and bingo caller. For instance, the transitive property says that if a = b and b = c then a = c. Yet, my dogs hate being put in a tub of clean bathwater, but adore jumping into a dirty pond. Particle theory contains rules for the spacing of matter based on composition and energy. So how is it that a dog one-third of my weight ends up with two-thirds of the space on a king-size bed? And if a cat's eyes can shift wavelengths to navigate in the dark, then why did one break the Limoges lamp I inherited from my grandmother? And why aren't there any seeing-eye cats?

My interest extends to life-forms other than just cats and dogs. In my kitchen there's an avocado plant and a colony of ants. Despite tremendous efforts to nurture the plant and kill the insects, I've ended up with a dead plant and a thriving ant colony. One equation I'm particularly interested in working out goes as follows: God has dominion over all things. Man has dominion over all the beasts of the Earth, including fish in the sea, and birds of the sky. Yet microorganisms can kill us all.

Like anyone descended from Ingmar Bergman's part of the world, I'm intrigued by death. It's puzzling how so many fitness gurus expired young while Irish grandparents in my neighborhood drank, smoked, inhaled diesel exhaust, never touched a vegetable, prayed the rosary as their only exercise, and lived to be ninety. When I was born, childhood was a perilous time as nurseries were stalked by polio, diphtheria, German measles, and scarlet fever. Thus it was practical to have spare children, and large families were the norm, especially in predominantly Catholic areas. Parents toiled round the clock in factories and kitchens to make our lives better than theirs and would have questioned your sanity if asked to organize a "play date." Yet it appears what future generations took away from this sacrifice was to not have nearly as many kids, since they clearly ruin your life.

Finally, we have human nature, and there appears to be a lot of that in all of us. It's no longer politically correct to say ladies and gentlemen. In fact, "women" isn't an acceptable designation anymore since it's just "men" with what sounds like "woe" tacked on, and we'd like to be called Estrogen-Americans going forward. Meantime, The LGB label has grown from sandwich-size to a Slavic last name. In my immediate family several people struggle with obsessive-compulsive disorder, and I'm wondering if it wasn't just plain cruel to put the acronym OCD in non-alphabetical order. Why not CTU for Continuously Tidying Up or ACT for Always Checking Things?

Otherwise, I'd like to consider this manifesto a public service. When I first arrived in Manhattan, I paid a guy (who, it transpires, was not operating in any official capacity) five dollars to ride the Staten Island Ferry (which, it turns out, is free), so now you won't make the same mistake, unless you always skip over introductions, which *A Theory of Everything Else* has just proven can be costly.

Section 1

QUADRUPEDS

All knowledge, the totality of all questions
and all answers is contained in the dog.

−Franz Kafka

Chapter 1

Can Dogs Tell Time?

Are dogs so pleased to see us when we return because they assumed we were gone forever? They can't tell time on a clock face, but do canines know how long we've been away, whether it was an hour, a day, a week, a month, or an entire year? This is the number one argument among companions to canines (Cats are well aware of how long you were gone but don't give a crap.) My black Lab, Maisie, knew to the minute when it was time for breakfast, dinner, walks, and treats. So actually my question is "Do dogs sense the passing of time?"

When I was a kid in the 1970s, before videography and surveillance became omnipresent with the advent of nanny cams and GoPro, I often wondered what my dog did while the family was out. One time after we left the house, I had my dad stop the car a block away so I could sneak back, climb behind the hedges, and peer in through the window. There was my poodle curled up with her despondent face turned toward the door. It was horribly sad, yet thoroughly satisfying: Fifi's entire existence revolved around me, and life as she knew it was on hold awaiting my return.

Most canines catch a panic when suitcases or large backpacks appear on the bed. If your dogs are sometimes included on trips, there may be a frisson of excitement as signs of car crates, airline animal totes, and travel bowls are eagerly sought out in the packing jumble. However, when a dog concludes this is a humans-only excursion, it will often attempt to cleverly conceal itself inside a suitcase, which is no small feat for a Labrador retriever. I had a five-pound Yorkie (what size brain is inside there?) that could tell by the dimensions and scope of luggage taken out how long a trip was intended to last.

Enter the Royal Academy of Canine Actors. If anything larger than an overnight bag appears, we are treated to a reenactment of the death scene from *Camille*. At departure time my dogs gather by the door wearing their funeral faces, looking like Chekhov's *Three Sisters* hoping to be swept off to Moscow. They take it as a personal affront when I leave on a trip without them. A meeting is called which always ends in the same decision: Let's all get sick. With a show of paws, they volunteer for vomiting, peeing, pooping, and explosive diarrhea. They become true philosophers and students of Gottfried Wilhelm Leibniz, who said the fact there is something rather than nothing requires an explanation. The only rule for creating a minefield of dog mess throughout the house is that it mustn't be done on any hard, washable surfaces such as tiles or a linoleum floor. They swear an oath. Soon after, the carpets, bedspreads, and upholstered furniture become empty canvases, unfilled dreamscapes, and hazardous dumpsites.

Clearly dogs are not colorblind, as they regularly select patterned carpets to express their maladies, where there's a much higher probability that people will discover the atomic waste by stepping in it. Oriental carpets are the catch-22 of animal companionship—while tremendous at hiding stains, they're even better at obscuring a fresh pet expulsion. And step in it you will, since you're so busy wandering around wondering, "Where is that smell coming from?" I highly recommend lying down on the floor and scanning the carpet at eye level for any three-dimensional patches rather than performing an inspection on foot.

I'm curious where dogs developed their affinity for carpeting and upholstery. Because I think most humans can agree that when vomiting, nothing feels better than a cold floor. Being descended from wolves, perhaps it reminds them of grassy meadows and forest undergrowth from their ancestral days in the wild. All I know is that if I give a dog a messy bone on the kitchen floor, it is immediately dragged onto the most expensive oriental carpet in the house. And if one of my dogs starts heaving on bathroom tiles or even a wooden floor, it will manage to drag itself onto a bed—or better yet, the sofa covered in cream-colored silk brocade—to vomit. I've seen with my own eyes a dog begin to retch on the cement floor of a basement, only to pull itself up a flight of stairs and lurch through the kitchen in order to expel on brand new wall-to-wall carpet. If I could be at one of those imaginary dinner parties that necromantic interviewers are constantly conjuring up, I'd want to ask Charles Darwin what sort of evolutionary adaptation this is exactly.

While dogs are able to determine if you're heading on vacation, off to work, or just leaving to run an errand, they completely disregard daylight saving time. As everyone else is dashing around changing clocks, looking like zombies, causing accidents, and showing up late for church, dogs have no intention of adjusting their timetables, much like Arizona and Hawaii. When it's time for a walk followed by breakfast, just try lying in bed and explaining to those eager faces that it's really only six o'clock because of a harebrained scheme begun in 1918 to make better use of daylight for people who don't live near the equator, and for this reason it's *actually an hour earlier*. They don't care.

*Mutt enjoyed traveling by car, but he was an
unquiet passenger. He suffered from the delusion,
common to dogs and small boys, that when he was looking
out the right-hand side, he was probably missing something
far more interesting on the left-hand side.*

−Farley Mowat

Chapter 2

Dog Is My Copilot

Traveling with pets can always be counted on for heart-stopping thrills and the kindness of strangers, even if it's just an offer to direct you to the nearest mental hospital. No one would ever look to an Outward Bound trip for adventure after going across the country with a couple of pets. My friend Neil had a Siamese cat named Ziggy who managed to meow all the way from New York to San Francisco. A spaniel named Roxy is by far my most intrepid passenger. The first time I went on a trip with Roxy, she decided the back seat was her domain, and we hadn't been on the road ten minutes before she had both windows down with the fumes of industrial New Jersey enlivening our journey, along with an easy way to leap out at exit 168. Did she have family in Ho-Ho-Kus? I raised the windows and applied the child lock so she couldn't do it again. Clever me. Problem solved.

What else could she possibly get up to? I stopped for gas and left my phone in the car. After filling the tank, I washed the windshield and we were on our way. My cell phone rang and it was Mom calling because she was worried I'd been taken hostage by a drug dealer or sold into slavery. Why ever would she think such a thing? Perhaps because the dog had just dialed her three times while I was pumping gas, and Mom was convinced it was some type of distress signal.

At the next stop I took my phone. What could possibly go wrong? I was in line at Moe's Southwest Grill when I heard a car alarm go off in the parking lot. Sure enough, hazard lights flashing and horn blaring, that was my car. How does one even activate the alarm from within? I thought it went off when people tried to open the car from outside with a coat hanger or crowbar. I dashed out and disengaged the alarm. When I started the car, it transpired that the dashboard had been completely reconfigured. Before me was a different set of monitors: the time was military; the fuel gage, temperature, and speedometer were in metric (or "Canadian," as we say near the border); and it was now blue and white instead of red and black. I spent the next hundred miles attempting to switch everything back but only succeeded in accidentally programming the satellite radio stations Hair Nation and Octane ("coming to you live from the trailer park capital of Illinois") as my favorites.

When driving dogs from New York to Florida, I usually need a break along the way since the twelve-hundred-mile journey takes about twenty-three hours in total. The first time I made the trip with four dogs, I could only find hotels with a two-dog limit. However, I decided it was possible to sneak in two since the spaniels look alike and the Frenchie enjoys curling up in a duffel bag. I parked the SUV on the far side of the hotel lot and went to check in, taking my keys and phone. Only this time Roxy discovered the button to open the back, leapt out, and met me in the lobby with the other three idiots following her like a Chuck Wagon dog food commercial. We found another hotel.

Nevertheless, what I hadn't factored in was that the dogs had slept all the night before, awakened at six in the morning, climbed into the car, and slept an additional twelve hours. They'd now been zonked out a total of twenty hours. While I tried to get some rest, they ran around like maniacs jumping from table to bed to chair. Having learned my lesson, I now roll to a stop in a parking lot, usually next to cars driven by guys named Rebel and Crazy Butch who are avoiding bounty hunters, tilt the driver's seat back ever-so-gently, and grab a cat nap. I also know that my travel gear, especially snacks, needs to be stowed securely. Roxy loves nothing more than unpacking every bag, not for consumption, but to spread around so the car looks like a rolling dumpster. She's talented at opening Velcro, hermetically sealed packages, and even zippered suitcases. However, Roxy's specialty is opening plastic containers that hold salads and burrito bowls and then giving them a twelve-inch drop for maximum spread. She missed her true calling as a crop duster pilot.

I've since realized that Roxy is like a roulette wheel. When you play poker and blackjack, the next hand is based on what previously happened, whereas each spin of the roulette wheel is an independent event based on nothing that came before. She always manages to stay one step ahead of me. Recently we were driving from a friend's house in Fort Lauderdale back to my mom's in Citrus Springs on the hottest day of the year. About an hour from home I spotted a farm stand and decided to make a quick stop for fresh corn and tomatoes. What could possibly go wrong? I switched off the car engine because I was raised during an energy crisis where we lived in cold and darkness for an entire decade, hopped out and bought some vegetables. The selection and purchase took a total of four minutes. In that brief interval Roxy managed to stand on the armrest and lock me out. The windows were all up, the keys were inside, and so was my cell phone. The car was in direct sunlight, it was noon, the heat index was 120 degrees Farhrenheit, and I assumed the dog would be dead within thirty minutes.

The farm stand proprietor lent me his phone, and I called AAA. They said it was a busy day and they'd attempt to be there in two hours. I explained the dog would be dead by then and they apologized for my loss. I could call my mom to come with the spare keys but she was an hour away and in the age of speed dial, I had no idea what her Florida phone number is or her cell phone. (Sadly, I'm old enough to remember when five-year-olds had memorized their home number and everyone over the age of ten knew between a dozen and fifty phone numbers of friends and family, plus one for the time and temperature.) Roxy was frantically leaping about inside the car, wondering why I was being such an idiot and not joining her inside. I had a thought—if she locked the door, then she must be able to unlock the door. I went to the window and frantically jumped around and she jumped about and finally *click*. Only I didn't grab the door handle in time, and she locked it again, and we were right back where we started. Once again, I began leaping about like a Mexican jumping bean, and she unlocked it. This time I was super-fast in grabbing the door handle before she could land on it again.

Another time while I was driving with Roxy in Florida, a state where not only is it *illegal* to leave an unattended pet in your car (since so many have suffocated) but it's *legal* to break into anyone's vehicle if you believe a "domestic animal" is in danger, I stopped to buy a newspaper. I left the car for three minutes in the morning of a not particularly hot or sunny day, but Roxy decided to reenact the death scene of the Wicked Witch of the West from *The Wizard of Oz*. When I returned with my paper *in three minutes,* a group of distraught animal lovers was gathered around the car, one phoning the police, one on the line with animal control, and one preparing to break the window with a tire iron. They insisted the frantic dog was "clearly dehydrated" and "locked in there for hours." My side of the story fell on deaf ears. Once again, the Oscar for Outstanding Performance in a Grocery Store Parking Lot goes to Roxy.

I've since put a BEWARE OF DOG sign in my vehicle. However, it doesn't face out toward people who might be peering into the car or tempted to knock on the windows. It's directly in front of me, the driver, reminding me to think like a mischievous spaniel and never let down my guard. I've also placed a corrugated yoga mat across the backseat. Whereas a beach towel or pleather seats will cause dogs to fly around like popcorn, they stick to the yoga mat like postage stamps.

The dogs enjoy being in Florida during the winter and avoiding the treacherous road salt in the Northeast. Between an increasingly litigious society and advanced chemical engineering, weapons-grade salt laced with various toxins now blankets New York City streets and sidewalks. This burns and cracks the dogs' paws, and when the dogs attempt to lick it off, they ingest a lethal brew. People who don't own dogs reasonably suggest using booties. Unfortunately, putting dogs in booties is akin to putting toddlers on stilts. There's an amount of standing stock still, strutting like a drum majorette, spasmodically twirling about, crashing to the floor, and then comes removal, one way or another. In other words, putting booties on most dogs is like that old adage about trying to teach a pig to think—it's a waste of your time and annoys the pig. But don't take my word for it, Google "dogs in booties compilation."

Northerners like to ridicule Florida, calling it "God's Waiting Room" and "The Handgun State." They joke about the Early Bird Specials, skinless boneless chicken, cataract sunglasses, headless drivers, and dermatologists on every corner. They say that most accidents happen in the Publix supermarket lot going five miles per hour. Liberals question the fact that maximum-strength pepper spray is sold in a large display next to the gator jerky at cash registers in convenience stores, and there's usually only one left. Truth be told, I'm no longer a liberal the minute my wheels hit the I-95, and firmly believe in waterboarding for anyone leaving their vehicle alongside the gas pumps at busy service stations while they shop for beer-boiled Cajun peanuts inside the minimart. Still, I've never heard any Floridians say that they're excited about retiring to Buffalo to enjoy shoveling, frostbite, and fishing for catfish, crappies, and perch. And Florida doesn't retest seniors who wish to renew their driver's licenses; the DMV relies entirely upon natural selection.

Otherwise, I have a travel tip for Yorkie owners. If you find out at the last minute that a vaccination certificate is necessary to cross a border with your Yorkie and don't have one, there's a workaround. Since puppies don't need shots until they're several months old, just say it's an eight-week-old sheepdog puppy. This has worked for me several times. The only challenge is that if it's an old dog you need a muzzle, because what comes out of its mouth is decidedly *not* "puppy breath"—it's what happens when you leave mustard-crusted salmon in the trash and go on vacation for a month.

There are no one-night stands with dogs.
–Diana Delmar

Chapter 3

Lying Down with Dogs

A popular subject of debate is whether you should sleep with dogs. Remember how for thousands of years authorities insisted that the Earth was the center of the Universe and then Galileo said no, that it was actually the sun, and the church placed him under house arrest for his trouble? Well, it's easy to forgive people for thinking of their bedroom as a small universe with themselves as the center star and their pets as planets that revolve around them, gravity drawing their four-legged friends ever closer. However, you'd be completely wrong, because it transpires that the bed itself is the sun, and even after you leave, dogs and cats are thrilled to continue basking in its warm embrace. Newton's law of universal gravitation states that larger bodies experience a stronger attraction, and this is why dogs over forty pounds almost without exception sleep in the exact center of the bed, sprawling outward until you're lucky to have six inches at the edge of the mattress.

I always find myself asking salespeople if the California king is the *largest* bed they sell. It just seems that no bed is big enough for two people and four dogs, and I end up frozen in one place all night like a police chalk outline. Sometimes I'm awakened at two in the morning (because a fluffy spaniel tail is feather dusting my face) and miraculously discover that I can move my leg several inches, or even turn over in this 3D jigsaw puzzle. I may be perfectly comfortable and not wish to do either of those things, but I seize the chance. Sleeping with dogs is like a football game where you're constantly in search of any yardage, as is the opposing team. It means waking up with at least two limbs dead asleep and a permanent back spasm. If the snoring Frenchie isn't pressed up against me like a sandbag holding back a flood, then an internal alarm goes off, and he pushes himself closer so I'm experiencing unbroken contact with thirty pounds of immovable object. I haven't shared a bed with cats since I was a teenager, but feline slumber expert Stephen Parker informs us, "Most beds sleep up to six cats. Ten cats without the owner."

There are plenty of news stories featuring dogs who rescue people, fetch emergency help, or visit their former owners' graves each day to stand vigil, so perhaps a more pertinent question than *Can Dogs Tell Time?* or *To Pee Or Not To Pee?* is *Will My Dog Eat My Dead Body?* In scientific circles, pets eating their peeps is politely known as "indoor scavenging." With regard to the argument of cats versus dogs, cats are a little faster to start the meal and prefer to focus on the fleshy parts such as your nose and lips, what they view as "facial pâté."

However, on balance, more "indoor scavenging" tends to involve dogs. Anthropologists like to remind us that dogs are descended from wolves, and if there's no other source of food around, they will dive into the nearest pot of flesh. In several cases, emergency workers have reported food in the bowls of dogs who had feasted on their owners, clearly working their way from the freshest and moistest course to the oldest and driest. In ancient Rome, crucifixion on a low cross rather than a high cross was considered to be crueler since it provided easier snacking for roaming canines.

For better or worse, there appears to be no correlation between a pet's devotion and how quickly it will switch from companion mode to consumption mode, so experts recommend that the best way to "save face" if you live alone with a carnivore is to make sure people check on you once a day, especially if you're older, or taste like chicken.

Try all you want to make your pet a vegetarian, but those pointy teeth point to predator all the way. Feeding the dogs left-over Thanksgiving turkey is always a mixed bag at my place. At first bite they look up at me adoringly, positively worshipful, clearly thinking what a great huntress and provider I am, and that this is the best home in the entire canine kingdom. However, they also see that the turkey goes back into the fridge, and consequently there arises a growing sense of impatience that perhaps they've been cheated. A staring contest results—eyes looking from me to the fridge and back to me. Surely there's been a mistake, and we should finish what we started. I leave the kitchen feeling the glares upon my back. Anger turns to edginess; they all become jittery as the turkey high wears off and they're jonesing for more bird. A clique of addicts forms in the kitchen waiting for anyone to provide a Snausage or whatever the equivalent is to methadone for poultry dependency.

Although I've had plenty of everything, I prefer dogs to cats. (That said, some of my best friends are cats.) The joke goes that the difference between pets and people is that if you lock your dog and your spouse in the trunk of the car, when you open it, your dog will be happy to see you. Dogs can run away, but none to my knowledge has ever consulted a divorce lawyer. As for the difference between dogs and children, obedience school is considerably cheaper than college, and whereas kids are always begging for a dog, a dog will never bother you about getting a kid.

Even if my dogs don't always come when I call, they at least want to know what it's about, whereas the cat usually says, "Leave a message and I'll get back to you. Or not." When people ask how old I am, I like to tell them that I'm on my tenth dog, or alternatively, give my age in months so they can stay sharp with their math. Still, I think most of us would be happy to see at least some of the billions of dollars that have been poured into the space program put toward having pets live as long as humans, rather than a vacuum tube for peeing in zero gravity. It's sad to see our beloved companions decline. While standing in the elevator, I said to a vet who lives in my building, "Wouldn't it be great if our pets lived as long as we do?" Her eyes widened. "Absolutely not!" she replied. "What if one is badly behaved? Now they're like a spouse you no longer like and you have to get a divorce or something." The elevator doors opened into the lobby, and she didn't elaborate on what the *something* might be.

Still, I love all animals, which is why I don't eat them, and I believe that you are what you eat and also whatever they had to eat, or the bumper sticker version: You are whatever you eat ate. I've always lived with a menagerie, purposely or otherwise. When I was a kid, during one particularly long and harsh winter, a family of raccoons snuck in through the eaves and took up residence in an abandoned doll's bed in my room. The poodle looked at this and thought, "Well, they're varmints and as a hunting dog I have a problem with that, but they're furry, and if they help keep us warm, I suppose I can look the other way until spring." The finicky cats made a note just in case we ran out of 9 Lives Ranch Supper and Fisherman's Stew.

Once when I was having some friends with children over for brunch, an eight-year-old boy who had no pets of his own informed me that he was allergic to peanuts. "Are you also allergic to dogs?" I asked.

"Do they have peanuts in them?" he said.

"They're nut free," I replied, without adding, "Especially since the Yorkie is gone." He was curious about the dogs and asked more questions, such as if eating raw food would turn them wild. Of course, the best way to find out would have been for the dogs to bite one of his arms or legs.

A terrific way to teach kids about dogs is by explaining that canines do most things that humans do including burp, cough, sneeze, shake, snore, have hiccups, and catch colds. They can be happy, sad, fearful, and angry (hence little dogs employing the bathmat as a toilet, or Yorkies who go straight for your pillow). If there is more than one dog, and toys or cookies are given out, the dogs are extremely concerned with what everyone else has and feel certain that it's better than what they received. Dogs also dream and have nightmares. Our Labrador's eyelids rippled in her sleep while her legs pumped away, accompanied by a high-pitched yipping. I assume she was in pursuit of squirrels, or better yet, an animal she has a history of actually being able to catch, such as a Pekingese. For her sake I hoped the reverie ended happily since my travel dreams always involve canceled flights and missed connections, and I wake up in a sweaty panic.

Obviously dogs fart. However, I possess a real miracle worker in the form of a French bulldog that can fart and snore simultaneously. When I drive Ollie from New York to Florida, the windows must all be down in an effort to evacuate the green smog. That said, he's a large-headed hypocrite as he takes unkindly to anyone else farting. If awakened from a sound sleep by anyone else's staccato blast he'll fix the perpetrator with a spiteful glare.

Our black Lab, Maisie, regularly embarked upon epic farting sprees. Maisie's farts were so toxic that when she let loose outdoors, the ants circled while the birds fled the trees, and the sky momentarily darkened. When Maisie farted in bed, she'd quickly leap up and exit the room, leaving us to fall asleep in a moist purple haze. In fact, her silent but deadly explosions led to a number of unfortunate incidents. I live on a high floor in an apartment building and while angelic looking Maisie and I proceeded down to the lobby in a crowded elevator and riders inhaled the toxic fart smell, it was immediately assumed that I was the perpetrator. The first few times I joked about how sweet my dog looked in comparison to the lethal nature of her gas. However, people glared at me as if I were trying to blame an innocent creature for my own noxious windiness. After that happened a few times, I'd wait for an empty elevator or alternatively a very full elevator. While waiting I often pondered what city dogs think about elevators since several times a day they walk into a box and then step right back out of the box. I've noticed that dogs visiting from the country are suspicious of the entire operation, as if it might be a trap, or else their initial instinct is confirmed, that people who choose to live in cities are just incredibly stupid.

I'm not a "love me, love my dog" sort of gal. If you don't like dogs or cats or any animals, for that matter, no problem, I don't like oompah bands or licorice. I'm happy to put my dogs in a back room while you're here if you promise not to play "In München steht ein Hofbräuhaus" on a trombone and ask for

Twizzlers. However, I'm often surprised by how little some people know about "man's best friend." While I was walking four dogs—a Frenchie, a golden retriever, a Tibetan spaniel, and a mutt—one passerby inquired, "Are they all related?"

I presume it was because the dogs were all what Clairol classifies as a "champagne" color, or else this person just had a lobotomy. "Yes," I replied, "cousins, and they all have the same middle name of Darwin."

Dogs' lives are too short. Their only fault, really.
—Agnes Turnbull

Chapter 4

The Circle of Life

Comedian George Carlin liked to say that pets are tragedies waiting to happen. Any human capable of basic computation would never take one home since, unless you're over eighty, there's a good chance it will end horribly with you in the fetal position on a cold antiseptic washed floor, sobbing and holding a frayed collar or empty crate. The only solace is that you won't need to explain your distress to anyone else in the room; they will politely step over you without staring, and through a stream of tears, it's hard to make out the twenty or so thousand dollars the vet has put on your credit cards over the past few weeks.

The End Times are something people don't always consider when deciding whether to bring home a big dog or a little dog. It's true that little dogs pee in the house more, bark more, bite more and are generally more annoying (they wouldn't be the first creatures to compensate for size). However, when small dogs enter old age it's much easier to carry them to the park and vet and put Wee-Wee pads near their beds to reduce outdoor excursions. Big dogs aren't as easy to scoop up in your arms and most don't fancy an indoor lavatory. Also, there can be bouts of heavy panting, so when you're on the phone with an old dog in the vicinity, callers automatically assume you have a pornography addiction.

My husband and I operated a canine assisted living facility for our black Lab, Maisie, the last few years of her life, and I was happy to do it, but it was also excellent training if I ever wish to become a firefighter. This is when living on the high floor of an apartment building is most punishing. As Maisie began pacing at three in the morning, which meant she needed to go out *immediately*, I had exactly sixty seconds to grab either pants or shoes or a coat to throw over my nightshirt while sprinting to push the elevator button and praying for its swift arrival. There wasn't enough time for all three articles of clothing so I eventually started leaving a pair of sweatpants and clogs in the path to the front door so I could dress as I dashed. Still, I'm surprised I wasn't arrested in Central Park, since more often than not I was absent at least one article of clothing required by public decency laws. And though I wasn't picked up for exposure, I was lucky not to die from exposure during the middle of winter.

This was also the year when, hearty and hale in my early forties, I caught a glimpse of my old age—disrupted sleep, rising for good at four thirty, napping before lunch, nodding off during dinner, and dreading evening engagements that could potentially run past seven thirty. It was hard to believe I used to watch late night talk shows (thank goodness for the DVR), and the idea that I'd pulled all-nighters in my twenties and been functional the next day seemed impossible. Now I had my bowl of soup at six, followed by half an episode of *Grace and Frankie*, and was comatose by nine o'clock. There was no danger of my binge-watching anything, or even making it through an entire thirty-minute show for that matter.

After returning home from that final trip to the vet and spending a week under the covers, you sadly begin to clear out the medications, pill pockets, special foods, treats, and Wee-Wee pads. You vow never to get another pet because yours was a one-of-a-kind animal companion. If economically feasible, you probably would have cloned the beloved pet, although the more you consider it, there were just a few bad habits, such as the predilection for dried cat turds. You wash or toss the beds and blankets with all the stains and pulls. You put away the paper towels and carpet cleaner and stow the bowls, bones, heating pad, blankets, sweaters, feeding mat, and plush toys. You give the leftover food and treats to a neighbor with dogs, but most animals are on a prescription diet nowadays so they kindly take it and throw it out when you're not looking. You remove the ramps, stools, steps, and benches that gave your pet access to all its favorite places.

Finally, you order new carpets and perhaps a new couch, armchair, and maybe even a mattress, pillows, and bed linens. Despite having sworn up and down that you're *never* going to get another pet because there will never be another Fido or Fleabag, and the heartbreak is too devastating, it's wise to follow some redecorating guidelines. The carpet store is always a bit of a tease because the displays consist of goods that would be ruined in a week by most pets. (Every experienced home manager can tell you, "Have children and pets *or* have nice things.") I grudgingly drag myself past the sumptuous Persian rugs and delicately muted Aubussons to a dimly lit corner in the back where there's a single book of industrial strength commercial carpeting intended for the break room in a chemical factory and upholstery for train seats; swatches that have been Scotchguarded and coated so as to wick moisture, and feel like you're walking across a Brillo pad. Basically, the next stop is Astroturf.

As previously stated, Oriental rugs offer little chance of seeing that broad catchall known in the carpet cleaning profession as "pet mess" prior to stepping in it. Yet they hide stains better than any plain, textured, or geometric patterned carpeting. I have Oriental rugs that started out as one pattern but, with scoured patches of vomit and diarrhea, have entirely new designs, though the casual viewer would never notice. It so happens that whatever stomach enzymes are in dog vomit blend nicely with flowers and medallions. A delicate yet busy paisley design can go a long way in camouflaging intestinal adversity.

Next comes the "choice" of color. The question is not what goes well with the room so much as what looks good with pee, diarrhea, and bile stains. Similarly, car and clothes shopping pose the question, "What goes best with fur?" My friend Neil's Siamese cat, Ziggy, shed his entire coat twice a day. As a result, to avoid looking like a hairball for fifteen years, not only did Neil dress in Siamese colors, but he purchased all his towels and linens in Siamese. I'm surprised that a company like Lands' End hasn't come out with a companion animal line called Furbulous that features colors named after short-haired breeds such as Abyssinian, Burmese, black Lab, chocolate Lab, yellow Lab, Weimaraner, Dalmatian, etc. It could make shopping for friends with pets much easier, since there's nothing crueler than giving a black shearling coat to the owner of a Russian white cat.

After redecorating, the place looks fresh and clean, just the way you always imagined it could while running around with Resolve in one hand and Bounty in the other. The carpets and woven cotton blankets are lovely and clean with no pulls, holes, stains, or chew marks, and you swear that this time it'll be different—they're going to stay looking fresh and new. Friends are no longer allowed to drink red wine or eat Chinese food in the living room. Everyone must remove their shoes no matter what the weather. Yes, life is quieter now, but you look at the bright side—no more heading out in rainstorms and blizzards, especially after you arrive home exhausted from a wedding. No more bolting upright in the middle of the night to the ominous sound of heaving and retching. No more being fast asleep while having your face slurped or nose bitten because you're not getting out of bed to put breakfast on the floor. No more heaps of towels by the door to wipe off dirty fur, faces, and paws. You're saving thousands of dollars on food, medication, pet sitters, and vet bills. Life is boring. It's weird. Time to get a kitten or puppy!

Outside of a dog, a book is man's best friend.
Inside of a dog it's too dark to read.

−Groucho Marx

Chapter 5

Making the Purrfect Match

How to choose a cat? One rarely chooses a cat. A cat is foisted upon you (often by my aunt) because it's lost or abandoned or else the owner is moving away or has joined the Heavenly Choir. A woman standing in the church vestibule with a box of adorable kittens just as we kids were pouring out of Sunday school led to the adoption of our cat Button. My mother was already vacuuming up after several pets, and my father was allergic. I don't think anyone spoke to the woman ever again.

What kind of dog is best? Or in puppy parlance, "Who's a good dog?" Just like there are people who collect old laundry wringers, matchbooks, and bottle caps, there are fans of every breed, crossbreed, and Heinz 57. Obviously, it's heroic to rescue a dog, and the Internet makes that easy to accomplish. If you can't decide between a shepherd, setter, or poodle, get them all by adopting a mutt. If, after watching *101 Dalmatians* and *102 Dalmatians,* the kids are still begging for a fire dog, then show them *Lady and the Tramp* and *Isle of Dogs* to demonstrate the glories of the mongrel.

When it comes to "dangerous dogs," most were trained to be that way, or else their aggressive behaviors are a result of harsh ownership. And because it's not necessarily their nature, this can be remedied with caring and kindness. Pit bulls, rottweilers, and dobermans come to mind. In fact, pit bulls have a history of being wonderful family pets and earned the nickname "nanny dogs" in England for looking after children.

Burglars agree that canines are the bane of their existence. Nevertheless, while a big, scary-looking pooch might deter home invasion, a good second-story man is happy to tell you that the superior threat is actually a small, yappy dog that hides and continues barking (where a Yorkie positively shines), and especially those smart teacup poodles that have been known to dial 911. An exception is the basenji, a smallish dog that doesn't bark at all but in fact yodels, which isn't scary so much as strange, and may only succeed in frightening off critics of *The Sound of Music.*

Don't be fooled by size—small dogs possess great fortitude. They were bred down from large dogs, which were formerly wolves. Only two canines survived the sinking of the Titanic, a Pomeranian and a Pekingese. Of course, they were traveling first class with their own luggage, since that's how small dogs roll. Training manuals like to euphemistically say that "small dogs are more challenging to train," but what they mean is that small dogs are actually no different from killer whales at SeaWorld— you find out what they like to do, when and how, and then you reward them not to destroy you. Small dogs can occasionally be calm and compliant. I have two twenty-pounders who are so submissive they lie next to each other on their backs both wanting to play while signaling, "You get on top," "No, you get on top."

Short-haired dogs and cats tend to shed copiously while long-haired ones not so much, which seems counterintuitive, like the fact that in a group of twenty-three people there's a 50 percent chance two will have the same birthday. Families who suffer from allergies should avoid shorthaired quadrupeds, and there's definitely more vacuuming and cleaning the lint trap involved with shorthairs. Otherwise, short versus long hair can work for or against you depending on whether or not you're a law-abiding citizen. In 1994 Shirley Duguay went missing and was found in a shallow grave by Canadian authorities. A blood-soaked leather jacket had been buried along with the body. However, the blood belonged to Shirley and was therefore of no help to police. But the jacket was also covered with something else—over two dozen white feline hairs. The Mounties recalled that Duguay's estranged common-law husband lived not far away with his parents, and they had a white cat named Snowball. Scientists developed a method to test animal DNA specifically to solve this case, and soon the cat was out of the bag. Douglas Beamish was convicted of second-degree murder and sentenced to life in prison.

Most pet owners concede that mutts are best because they were the last ones picked for dodgeball and spend the rest of their lives trying to compensate. However, I'll offer a few observations with regard to the canine selection process. First, dachshunds (a.k.a. wiener dogs) are indeed adorable, and what breed is more fun to dress up in a hotdog costume, but don't be fooled by the name. A dachshund is a *terrier*. It was created to flush out prey. "Dachshund" isn't German for "dashing dog" but for "badger dog."

As for Yorkshire terriers, I'm pretty sure they're the only dog breed with support groups for their human companions, and I know for a fact that I'm not the first person to ever describe myself as a "recovering Yorkie owner." When I say "seventeen years," other survivors put a comforting hand on my shoulder while those with young Yorkies burst into tears. Conspiracy theorists like to argue that there is a secret agreement between state surveillance and Silicon Valley, but I propose there may well be a quid pro quo between Yorkie breeders and psychotropic drug manufacturers. I'm aware that plenty of people adore their adorable Yorkies, and that's wonderful. If we're going to be honest, I like bagpipe music, to a point. Since it would be easy to use up the rest of this space on the subject, I'll offer just one Yorkie story. A piece of kibble dropped and skidded underneath the refrigerator. The rogue kibble was impossible to remove, even by fishing around with a hanger or a yardstick. My persistent Yorkie stood in front of the fridge whining. On day three of this high-pitched solo performance, at about four in the morning, she was still scratching and fussing at the fridge, so I rose out of bed completely exasperated and with the kind of brief Herculean strength *Reader's Digest* describes in stories about mothers experiencing a surge of adrenaline to lift cars off their children, I moved the fridge and managed to extract the single piece of food the size of a Skittle. The Yorkie sniffed, decided it was too dusty, and clambered off to bed. So if you decide on a Yorkie, just be sure to also get the name of a good therapist and one of those white noise sleep machines. In fact, I was recently dining at a fancy restaurant in the new Hudson Yards neighborhood in Manhattan. Normally I'm more of a burrito bar gal, but a friend and I had just seen a production at the Shed that was so confounding we needed to sit down. A tiny Yorkie in a plaid jumper came hurtling down the banquette seat and startled my friend. She said, "I didn't think they allowed dogs in restaurants." The Yorkie owner replied that it was her emotional support animal. I laughed out loud. When has a Yorkie ever made anyone *less* crazy? Try again.

While on the subject of terriers, I once went horseback riding with a woman who had a Jack Russell puppy. I told her about a friend whose Jack Russell ate all the molding in her living room, including long strips several feet off the ground. The woman replied that her Jack Russell had eaten two living room sets. "Two?" I exclaimed. She thought he was finished after the first one and foolishly ordered another. It all depends on what you want your dog to be famous for—which dog breed do you think holds the record time for popping one hundred balloons? That's right, forget those dancing poodles in flamenco skirts and spaniels who play dead when you point a finger at them, it's Jack Russells that are hardwired to snap the necks of unsuspecting rats. Inflate a hundred small balloons, toss them into the living room, release a Jack Russell, and paws down it has the best party piece. The expressions "dogged pursuit" and "dogged determination" were definitely created with the terrier in mind.

Do you ever find yourself thinking how cute it is when a dog carries around a floppy stuffed animal, such as a golden retriever with a teddy bear? Notice the way they grab it, shake it, and clench it in their jaws. Now imagine that stuffed animal is an actual squirrel or rabbit, because those are the instincts at work, and the shake is the neck-snapping portion of the fun. I only mention this because I have two friends who lost birds that were beloved family pets to "hunting accidents"—upon spotting a parrot, the dog had enough spaniel, setter, or pointer to be overcome by its seek-and-destroy instincts. And while ferrets and other pets in the weasel/rodent family will likewise excite a hunting dog, most varmints still possess their natural flight instincts, whereas a pet bird's wings have usually been clipped.

Despite the avian executions happening incredibly fast in both cases, so we can assume the birds didn't suffer much, the children were still traumatized. I sincerely hope you never find yourself in such a situation, but I'll add from unfortunate personal experience that a good homeowner's insurance policy will pay to replace the bird, so definitely keep the receipt.

Now French bulldogs are the farthest thing from killers, so long as farting doesn't count. These friendly and adorable big-headed canines are having their moment on Instagram—poking out of backpacks, wearing prison stripe onesies, and sporting biker jackets. However, they are the only dogs that, when Googled, the first article to appear isn't about feeding and training but rather "Seventeen Health Issues You Need to Know About." Because your delightful invalid may have anything from hip dysplasia, cherry eye, stenotic nares, patellar luxation, entropion, and Von Willebrand's Disease (VWD) to distichiasis, cataracts, laryngeal collapse, an elongated soft palate, tracheal stenosis, invertebral disc disease, and brachycephalic respiratory syndrome. And how is there no mention of noxious farting? In short, this is a dog for the childless and independently wealthy. After we somehow inherited an eighteen-month-old Frenchie during a dinner party that took a strange turn, the vet gazed at that loveable face and advised, "Give it away immediately, while you still can." When I replied that we were keeping Ollie, Dr. Miller looked horrified and advised us to get the best insurance policy possible or be prepared to live on the street.

Finally, when adopting a dog, don't be alarmed if it has a blue tongue. The blue-tongued chow chow is genetically one of nine most wolf-like breeds and can be found in paintings from the Han dynasty (206 BC–220 AD). In addition to hanging on walls, chow chows were sometimes served for dinner, and probably named after the Cantonese word *chow* which means "to mix," as in *chow mein*. Chows are protective, so they make good guard dogs, but are also stubborn and notoriously difficult to train, which may go a ways in explaining why they ended up as an entrée.

One last thing, and I'm sure this won't happen to you, but be cautious when adopting a Tibetan mastiff. A few human companions have witnessed their cuddly pups burgeon upwards of 250 pounds and start walking on their hind legs, which just happen to be signs that, instead of a dog, you've brought home a bear.

It is impossible to keep a straight face
in the presence of one or more puppies.
—Unknown

Chapter 6

Dognition

Bringing home a puppy is a lot like babysitting after not having kids in the house for a decade, and in addition to the crying and colic, you somehow forgot about the diapers, formula, crib, and paraphernalia filling every room along with doing a load of wash every hour. It immediately becomes clear that you've basically been living in a retirement community, sitting around yelling at the TV, leisurely reading eight-hundred-page books, taking three pleasant strolls a day at specific times, and heading out for dinner and a show without a care in the world. You and your dog were like an old married couple, ensconced in your routines, finishing each other's sentences, or better yet, merely trading glances to mean it's time for dinner, a walk, or bed. You loved all the same programs and snacks and shared a nap schedule. You both hated the neighbor's cat and waited for the mailperson. Heck, if you became busy on the computer and forgot that it was time to eat or go outside, Old

Faithful reminded you by dropping the bowl or leash at your feet.

Suddenly there are gates to trip over, Wee-Wee pads to slip on, and squeaky toys strewn about like beer bottles during spring break. The entire house needs to be puppy-proofed by stowing potpourri dishes, shoes, electronics cords, and basically anything else you don't want destroyed. Still, lamps and laptops crash to the floor. The mixed-up pup seems to pee either right before being taken outside or directly after returning home. Why can't you even remember house training the last one? You Google "housebreaking a puppy"—sounds easy enough the way they explain things. Why is the system not working?

The finger-chewing is cute until those needle-like baby teeth give you welts. The water bowl becomes a swimming pool. Poop is mistaken for lunch. Why doesn't puppy walk on a leash instead of rolling around and gnawing at the collar? Being put inside the crate results in heartbreaking wails. There's a vaccination list a mile long. You dash to the store for training treats and arrive home to a downed gate or crate escape, and there's diarrhea all over your brand-new carpets, and not just in one place, but as if a miner left a trail blazing through the Yukon. You rise from a warm, cozy bed and a sound sleep to go outside at one in the morning and again at four. Puppy wants to play after these outings. It's like having a newborn baby in the house or being in a hospital. Seriously, you don't remember *any* of this. Do you have Alzheimer's? Why didn't someone warn you? For the same reason women regularly say that you don't remember the pain of giving birth. If you did, you'd never do it again.

Still, the power of puppy therapy cannot be denied. Have you heard the expression, "If he didn't have bad luck he wouldn't have any luck at all"? That was my friend Mary from 2012 until 2018. A regular chaos magnet. It started when her youngest daughter, Erin, was hit by a car and killed while crossing the street between their suburban neighborhood and the school playground. You'd think they might want to have a traffic light there, and they finally do now thanks to the persistent and valiant efforts of Erin's parents. When the town told them there was no money for a light, Mary and Jerry raised it by organizing special events.

Two years after Erin passed, Mary's brother Steven died in a car accident at age fifty-two. Steven was closest in age to Mary. He was number eight and she was number nine, if anyone was still counting at that point. Steven was the ultimate escape artist, the wheeler-dealer, motorcycle riding, too fast to live and too young to die James Dean of the neighborhood. He was generous, kindhearted, and funny and could joke his way out of most anything, even if witnesses were involved. Still, we were so astonished when he turned fifty unscathed that apparently we all stopped praying for him at once, assuming he was invincible, when we should have adjusted our prayer window upward to fifty-five. At his funeral was an interesting assemblage of churchgoing neighbors, professionals, and leather-jacketed Harley Davidson enthusiasts with an array of colorful tattoos, but everyone got along just fine and a few business cards were even exchanged.

Many marriages don't survive the death of a child and Mary's was no exception. She and her husband divorced after twenty-six years. At age forty-eight, Mary had a hip replacement to repair an irregular socket that had been a time bomb since birth. Then Mary's mom died at age eighty-eight after struggling through a decade of dementia. The following year her father passed at the age of ninety-two. The dog that had so faithfully seen her through all this misery was diagnosed with a spinal tumor and had to be put down. That's a lot for any one person. To cap things off, so to speak, all her gorgeous red hair fell out from alopecia, an autoimmune disease that attacks the hair follicles and can be triggered by stress.

Mary was cracking up—who wouldn't be?—and asked me to come home to Buffalo. I was happy to go, but what could I possibly do without a magic wand to bring back her daughter, brother, and hair? We bought some wigs, big earrings, headscarves, and what are called "chemo scarves" because they don't have a hole in the back. We went makeup shopping, for spa treatments, and to our favorite restaurants.

Still, she was miserable. We both were. What I really needed was a time machine. There was only one thing that could possibly bring the slightest smile to this situation. I called every breeder in a six-hundred-mile radius looking for a hypoallergenic dog (as her two remaining children have sensitivities). The puppies had either already been sold or wouldn't be old enough to leave their mothers for several more weeks. I went to the wonderful new 52,000 square foot SPCA in nearby West Seneca. No luck.

In a last-ditch effort, I sat in the parking lot and Googled "puppies near me." The address of a nearby pet store appeared. In this day and age, it's of course anathema to buy from a pet store—they're notorious for using puppy mills, and so many abandoned dogs need homes, etc. I knew and agreed with all the reasons and have rescued a number of older cats and dogs myself, but at that moment I would have gladly purchased a puppy from a dealer named Headlock, Snake Eyes, or The Enforcer in a back alley by handing over a bag of nonconsecutive hundred-dollar bills.

At the pet store was the exact breed of dog that Mary had

recently lost, only a male instead of a female. Perfect, I thought. An employee allowed me to play with him in a pen where he proceeded to chew my hand until it looked like a pink sponge and even after presented with a bone continued to use me as a chew toy. He was a delightful little fellow but not exactly what I had in mind. However, a gorgeous yellow goldendoodle had caught my eye on the way in. She was sweet, calm, and comforting. Puppy and I hopped in the car and returned to Mary's house. We went from weeks of uncontrollable sobbing to a big smile. I'm not saying puppies can solve every problem, but occasionally they can succeed where mere mortals cannot, especially when you're certain there's a dog lover in your sights.

But don't take it from me. *The Curious Incident of the Dog in the Night-Time* is a book that became a blockbuster play in London and on Broadway. The members of this family are all difficult or unlikable for various reasons, and after two and a half grueling hours of bad behavior, an adorable puppy arrives on stage and fixes everything. I rest my case. Though I suppose the cat people will argue that Nobel Prize winning poet T.S. Eliot did not publish a collection of light verse that became a worldwide musical sensation called *Dogs*.

Life has improved in other ways. Mary's son became engaged to a lovely local girl. Nowadays, the gals tend to foregather to do their hair and makeup, and my understanding is that this can take on a celebratory atmosphere. The effects of this were in evidence when the maid-of-honor began to sway while standing on the altar. They stopped the ceremony, sat her down, and sent for a glass of water. However, moments later the bride slumped onto the kneeler directly in front of the priest. Much like a contagion of church giggles, it didn't stop there. To the priest's dismay, girls began toppling over left and right. Apparently dieting for several weeks to fit into dresses followed by mimosas is a recipe for being horizontal during the actual ceremony. An intrepid athletic coach ran to his van and brought in a case of Gatorade. The priest looked at his watch and said we'd have to wind this up since another function was beginning soon. A dozen chairs were placed on the altar and the only one to remain standing through the rest of the ceremony was the priest. But everything worked out fine. It's three years later and Mary is grandmother to a beautiful baby girl whose middle name is Erin. And her gorgeous hair has grown back.

Histories are more full of examples of
the fidelity of dogs than of friends.
−Alexander Pope

Chapter 7

And a Dog Shall Lead Them

Nowadays animals are employed across a wide spectrum of vocations. Dogs in particular can earn their living in a variety of fields including bomb sniffing, tracking, rescue, herding, hunting, security, therapy, and acting. Then there are team mascots, sled dogs, seizure alert dogs and, of course, guide dogs.

My Buffalo gal pal Julie became a puppy raiser for an organization that trains seeing-eye dogs. This requires an enormous amount of time and dedication, which is why penitentiaries are often good places to raise them. It takes almost two years from the time a pup is weaned from its mother until it can begin working with a blind person. The puppy comes with a manual about two inches thick, while you and the dog must also attend classes several times per week or month depending on your progress.

And a Dog Shall Lead Them

At the school, 90 percent of the dogs were Labrador retrievers colored yellow, chocolate, or black. About 10 percent were German shepherds. The shepherds were the frustrated poets, issuing mournful existential yowls apropos of nothing during training exercises. And with that stealthy shepherd crouch, they appeared to be stalking a murderer rather than helping a blind person cross the street, which I guess is why they're the number one choice for police dogs around the world. I've heard that some guide dog schools use golden retrievers, but I can't imagine a golden retriever choosing to help a blind person over playing a game of Frisbee. It's my understanding that poodles are the smartest dogs, and yet I've never spotted one leading a blind person, so I can only assume they view it as the factory work of the animal kingdom, or at least in New York City they hold out for celebrity roles in circus acts and the fashion world.

Border collies are, of course, exceptionally intelligent and trainable, but if the work doesn't involve harassing sheep, it's difficult to capture their interest on any kind of long-term basis. Corralling sheep also requires a particular glare which border collies specialize in, and I don't think blind people want their dogs staring down coworkers, airline personnel, and potential romantic partners. Beagles regularly sniff for contraband at airports, so clearly they're not lazy or stupid. One cute green-vested beagle plopped down next to my husband at John F. Kennedy airport upon his return from South Africa. My spouse thought this was adorable, and while he was trying to make friends with the little cutie, his suitcase was hauled off by inspectors. Indeed, he was smuggling biltong, which is South African beef jerky and also happens to be contraband. My husband, who trained as a lawyer, claimed the fact that it was vacuum-packed allowed him to skirt the foreign meat ban. The beagle knew better.

43

The two-hundred-page seeing-eye dog manual contains a directory of commands that will ensure everyone is communicating with the trainee in the same way—from the service dog center staff to the puppy raisers and eventually the recipients. For example, in our manual "lunch" meant any kind of meal, "easy" meant to stop pulling my shoulder out of the socket, and "get busy" meant it's time to poop. "Wow!" meant the dog did something so terrible that if you were married it would require a divorce on the spot. "Wow!" is most often employed when the puppy has eaten a dinner off the counter that was supposed to serve six people while you were in the next room folding towels.

There are the obvious commands like "sit" and "down." "You're free" means the dog can stop obeying the previous command, which I always thought was a little cruel on the prisoners training dogs, especially New Hampshire convicts who paint license plates that say "Live Free or Die." The command "leave it" means stop chewing on the dead squirrel with the wormy intestines hanging out. "Off" tells the black Lab to get off the white furniture and the yellow Lab to get off the dark furniture. Labs excel at the army crawl and while in the "down" position can still manage to consume every single Cheerio the baby dropped throughout a two-story house with a finished basement while never rising more than an inch above the ground.

It's important for seeing-eye dogs to learn to negotiate all sorts of transportation options and activities of daily life, so on weekends Julie and I would drive around with the dog and always end up at Krispy Kreme donuts. Krispy Kreme is a favorite of old Buffalonians because the glazed donuts are similar to the beloved Freddie's Doughnuts (and conspiracy theories about a stolen recipe abound) from our childhood, which has long since shuttered. Part of the dog's training was to watch us eat hot, delicious doughnuts without being given any. However, you wouldn't be tempted to feed a Lab anything but dog food after witnessing what happens when they go off their regular diet. I never understood how my Pekingese could ingest staples, cement chunks, and cake frosting without so much as a hiccup, yet the minute the Lab swallowed a jellybean, there was a gastric blast.

Lab puppies are delightful, and after raising one for almost two years, it's impossible not to become attached. Of course, puppy raisers know going in that they will eventually have to give up their dog, whether for service or breeding, and even if it does ultimately become a "release dog," they may not be next on the list for one. Julie became exceptionally devoted to a dog named Cosmo and went into crisis mode two days before parting. Julie had been a star soccer fullback, playing in Europe against forwards raised from birth by the Communist Athletic Complex with no other purpose than to shoot and score, and was not prone to histrionics. But when it came to losing Cosmo, there was anguish, tears, and schemes to flee the country. Having grown up in Buffalo, five minutes from the border, Julie was fluent in Canadian and already enjoyed pouring vinegar on her French fries.

On the final morning, Julie planned to take Cosmo for a long walk in the park. It was late autumn, and the weather was perfect for Labs and Buffalonians, who find temperatures above fifty degrees Fahrenheit to be on the hot side. At sunrise the park was quiet and a cavalcade of red, green, and gold. Cosmo tore off into the leaves and disappeared for a few minutes. By the time Julie caught up with her, Cosmo had consumed the majority of a rancid pigeon, bones and all, whose decomposition one could smell from several yards away. Julie panicked, knowing full well that small bones pierce the intestines of dogs and kill them in short order. She called the seeing-eye dog center and was told to feed the dog "Vaseline sandwiches"—two pieces of bran bread with an inch of Vaseline in the middle. Julie scrambled around the Upper West Side to find a tub of Vaseline at seven in the morning, then picked up a nine dollar loaf of bran bread and began making "sandwiches."

We both thought the same thing, "No dog would eat this!" We were wildly mistaken. A Labrador is indeed omnivorous, and the Vaseline sandwiches went down one after the other. Two hours later we drove to Westchester and turned in the dog with the pigeon still inside it. Despite being sad, we both had to agree that the pigeon episode had lessened the trauma of giving up Cosmo. We were in our twenties then, with many dog and human relationships still to come. Whenever we broke up with a friend or lover we commiserated and took the other out for Krispy Kreme donuts. However, if the person we'd broken up with had committed some egregious or thoughtless act right beforehand, which just happened to render parting that much easier, we henceforth referred to it as "eating the pigeon."

You may have a dog that won't sit up,
roll over or even cook breakfast,
not because she's too stupid to learn how
but because she's too smart to bother.

−Rick Horowitz

Chapter 8

Häagen-Dazs Retriever

After being a puppy raiser for several years, my friend Julie was on the list to receive a "released" seeing-eye dog. A dog can flunk out of the program for a number of reasons. They must pass rigorous tests including crossing heavily-trafficked streets, encountering other animals, having an umbrella opened in front of them, and standing next to a person with a slice of pizza. The released canines make marvelous household pets since they're healthy and well-trained, with excellent temperaments. This is different than taking a retired seeing-eye dog, which is usually around eight years old and has finished working with a blind person. These youthful re-careered dogs ("failed" sounds so negative) are usually between two and a half and four and may have been employed in the breeding program, but after not passing the tests to become seeing-eye dogs or else trying the job and not succeeding, they weren't able to perform any other type of service such as drug or bomb sniffing. Julie's first dog, Cosmo, was extremely motivated by food (as we witnessed first-hand during the pigeon episode) and ended up working with the Bureau of Alcohol, Tobacco, Firearms, and Explosives (ATF) at the Australian Olympics.

When Julie's name reached the top of the list to receive an unsuccessful dog, she was pregnant, and so she accepted the dog but secretly passed it on to my husband and me. I didn't feel at all guilty about this deception, since I was the one with the car who had been driving dogs to Krispy Kreme every weekend the past four years, and from Manhattan to Westchester for puppy classes on Wednesday nights. Our dog was named Indigo, but the release manual said it's fine to rename them at age two and a half since they're *that* smart. Whereas I name all my dogs after old strippers, my husband, who went to college in the UK, names his dogs after English schoolchildren, so Indigo became Maisie.

Labrador retrievers are the most popular dogs in the US, UK, and Canada, though Canada is the only country to go so far as to name a province after the breed. In my experience they also shed the most, and covering the world in Labradors may very well be a capitalist plot by the makers of Dyson vacuums. People think Labs are one of the friendliest breeds, and this is true, but their motivation isn't necessarily kinship. A Lab that approaches and you believe is saying, "Hello, I really like you, let's be friends," is actually saying, "Do you have any extra food? Anything at all you don't want? What about that sandwich I smell in your bag?" One thing that characterizes people, the French philosopher Descartes famously told us, is that "people think." Well, dogs think too, and Labs think mostly about food.

A Lab always sits next to people while they eat, especially children and other pets, in case there's any "extra" food. It's always a surprise to discover that dogs know inferential statistics, but Labrador retrievers are particularly talented when it comes to probability theory. Maisie knew that if she parked herself in the geometric center of the kitchen at eight o'clock on Thanksgiving morning, there was a 99.9 percent chance of getting plenty of food to eat by eight in the evening. In addition to whatever goodies were dropped, she was guaranteed the pre-wash cycle on at least two loads of gravy-laden dishes.

However, Labradors need an enormous amount of exercise, especially when they're young. Consequently, city folk must be prepared to throw balls several times a day in all types of weather and wash muddy fur, shoes, and clothes. There's no need to enroll in any "Tough Mudder" events if you're an urban dweller with a youthful, medium-to-large canine. I've had countless New Yorkers tell me over the years that they have a dog with behavioral problems, and 95 percent of the time it's because the creature isn't getting enough exercise. This is also the case with Manhattan children—for best results you need to run them hard at least three times a day.

Much like humans, dogs exhibit different levels of intelligence and also judgment when it comes to putting things in their mouths. Maisie repeatedly ate poisonous acorns and then vomited them up an hour later. My husband teaches business strategy at Columbia University and basically lost his mind when this happened, running around the house with paper towels, arms flailing, and yelling, "Where is the learning?"

We weren't told exactly why Maisie had flunked out (and why should one bad reference follow a dog throughout its career?), but I can guess. Despite two years of being taught how to cross streets, board buses, and ride in cars, where Maisie truly excelled was in taking ice cream cones from toddlers. Because we live one block from an entrance to Central Park, where a vendor is stationed throughout the day, she had a dependable supply. If a child was given an ice cream cone, Maisie was diligent about first ingratiating herself with the entire family and posing for photos. Then she'd zero in on befriending the cone-carrying child until a look of sheer delight crossed the toddler's face and ice cream ran down its hand. Maisie would lick the child's palms and wrists clean as if performing a public service. The child would giggle with happiness while the parents took photos for the grandparents and discussed how they just had to get a family dog. Meantime, Maisie worked her tongue toward the cone and gently plopped the ice cream into her mouth as if doing the child a favor while everyone beamed at this cute moment. Indeed, she taught many young people the joys of sharing. So it transpires that Maisie fulfilled her purpose as a service dog after all. It just takes some of us a little longer to find our true path in life. What was once classified as a "learning disability" that prevented her from passing on ice cream-stealing genes to future generations turned out to be a higher calling.

In the meantime, Julie had the baby and then another one. Despite reading a stack of parenting books she ended up using the two-hundred-plus page seeing-eye dog manual to raise them, since after a decade it was hardwired into all our vocabularies. You'd be amazed at how well seeing-eye dog commands transfer from puppy to baby, especially sit, stay, off, easy, leave it, let's go, you're free and *wow*! Still, I was relieved she didn't crate them at night.

There are two means of refuge from the misery
of life, music and cats.
—Albert Schweitzer

Chapter 9

The Tell-Tale Meow

People often ask if I'm a vegetarian for my health. Actually, it's for the animals' health. Other living creatures seem to thrive when we don't slaughter and consume them. When I was a kid working on a farm, I found the pigs to be especially playful and intelligent, just like a lot of dogs. They easily recognized me as I approached the pen and excitedly ran around squealing. (It may have helped that I was carrying a white slop bucket.) I couldn't see the difference between eating a pig and a cat or a cow and a dog, or those animals who uneasily tread the divide of companion and cuisine such as horses and rabbits. The chickens were also amiable and had their own personalities. For several years I stopped eating eggs but started going to bed at eight o'clock and leaning toward the light when I was awake, so I took the view that chickens feel better after laying eggs. People tease me about being a vegetarian, and my dad artfully made it into his full-time job during retirement. But I've asked several heart surgeons how many longtime vegetarians they've performed angioplasty on and thus far haven't heard of any.

As a result of having so many dogs and being outside with them in all sorts of weather, I'm often mistaken for a dog walker. People regularly ask for my card, rates, and "range"—will I go as far down as 79th Street—and whether I work on holidays (yes, I do!). I explain that I'm out with my own dogs but will keep them in mind if a career change becomes necessary. I'm definitely not insulted to be thought of as a dog walker, as it's a noble and necessary calling, like being a clown at children's birthday parties. In Manhattan people regularly feel obligated to comment on the passing canine parade and even take photos. One man decided it was essential to tell me that I looked exactly like his golden retriever. Indeed, we are both big-boned and large-nosed with a generous amount of strawberry-blond hair. Clearly he meant this as a compliment, and I took it as one, but I can understand how some women might not.

I enjoy walking my pack, at least when the wind in front of my building isn't 40 mph, causing the spaniels to become weaponized and take flight. Still, despite mostly working from home, there's travel, meetings, and destination weddings, so I need to employ a dog walker. Olga used to be a nanny in my apartment building but soon decided she liked pets better than people, which I assume is true for a lot of New Yorkers based on the many rows of single serve items available in every store. The steadfast and indefatigable Olga walks dogs 365 days a year, which includes holidays, hurricanes, blizzards, and transit strikes, not only without complaint but with exuberant pride. In fact, the only time she ever misses a walk is when detained in a holding cell down at the local precinct. Because Olga has memorized all the many rules regarding pets in New York City, and the beat cops have not, she remains incarcerated while the regulations are consulted, usually after she's become obstreperous in her unflagging certitude. For instance, you're allowed a five-foot radius when walking a dog in Manhattan, so if some idiot invades that space (like the one who did so on a skateboard) to hassle a dog, and that dog snarls or bites the individual, the dog is within its legal rights.

Olga is from Bavaria, and when the police hear her accent they assume she might have immigration issues and will therefore be intimidated by law enforcement. They are wrong. Her "papers" are completely in order. Furthermore, Olga's father trained police dogs in Germany and regularly employed her as "the suspect" in drills, or I guess "bait" or "chum" might be the better word for it. This happened without modern-day protective clothing, and she's happy to show you the multitude of scars. She's also extremely lithe and fast for a seventy-year-old. Olga has a lifestyle philosophy she describes as "The German Way" that revolves around simplicity, hard work, and following rules. I must admit I never took much notice of Olga's short hair, practical outfits, and sturdy shoes until a recent trip to Germany when it struck me that all the women over age sixty look exactly like Olga.

In addition to being a responsible pet caretaker, Olga raised two boys of her own, and in her fifties, rescued a boy she found living under a bench in Central Park. Steven was eight years old and fending for himself, his mother being a drug addict in Harlem and the whereabouts of his father unknown. Olga engaged a lawyer to complete the adoption process so the new arrangement was entirely legal, and the boy grew up (in accordance with "The German Way") to be a wonderful man who now has a son of his own.

A Theory of Everything Else

The only thing I would change about Olga is that she reports on my house guests, of whom there are many. She grades them for cleanliness, especially pertaining to the kitchen, bathrooms, and laundry area. Dishes left in the sink cost a lot of points. Olga similarly assesses what kind of schedule they keep and prefers early risers. But whatever the timetable, she likes it to be regular. When Olga texts me dossiers on my guests, I tell her that she doesn't need to spy on people staying in my apartment. I'm not running an Airbnb, so they are all friends, family, or Unitarians in town for church functions, and I don't maintain rigorous standards when it comes to housekeeping. Olga's response is always the same—"It's no problem, I like to do it." Apparently you can take the gal out of the Stasi but you can't take the Stasi out of the gal. (A German friend once explained, "You cannot keep a German from *vorking*.") So I warn guests that they're being monitored and inform them that only my friend Neil has ever received a passing grade. Some visitors are competitive or desire tips for living "The German Way" in order to be as ever-sensible, upbeat, and fighting fit as Olga; they are eager to know Neil's secrets and more important, his schedule. Olga has now been overseeing my place for two decades, and I hate to say it, but on balance it may be a win-win, since anytime I've arrived home early from a trip or popped in to pick up a winter coat between airports, everything is always shipshape. Even the dogs know to clean those bowls, tidy up their toys, and be in bed with the lights out by ten o'clock.

I happily consider myself a "dog lady," but of course the missing word here is "crazy." I've decided that the definition of a "crazy dog lady" is a woman with one more dog than however many I currently have. The term "cat lady" is more mystifying because there's no "cat man," much like we have "Valley girls"

54

but no "Valley boys." In popular culture "cat girl" is a female character with cat traits while a "cat lady" automatically suggests a single gal with lots of felines. Maybe it's just a rebellious term as dogs are historically known as "man's best friend." However, "cat lady" brings to mind a woman who doesn't want the kind of man around who stays out all night, doesn't come when he's called, and doesn't pay attention when spoken to unless it's about dinner, yet this is exactly what you get in most cats, so we may want to rethink the term.

Although Dogtown is the name given to over a dozen ghost towns and old mining camps throughout North America, there is only one official Cattown. The Fly Creek Area of Otsego County in Central New York State is home to Bedbug Hill, Panther Mountain, and the hamlet of Cattown. Bedbug Hill was inspired by a nineteenth-century migrant hops picker who insisted he would not return to the area because local bedbugs were "as big as squirrels," and Panther Mountain was named after a Native American who lived alone. Unfortunately for one feline, Cattown Road was designated thusly after a man dropped a cat down the chimney of a house to break up a meeting his wife was attending, because dinner was not on the table.

Whereas you can't normally identify a "cat person" on the street, "dog people" are more conspicuous, yet simultaneously members of a secret society. For instance, when they smile and describe their dog as "moody" or "opinionated" or as having "shared space issues," this means if you come one step closer it will bite your face off. Instead of Skull and Bones we're more like Bag and Bones. New Yorkers must carry poop bags since this isn't a city with dispensers in convenient locations. Heck, we're excited to have recently been given back (some) trash cans on subway platforms. The geniuses at the MTA decided back in

2012 that removing waste receptacles would reduce both trash and rats. The result was more litter covering station platforms, an increase in track fires, and triple the rats. No—you're kidding!

But back to poop. Dogs tend to be reliable poopers in that you have your one-poop-a-day dogs and your four-poop-a-day dogs, and then there's my little philosopher Penny who is what I call a "traveler" and drops a trail of poop that requires six pickup locations and reminds me of Dad taking a newspaper into the bathroom for half an hour. I always have at least one small dog that refuses to use papers inside the house, like Americans not wanting to use the bidet in France—it's weird and they just don't like the idea; yes, 67 million people can be wrong. So a dog person gets in the habit of carrying a certain number of poop bags; but every once in a while you forget poop bags or run out, in which case it's necessary to stand on a street corner asking passersby for a poop bag like a hobo bumming a cig in the old Bowery. We've all been there, so usually it isn't too long before another pet companion is happy to "pay it forward."

My aunt Sue proudly wears the "cat lady" badge. In fact, her life with cats would make a good reality TV show. This story begins like your typical sitcom, with a minor plumbing problem where the woman wishes to call a trained professional but the man suggests he can fix it. Cut to a shot of water spraying everywhere and the woman getting an estimate of several thousand dollars from a plumber.

One cat is locked in the guest room and the other rarely comes out from under the bed, so that's not an issue. The plumber leaves the door to the outside open while going back and forth to his truck for various implements. Four hours later, the wall has been broken, pipes are refitted, and the wall is patched. The plumber happily leaves with enough money to purchase a new truck, while Aunt Sue once again has a functional toilet. One cat is released from the guest room but Under-the-Bed Cat is no longer under the bed, or anywhere else for that matter. Aunt Sue organizes a search party and hangs missing cat signs throughout the neighborhood, which is also home to several varieties of cat-consuming wildlife, including foxes and vultures.

After four days of scouring the streets and fields and four sleepless nights, a faint meow is heard. Only the meow is coming from inside the house, or rather inside the wall of the house. Aunt Sue was an English teacher, and Edgar Allan Poe's short stories "The Black Cat" and "The Tell-Tale Heart" come to mind. Seven friends and neighbors squeeze into the clothes closet and discuss how to best remedy the problem.

The plumber is immediately called back to chop down the brand-new wall. Freshly roasted chicken is placed inside the wall and everyone waits. Nothing. But in the morning the chicken is gone! More chicken is put down, this time inside the bathroom. Recalcitrant kitty comes out from behind the wall and the plumber seals the wall free of charge. The pussycat is now back under the bed and the toilet remains functional.

People tend to think cats are pessimists since they're often cynically portrayed in literature: the Cheshire Cat, the tattletale Mrs. Norris in the Harry Potter chronicles, cartoons featuring Garfield, and Grumpy Cat on the Internet. Conversely, dogs are depicted in popular culture as being the optimists—overly-eager and intrepid—such as Toto, Benji, Astro, and Scooby-Doo. Surprisingly, the truth is just the opposite. When the weather is bad, anything from a blizzard to extreme humidity, my dogs do not want to go out. However, I've had cats who check the weather at the front door and, if it's not to their liking, insist on being let out the back on the assumption that it will be better in the yard.

Despite the heartbreak of loss and occasional catastrophes, numerous studies show that pet owners live longer than those without pets. This makes perfect sense to me when I consider the rigors of being a dog person—the walking, cleaning, bending, and shouting "No!" So how is it that cat people live longer than dog people? Cat owners are 30 percent less likely to die from a stroke or heart attack than "people who had never known the love of a cat," according to a twenty-year study done by the University of Minnesota. Cat persons experience fewer instances of high blood pressure, colds, and doctor visits. Adding insult to early demise, cat owners are more intelligent than dog owners and in possession of more college degrees, according to a University of Bristol study. Certainly, whomever stated that "If the Earth was flat cats would have pushed everything off it by now" had a superior education. As much as it hurts to discover that cat owners are smarter, I can accept the logic here, as I don't see cat owners standing outside holding a leash in torrential downpours or blinding blizzards. And honestly, in our busy, modern age, who is the idiot—the person with an animal that can't be on its own for more than eight hours, or the one who adopts a pet that's perfectly fine being left for a week with a bowl of food on the floor? However, if you're still not prepared to embrace feline companionship, it's been demonstrated that simply watching cat videos can make people feel more energetic and reduce anxiety.

Of people hospitalized for a heart attack, those with pets were 23 percent more likely to be alive one year later than those without pets, according to a Brooklyn College study. Good news: when a study was done fifteen years later specifically with dogs, it transpired that dog owners were significantly less likely to die in the year following a heart attack than non-dog owners. However, these studies do not include tripping over your dogs and breaking a hip. Evangelical Christian minister Billy Graham was hospitalized after falling over one of his dogs in his North Carolina home. Does everything happen for a reason? Was this part of God's plan? He lived another decade, until the Old Testament prophet age of ninety-nine.

Cancer patients have ranked visits from therapy dogs to be as comforting as human visits and more likely to make them feel better. These dogs have proven effective treatment for a vast range of physical, emotional, and psychological conditions and occasionally more effective than drugs. Perhaps insurance will soon cover "pet addiction."

Many automobiles are named after animals, right down to the lowly beetle. However, cats also fare much better than dogs when it comes to branding cars. There's everything from the bobcat, jaguar, cougar, and cheetah to the tiger, puma, lynx, and wildcat. But where are all the cars and trucks named after canines? When have you ever witnessed a cat chasing a car or begging to go for a car ride? When have you seen a cat with its head out the car window or asleep in a truck bed? Dogs are about reliability, steadfastness, trustworthiness, and dependability in all sorts of weather, and in the case of Yorkies, a vision of downright tenacity. Where are the Toyota Husky and Pontiac Chihuahua? Why has Dodge produced a Super Bee but no Stellar Yorkie?

Footwear seems more impartial, as there's a brand for cats as well as dogs, but it depends on what type of customer the manufacturer is courting. A puma is one of the fastest and most powerful cats on Earth, and the eponymous sneakers are popular with athletes. Meantime, Hush Puppy shoes are commonly found on old hippies, geometry instructors, and Spear Carrier #2 in the theater, while the name also moonlights as a fried food.

However, it's worth noting that a pair of suede Hush Puppies are credited with saving the life of Rolling Stones musician Keith Richards at a 1965 Sacramento concert when his guitar touched an ungrounded microphone. Richards was knocked unconscious, but medics claim his thick crepe-soled shoes halted the charge of what otherwise would have been a death blow. This case of near-electrocution may also go a long way in explaining all the electrifying photographs of Richards which have appeared since the episode, and perhaps inspired the songs "Heaven," "Let Me Go," "Let it Loose," "Hot Stuff," "Rough Justice," "Hand of Fate," "Jumpin' Jack Flash," and, of course, "Start Me Up."

The real tie-breaker might be whether dogs or cats go to Heaven. Other than as lions or leopards, cats aren't mentioned in the Bible even once, whereas dogs make over two dozen appearances. That said, the references aren't all that flattering. For example, Proverbs 26:11 states, "As a dog returneth to its vomit, so a fool returneth to his folly." The good news is that when God demeans dogs in the Bible, he's actually referring to humans. Furthermore, there's no reference anywhere about dogs going to Hell. However, in the 1800s, Pope Pius IX officially declared not just cats and dogs, but all animals "soulless" and unable to enter Heaven, even on a leash. But a century later Pope John Paul II had a revelation and professed that animals must have souls since they were created by "God's breath." Twenty-five years after that, another reversal occurred as Pope Benedict XVI stated unequivocally that God gives only humans access to Heaven. Lest that be the end of it, Pope Francis declared in his encyclical *Laudato si'* that animals will indeed join humans in the hereafter. (After choosing the name Francis, wouldn't it be awkward to rule otherwise?) "Eternal life will be a shared experience of awe, in which each creature, resplendently transfigured, will take its rightful place and have something to give those poor men and women who will have been liberated once and for all." So my packing for Heaven advice would be to wear galoshes and bring lots of shark repellent, mosquito netting, a snakebite kit, and a bucket of liver treats.

Otherwise, despite their quarrels and competitions, dog people and cat people have a lot in common. Most of us have housed both species at one time or another and occasionally mix it up to this day. I'd say even the most ardent cat lover or devoted dog person is still part of a big mammalian family where we argue with one another but know when it's time to team up against the outside world. For instance, I think that when we heard how literary lion John Updike's mom died, and rather than find homes for his mom's cats among his friends and fans, he immediately called the humane society to collect them, we all stopped purchasing his books. Similarly, when we learned that in his old age composer Johannes Brahms was cranky with most townspeople but kind to dogs, we played more of his music.

In general, animal lovers tend to trust other animal lovers. In school my class was tasked with writing an essay on whether George Washington or Abraham Lincoln was the greater US president. Many chose Washington because he'd distinguished himself in battle. Some flipped a coin. When I learned that as a boy Abraham Lincoln had a pet pig and carved a cradle for it, he was my man.

Our perfect companions never have fewer than four feet.

—Colette

Chapter 10

Having Pets on Five Cents a Day

There wasn't any disposable income, a.k.a. "extra money," when I was growing up in the Rust Belt during the 1970s. Local manufacturing had bolted overseas, and the country was in its biggest recession since the Great Depression, suffering from an oil crisis, stagnant wages, and raging inflation. Fleece had yet to be invented, heat was scarce, and the biggest blanket we had was of snow. In addition to plenty of influenza, bronchitis, and frostbite, there was a bad case of disco fever going around. Lighted dance floors featuring brightly-clad, hand-clapping youth gyrating to "Freak Out" were popping up like corpses in English country houses.

Whereas my parents enjoyed the Fabulous Fifties and Swinging Sixties, authors and advertisers didn't even bother to name the 1970s. If they had, it could have been one of several oft-heard catchphrases such as, "Who is going to pay for that?" "Does the salad come with the meal?" or "Jump up and down if you want to feel warm." In the hard times of Lucky Strikes and lost chances, the best gift you could give anyone was a lottery ticket or "a scratcher" as they were known. Church raffles were commonplace, but the prize wasn't a car or vacation. It was either a snow blower or meat. Indeed, the "meat raffle" is still a popular fundraiser in Western New York. The winner of one before Easter could hope to go home with a ham, Polish sausages, pork tenderloin, and some hotdogs and hamburgers for the kids.

Another way to gauge the lack of disposable income is by the fact that there wasn't any bra-burning in Buffalo to bring attention to feminism. We had petitions and protests and placards, but no one was willfully setting ablaze even the cheapest of undergarments. There were fires burning all over—Molotov cocktails were thrown in protest, businesses torched for insurance, spontaneous combustion on Lake Erie, old wooden houses regularly went up in flames (complete with shoeboxes full of cash in the rafters), deep fryers caught fire, kerosene lamps started blazes, and I saw draft cards burned with my own eyes. Radios blared The Rolling Stones' "Play with Fire," Bob Dylan's "This Wheel's on Fire," and The Doors' "Light My Fire," yet no woman in her right mind torched a perfectly good brassiere.

If the collapsing warehouses, shuttered factories, and rusting grain elevators that cast hulking shadows over Lake Erie weren't enough of a gritty ambience, add an unpopular nineteen-year war in Vietnam that we were clearly losing. Marvin Gaye crooned, "What's Going On?" across the airwaves while angry protests, which escalated into a war against the war, were matched by anti-abortion demonstrations, since Buffalo was 80 percent Catholic and considered fertile ground for reproductive activism. The area was so Catholic that when the first *Star Wars* movie came out in 1977, every time someone on the silver screen said, "May the Force be with you," the entire audience dutifully chanted back, "And also with you." Buffalo was so Papist that even the atheists and Unitarian Universalists were Catholic in that the God we did not worship was a Catholic God.

The good news was that a family didn't need to have money to keep pets. Back then it wasn't obligatory to buy designer clothes and specialty food for your dog, and puppies didn't come with vaccination sheets longer than the tax code. Pets with loose morals regularly snuck out on dates and produced offspring of dubious lineage, and therefore one frequently saw homemade signs offering free mutts and kittens. Otherwise, strays often appeared in the neighborhood to a chorus of kids shouting, "Can we keep it?"

Anyone could afford a dog by feeding it table scraps, and thus they were employed by most families as entertainment for the kids and a free security system. The idea of buying dog beds, toys, and biscuits was ridiculous. If meat was being served, the dog might get a bone. Otherwise, "cookies" were ice cubes from the freezer, and most dogs were excited to get those, especially after seeing how happy kids were to have homemade Kool-Aid freezer pops.

Meantime, with runaway inflation devaluing pension checks by the day, senior citizens could no longer make ends meet. Money wasn't the problem, but the solution; the problem was how to get it. Widowhood and divorce had forced numerous older women into poverty because they'd gone from high school to housewives and didn't have the necessary skills to enter the workforce and qualify for much above an entry-level job. The news constantly reported stories about indigent seniors forced to eat cat and dog food, which makes no sense to us now since pet food costs a fortune, and a Wall Street pal is hoarding cans of Halo dog food in case the banks collapse. But back then you could find a sale on Alpo of ten cans for a dollar, while many cats were in the habit of going outside to hunt for their dinner. In fact, when a neighbor lady fell in her kitchen and was stuck there overnight, she was at least able to cadge a meal from a nearby bowl on the floor since the cat had gone out on the prowl. Best of all, it was creamed liver, because she'd already removed her teeth for the night.

The only downside of housing pets on a restricted budget was that they had to sleep off most illness and injuries. Adults explained to us that when a dog becomes sick it goes under the house until it feels better, and I sensed the implicit message was that we kids should do the same.

The dark side of pet ownership on slender means is that many beloved cats and dogs were "put down" by Dad. While no one is prepared for a single gunshot in the backyard, it was the era of sad animal books and movies including *Bambi*, *Old Yeller*, *Sounder*, *The Yearling*, and *Charlotte's Web*. These helped to educate us about the circle of life and its inevitable sufferings, although I know at least one person still in therapy over a gangland-style dog execution. Thus it was actually a relief when Mary's mom, a.k.a. The Coupon Queen, who had nine children to feed, called every vet in town to find the best deal on euthanasia for Charlie the family dog while we had our after-school snack at the kitchen table.

Fifty years ago, children weren't sheltered from negativity as much as they are today; there weren't any pet cemeteries, tiny monogrammed boxes of ashes, plaques with paw prints, or animated films called *All Dogs Go to Heaven*. Generally speaking, childhood was much more violent back then, as evidenced by the most popular parental threats—"I'll break every bone in your body!" "You won't sit down for a week!" "I'll give you something to cry about!" There were no helmets unless you were going off to war. Reaching adulthood was a riskier proposition in general. Parents drove station wagons while kids stood between them on the front seat or stuck their heads out the windows like collies. If you sat in the back while my dad was driving, there was a fifty-fifty chance a lit cigarette was going to land in your crotch after he'd tossed it out the front window. Who needed amusement parks?

Dogs and cats were considered amazing playmates for children during the 1970s when computers hadn't yet been invented, and not much was happening on TV aside from *Bowling for Dollars* and Christian Broadcasting Network's flagship program *The 700 Club*. We had a total of three network channels that ran soap operas all afternoon, and the bizarrely named UHF, which suggested an interplanetary frequency, and just happened to show *Twilight Zone* reruns. There was also PBS, where Mom liked to watch Julia Child basting and braising up a storm, or the Irish Rovers sweating in their white cable knit sweaters under hot studio lights while plucking out "The Unicorn."

With such limited indoor entertainment, everyone was outside shoveling, playing, gardening, mowing the lawn, or just stoop sitting. Looking at what neighbors hung out to dry on their clothesline often made for good conversation; on the downside, when it was loaded with sheets, this obscured our view into their yard and windows. Dogs and cats freely wandered the neighborhood, and we knew most of them. Kids were as abundant as dandelions or snowflakes, so there was always a game of one sort or another underway. When the boys were off running in their feral gang, girls entertained themselves with jump ropes, hopscotch, and roller skates. Or we'd make clothes for our dogs and cats, dress them up, and create pageants. This explained the large number of cats in high branches of trees wearing tutus and tiaras.

Farms employed dogs for security, more to guard against foxes than humans, and cats to keep down the rodent population. As a youth I worked at a farm that doubled as a day camp where we engaged children with games, rowing, swimming, amateur theatricals, and English style horseback riding. We had kids aged five through twelve, though we didn't require birth certificates, and desperate parents were constantly sneaking in sticky four-year-olds who weren't altogether dependable when it came to using the toilet and blowing their noses.

One summer morning, just after a torrential downpour, my group ran across a chicken stuck in—what else?—chicken wire. During the struggle to become untangled, her feathers had gone from bronze, black and white to a mucky gray, and her fleshy red comb sported a layer of mud icing on top. I eventually worked her free, and several eight-year-olds took Henrietta over to a spigot mounted three feet above the ground that we normally used to fill watering pails. After a few minutes I heard the chicken choking and the kids screaming. She'd stopped breathing after water had flooded the two nostrils atop her beak, and the kids were horrified at the prospect of having killed the just-rescued chicken. Being the daughter of a nurse (one who is an aggressive force in public health care to this day), I opened the chicken's beak and blew air into it while massaging what at the dinner table is called her breast. Fortunately, the chicken promptly returned to life, and the campers were relieved. I quoted them Mom's favorite saying, "When it's not your time, it's not your time."

The following summer, a camper had a boy from Mexico named Nestor with him as part of an exchange program. Nestor told our merry band that kids in Mexico kept flies as pets. He proceeded to demonstrate the Zen art of capturing a fly with your bare hand—lightly shaking it so the fly was stunned but not concussed, then tying a long hair around it. When the fly rose again it was on the end of a leash. Hundreds of dollars' worth of rowboats were left overturned on the banks of a manmade pond while all my boys and girls diligently applied themselves to acquiring a pet fly. By the end of the day you could hear my group coming from a half-mile away as we were preceded by a buzzing symphony of three dozen flies. Meantime, I was lucky not to go bald once the campers discovered my blonde hair was not only long and extra-strength with regard to durability, but it disappeared in the sunlight, so it looked as if the flies were following the kids of their own volition or had perhaps been hypnotized.

Fast forward ten years after life as a camp counselor and barnyard paramedic. Having taught horseback riding all those years ago, when I walked the bridle path in Central Park, I enjoyed randomly barking at lazy riders, "Heels down, shoulders back, squeeze with your knees, hands together, thumbs up." One morning the rider turned out to be Jackie Kennedy Onassis, and fortunately she just laughed. I'd heard that she often answered the phone in Spanish, pretending to be her own housekeeper, so clearly she was a bit of a jokester herself.

With some regularity, a riderless horse would come around the bend at a full gallop, and since Central Park is surrounded by heavy traffic on all sides, this can be a problem, so I always call 911 to report any renegade quadrupeds. One emergency operator sounded like she was a Queens native, and when asked the location of the horse, I suggested it was best to send police to manage traffic around 90th Street and Central Park West, since that's where the animal was heading. She asked me how I knew where the horse was going and I replied, "Because that's where Claremont Riding Academy is, and a horse always returns to the barn." She asked me how I knew that and I said, "Because we all like a drink after work."

Section 2

BIPEDS

That will do extremely well, child.
You have delighted us long enough.
—Mr. Bennet in Jane Austen's *Pride and Prejudice*

Chapter 11

Stayin' Alive

In the 1970s, an era best defined by famous serial killers and slasher films, most schoolyards resembled *Lord of the Flies*, and there were no "participation" trophies. In every gym class, two athletically gifted children were designated "captains" and tasked with selecting their teams one by one until only two ungainly kids were left, and the teacher would charitably assign one to each team to avoid anyone being picked last, which was the same thing as being picked last.

With no video games or cable TV, no play dates or tutoring, little homework and no private lessons, we had considerably more time on our hands. There were no helicopter parents, pharmaceuticals for children (aside from candy cigarettes), or self-help books for our souls. Nowadays, there is rampant exceptionalism and a preponderance of straight-A report cards, along with an expectation of unconditional happiness. For better or for worse, we found meaning in the sometimes sad, harsh, and tedious boredom. Life was one long French movie that didn't need to be paused for fear of missing anything when you went to the bathroom.

In those days, parents were to be avoided at all costs. Fathers arrived home exhausted and irritable from putting in long hours on factory floors, in office parks, or at civil service jobs, while mothers slaved away caring for large, extended families, using limited resources and operating at ground zero for flu epidemics. By large families, I don't mean five or six children, I mean eleven or twelve, all close in age. There was an abundance of twins who were inexplicably given similar names like Sammy and Sally or Tommy and Timmy. Parents were already verbally tripping over who was who, so I still haven't figured out why they made things even more difficult for themselves.

The result was that in a community bursting with hundreds of kids, small humans weren't considered to be all that special. When neighbors spotted another newborn being brought home they were more likely to say "ugh" than "aww" and gaze hopelessly at their trampled lawns. In such a Catholic area, it was a well-known fact that first babies always came early, and not uncommon for babies two months "premature" to weigh in at nine or ten pounds. I'm surprised more studies weren't done about this medical miracle peculiar to the Buffalo area. Or perhaps scientists guessed that a lot of Wite-Out was used on marriage licenses while parents were often winking on their "anniversary."

Because television was so underwhelming compared to current standards, parents began procreating when they were much younger than they do now, and thus were aware that if anything happened to the first half dozen children, or if they didn't like them very much, they could just have more. There was no need to be overprotective or waste valuable time shaping offspring into beacons of society. We were told to walk off any injuries and sleep off any diseases. Every father and grandfather had been in some war or another, while every grandmother had given birth at home and had at least one close call with a laundry wringer (portentously called a "mangle"), so there was a white-knuckle attitude toward pain. Most families experienced at least one pressure cooker explosion and lived to tell the story (videos are now available on YouTube). Sometimes they informed us a sprained ankle was all in our head, and we were lucky to get a scoop of ice cream out of a concussion.

Mothers all suffered from similar medical complaints. Most often they groaned about "splitting headaches"– hey, maybe try not yelling at us all day. They continuously reminded us that we were exhausting their patience and driving them to a collective nervous breakdown, even though they were the ones using psychological torture on us! For instance, "This is the last time I'm going to tell you to make your bed," did not mean you were released from the task and the subject was now thankfully closed. Mothers of toddlers, tweens, and teens pioneered the phrase, "Look at me when I'm talking to you," which was co-opted by a protester confronting Arizona Senator Jeff Flake during the Kavanaugh Supreme Court confirmation brouhaha. There is *no way* to say that and make it sound like a friendly or casual invitation. The fact that moms all had early onset dementia was clearly evidenced by regular queries such as, "Who do you think you're talking to?" "Do you know who you're talking to?" "Who do you think you are?" and working up to the big finale "You're not my child!" This was obviously before DNA testing. Meantime, birth certificates, like marriage licenses, were typed and not all that hard to change.

Parents didn't have much impact on how their offspring turned out, since after the first few kids, subsequent additions were raised by siblings and neighborhood kids. Adults were severely outnumbered and left to play defense as a critical mass of toddlers and tweens moved into their teen years under each roof. Threats and bribery were the basic tools of parenting. The favorite lecture in every home was called JOBS and went something like this: Dad's JOB is to work, Mom's JOB is to take care of the house and all the ingrates squatting here, and your JOB is to go to school (in addition to chores such as bed-making, dishwashing, vacuuming and lawn mowing). Everyone has a JOB to do! The subtext was evident—the boss was willing to fire people for underperformance with little notice and no annual review. The idea of an allowance brought howls of laughter and a reminder of who put food on the table and a roof over your head, the upshot being that you actually owed them money, and if you didn't do your chores, they might very well try to collect. It was continually suggested that you should have a backup plan for living if you fell from the good graces of the Boss, even at age eight.

Cleanliness went with godliness just like peanut butter went with jelly for us kids and gin with tonic for our folks. Mothers didn't want their progeny to appear unkempt, since this supposedly reflected poorly on childrearing and housekeeping skills, so there were constant edicts about hair combing, appropriate necklines, and clean underwear. A mother's worst nightmare was that you'd be in an accident and while attending your broken bones and/or collapsed lung, the paramedics or someone they knew in the emergency room would see stained or torn underclothes. Recently I was working on a play, and the young actors didn't understand the obsession with starched and spotless undergarments since they'd come of age after discount stores had made affordable underwear widespread and practically disposable. Prior to cheap imports, it was an item you washed carefully and mended since clothing was much more expensive and took a considerable bite out of the family budget.

One neighborhood mother of a large brood took pride in turning her gang out for school on time and perfectly dressed and coiffed with lunches and book bags in hand every single morning. Even during the dead of winter when it was necessary to don sweaters, hats, and mittens. What was her secret? I discovered it one morning in gym class when I spied her daughter with an abundance of wrinkles on the back of her white cotton blouse—it appeared that she'd slept in her clothes. Indeed, she admitted that she had. They all had. Not only was this a way to save on heating but it saved time—the kids just had to put on their shoes and coats and they were ready to head out the door.

Sociologists were proclaiming that car culture was breaking apart tight-knit communities, and while advertisers sexualized and sensualized automobiles, the clergy despised them. One can easily see why—those wide banquette style seats, unbroken by armrests and cup holders, with safety belts buried in the crevice, were more like sofas. Couples would venture off down back roads and park along lover's lanes. In heavily Catholic Buffalo when people talked about having an accident, they didn't necessarily mean a fender bender but oftentimes a child born unto thee nine months later. Most were named Mary, John, and Joseph, but they could have just as easily been called Chevy, Ford, and Lincoln.

Hearing nuns' confessions is like being stoned to death with popcorn.
—Venerable Fulton J. Sheen

Chapter 12

Leave it to Jesus

Buffalo has tilted Catholic going back to the missionary priests and French adventurers scouting the Niagara Frontier in the late seventeenth century. Once the Erie Canal opened for business in 1825, it brought prosperity along with massive immigration to the western terminus. People from Poland, Germany, and Italy tended to be Catholic, as did the enormous influx of Irish who were fleeing the devastating Potato Famine. Immigrants usually went through Ellis Island in New York harbor and hopped a train or boat to Buffalo because of all the jobs waiting at factories, mills, and plants along the Great Lakes.

Churches went up constantly in the early days, and most Catholic ethnic enclaves desired their own; in addition to Polish, Italian, German, and Irish there were Ukrainian, Lebanese, Hungarian, and Slovak. A large Greek population fueled the rise of dozens of Greek Orthodox churches and really good diners with encyclopedic menus and revolving dessert cases. These immigrants were accustomed to worshipping inside imposing structures that dominated the skyline and served as a focal point for their community. They wanted edifices built to last and made primarily of stone, and they didn't spare the flying buttresses, stained glass, copper bells, or crucifixes. In addition to storm clouds and smokestacks, the skyline filled with crosses and spires.

However, most of these majestic churches didn't rise because people pledged money and hired contractors. No, people labored in factories from seven until three, went home, had something to eat, and then worked on their churches until nine or ten at night. They were lovingly built by laborers who took showers after work rather than before. So when you sat in a pew on Sunday, you were worshipping in a building that you'd constructed yourself. And if you were a carpenter like Jesus, you could gaze up at God's son with great pride and satisfaction knowing that you'd nailed him to the cross with your own two hands. Hang in there, buddy, Easter is coming. Which rather begs the question, Who decided Jesus had six-pack abs, especially among the beer bellies in my neighborhood? I mean, it was decades before jazzercise or CrossFit, complete with its donkey kicks and sumo squats.

Most people had New Testament names: Michael, David, Matthew, James, and John for boys and thirty variations of Mary for girls–Maria, Maureen, Miriam, Maryanne–and then your doubleheader Mary Beth where you get the mothers of Jesus and John the Baptist rolled into one. The only name to top that was Virginia, since you basically came with a guarantee. As kids, we had several dozen guys named Jack in our lives: Uncle Jack, Grandpa Jack, Big Jack, Little Jack, Fat Jack, Cousin Jack, Jack the TV repair guy, and Father Jack. Add to that Jack the family dog who was half Jack Russell terrier and half not. Now imagine our surprise when Grandpa Jack joined the Heavenly Choir and we saw the name "John" on a Mass card at his funeral. Who the H-E Double Hockey Sticks was John? If you're Catholic this is, of course, no mystery. All the Jacks were secretly Johns because you couldn't name a child Jack for the simple reason that Jack was not a saint.

Catholicism seeped into the warp and woof of everyone's daily life. Lunch ladies liked to warn that if we ate another Little Debbie Nutty Buddy, the angels wouldn't be able to carry us up to heaven. My chorus teacher cautioned girls that when they went out with a boy, they shouldn't wear white bows or order ravioli since this would make the boys think of pillows—and we all know where that leads! My favorite was, "Lent is coming, get your ash in church." If you got in trouble and tried to impress a teacher with a little scripture such as, "In the Bible God says that children are a blessing and a gift," you were likely to hear back, "Knowing the Bible is one thing, knowing the author is another." We called these nun sequiturs.

Apart from a majority of Catholics, the area was home to some Jews and Protestants—mostly Methodists, Presbyterians, and Episcopalians—plus a smattering of Jehovah's Witnesses. Aside from Protestants having a coffee hour, ordaining women, and not requiring celibacy, the main difference between Catholics and Protestants is that when Protestants need a miracle they go straight to the top and ask God without so much as an appointment, often without entering a church, and definitely without getting down on their knees, as if sanctification through grace can be mail-ordered. Catholics, with their multitudes, are accustomed to queuing up, bowing down, and enduring the chain of command, whether it's praying for help, begging forgiveness, or making a plate at the pancake breakfast. There is a hierarchy, not only in management, but also when it comes to angels, saints, values, truths, sins, penances, and even choirs. Or perhaps I should say even hot cross buns—the best are made with fresh spices and iced directly before eating while the worst have been frozen. Buffalo Irish Catholics, of course, have a recipe that includes plenty of brandy and rum. "Half for you, half for me, between us two, good will shall be," the old rhyme goes.

When seeking celestial assistance with life's vicissitudes, you start with your guardian angel, which is located over your right shoulder. Your left shoulder is reserved for the Devil, and this is why left-handed children attending Catholic schools were switched to being right-handed either by tying their left hand behind their back or by smacking the dominant hand with a ruler every time it reached for a pencil. This practice eventually stopped in the 1960s, but as a result, Buffalo still has a large number of ambidextrous senior citizens, so don't think Grandpa won't switch hit, or Grandma can't give you a left hook while cutting cabbage with her right hand. There's also a handful of changelings who never recovered from the process and are bed-wetters to this day. "What's wrong with being born a south-paw or choosing the left-handed lifestyle?" those deprived of a proper religious education might ask. Put simply, lefties were servants of the Devil, and right is right. For example, in the parable of the sheep and the goats, the sheep are set on Christ's right hand and the goats on the left. Sheep are good, hence "the flock," while goats represent the Devil in the Good Book, in the same way as Jefferson Airplane's "White Rabbit" denotes altered states. Those on the right inherit the kingdom of God while those on the left depart into everlasting fire. It was too late to change the Bible, so instead the church would just have to switch all the lefties. How's that for an idea straight out of left field? In Eastern religious communities, the right hand is used for eating and greeting while the left is used for wiping after using the toilet and considered unclean. Meantime, no one refers to previously enjoyed food as "rightovers." In my thesaurus the first word under "leftovers" is "residue," and oddly there isn't another word for "thesaurus."

Moving right along, if one is Catholic, the next stop for assistance is a patron saint. Even butchers, psychiatrists, bell-makers, software engineers, and gamblers have their own heavenly protectors. Everyone in Buffalo knows that if you want to sell your house, you bury a St. Joseph statue in the yard next to the FOR SALE sign. Joe should be interred upside-down and facing the house so he's more motivated to get out and move to the new home. I should think that would be obvious. In my day you then threatened him by proclaiming, "I will keep you with your head down in the dirt until you sell this house for me." Much like spanking children and calling waitresses "Sweetheart," this has become passé, and now you pray for his good will in overseeing a fast, smooth, profitable sale and not letting the inspector find mold. For heaven's sake, don't forget to dig up Joe following the sale and give him a place of honor in the new home, at least if you'd rather the roof not cave in or the basement flood.

If you still find yourself in need of a miracle after exhausting the saints, you can pray to Mary, the mother of God. Everyone knows it's always better to ask Mom than Dad. Then there's Jesus. In Buffalo Jesus tended to be blue-eyed with long blond or light brown hair and pale skin as a result of not getting much sunshine due to our long winters (hence the nickname "God's Frozen Chosen"). The statues always made him look so sad you felt like you didn't want to bother him, even on his birthday. Never mind the Holy Ghost, since that was always a bit squishy, what with chaperones at socials going around separating young couples during slow dances, reprimanding them to leave room for the Holy Spirit.

Next stop is headquarters, which in this case is the Vatican. (Although in the Bible I can't find any job description for a Pope, archbishops, cardinals, or chocolate rabbits.) In addition to communicating with the flock on Twitter, Facebook, and Instagram, and being available as an action figure or bobblehead, Pope Francis answers questions from children. So if you're not a child, perhaps find one to put your missive through the way we employ them to set up our electronics (and the way they use us to buy alcohol). One girl asked Papa Frank if people who aren't baptized are children of God. He replied that God created everyone, even the Mafioso.

Finally, you've reached the big guy. If you can't contact God directly, it's possible to look up his thoughts on a particular matter in his self-help manual. The Bible is the bestselling book of all time, just barely beating out Harry Potter. I'm surprised the Devil doesn't have his own book, *Hell is for Real*, at the very least a paperback or an Audible version. When squeezing everyone on the bleachers, the nuns always said, "Leave no gaps for the Devil," so I think we have our sequel right there. Plus we know a lot about him, and he's popular in movies, but his story has never been properly told. For instance, The Book of Johnny would start, "The Devil went down to Georgia, He was looking for a soul to steal," The Book of Rosemary would contain recipes for tannis root, and The Book of Dorian Gray could comment on the aging process. Since the Devil used to work for God, there must be a tell-all along the lines of, "Take This Kingdom and Shove It!" I'm surprised an artist hasn't done a companion piece to the popular *Last Supper* called *The Last Dessert*. What's better than Devil's food cake?

The problem with asking for miracles, favors, or intercessions is, of course, that if God has a Plan, then you're basically asking him to change his Plan to suit your own plans. However, I found growing up in a Catholic community good preparation for investing in the stock market, since praying works about half the time.

Forgive, O Lord, my little jokes on Thee
And I'll forgive Thy great big one on me.

−Robert Frost

Chapter 13

Religious Olympics

Would it cut back on wars and terrorism if we had some sort of event every few years to decide which religion is the best?

I've always thought that if Catholicism were a sport, it would be wrestling. Adherents were always said to be wrestling with the Devil or wrestling with your conscience or wrestling with your mother over an outfit. If you were a boy, every time you did something wrong, your parents wrestled aloud over whether to send you to Father Baker's orphanage. Some parents would go so far as to order their little sinner to pack a bag for the trip and perhaps get in the car. My nonagenarian great aunt, who worked in a church office, privately referred to the rectory as The Home for Unwed Fathers. She was also fond of saying that the difference between a terrorist and a liturgist is that you can negotiate with a terrorist.

If being Quaker were a sport, it should probably be golf.

They like to wear hats with brims and not a lot happens. Have you ever been to a Quaker meeting? I went once, and nobody said a thing for almost an hour. It was like sitting in the waiting room of an infectious disease clinic with everyone looking around thinking, "I wonder what she's got?" Yet, directly following the silent service was a garrulous social hour; go figure.

Remember the Shakers? They came from England and settled in New York State where they practiced communalism and celibacy, which sounds like an oxymoron, especially for those who remember Woodstock. If the Shakers were a sport, I think it would be cliff diving. I mean, celibacy just isn't a good business model for growing a religion. All that's left of them is a museum and some furniture best described as durable. The hard-backed chairs go a long way in explaining the apparent lack of sexual congress.

If being Jewish were a sport, it would definitely be cricket. There's a big book of confusing rules, such as Leviticus telling you to eat the pan-seared salmon but not the shrimp cocktail and that you can wear cotton but not Lycra. They have umpires whose full time job it is to study the rules all day long and argue about them. If you don't believe me, watch the movie *Yentl* or else the vegan version *Lentil*.

Buddhism would be badminton. Anyone can play. You wander off for a few years and then just as suddenly pick it up again. It doesn't matter if you know anyone else on the team. Wear whatever you have on. Watch the birdie. Whoosh. The Buddha taught mindfulness and meditation. However, his mom died shortly after he was born, so it's worth noting the Buddha never had anyone asking, "Is *that* what you're wearing?"

Evangelical Christianity could be fishing. They're pretty much waiting around for The Big One. Side note, it's very hard to run a successful church capital campaign if you're preaching that the world is about to end. It's, shall we say, counterintuitive to investing in infrastructure. Being evangelical might also qualify as beach volleyball, since if the ball bounces the wrong way, there's the potential for things to get extremely hot.

If Sufism, with its whirling dervishes and loose clothing, were a sport, it would probably be curling. No one knows what's happening or why. "He's sweeping the ice and pushing a cement tire across it with a hoe. And the crowd is going wild!"

Mormons would be a marching band. Everyone is pointing in the same direction, playing the same tune, chins up, smiling, good skin, rosy cheeks, and sporting crisp uniforms.

Jehovah's Witnesses look like a track and field team. They can't smoke or drink and wouldn't need time off from practice for holidays. Only it might be a problem when they divide into age groups since they don't celebrate birthdays. Long wait times between events could be used for recruitment.

The Wiccans clearly own Quidditch.

Rastafarianism would be Ultimate Frisbee. No referees—it's all about the spirit of the game, meeting in the park, being free to play any position. A boom box and some weed on the sidelines. Yeah man.

If being Amish were a competition, it would definitely be ice dancing—you're up early every day, working out in the cold, and it's an all-consuming lifestyle. We like to watch ice dancing on TV, but no one is running to sign up the next day like right after a marathon, or the way watching *The Fast and the Furious* makes everyone want to drag race.

Unitarian Universalists might be mountain climbers. Or perhaps the debate team. Who else has a "talk back" following the sermon where you can disagree with the minister, request references, and correct grammar? I love when people raise a hand and say, "My question has six parts." Maybe UUs are surfers—riding a wave and then getting dumped and pummeled. It's no coincidence that our favorite Bible verse is Genesis 13:9 where Abraham says to Lot, "If you go to the left, I'll go to the right; if you go to the right, I'll go to the left."

Despite all the UU's success fighting for social justice, our hippy-dippy reputation lends itself to plenty of good-natured (I hope) ribbing. If you're wondering what the difference is between a Subaru dealership and a UU church parking lot, that would be potholes. And if you want to know who the transvestites are in UU congregations, they're the ones wearing heels.

Some years ago, my minister, the Reverend Forrest Church, was asked for his upcoming sermon title so it could be printed in that Sunday's *New York Times*. A deadline daredevil, he gave the secretary a placeholder, "Trees I Have Known and Hugged," fully intending to replace it with the actual title the following day. He forgot and the newspaper of record announced to millions of readers that "Trees I Have Known and Hugged" would be the homily at the Unitarian Church of All Souls. Not a single person arrived at church wondering if there had been a mistake. And I'm fairly certain that people of other faiths who may have read the title likewise thought it was just another Sunday for the UUs.

I know my humor is outrageous when it makes the Unitarians
so mad they burn a question mark on my front lawn.

–Lenny Bruce

Chapter 14

Church of the Free Refill

Most religions are instantly recognizable by their art—a cross, six-pointed star, Buddhist wheel, Muslim crescent moon and star. When one hears Unitarian Universalist, I suppose a unicorn comes to mind, but our symbol is a flaming chalice. Yet whenever I order a cake for my UU Church and bring a picture of a flaming chalice, the baker always assumes we're ghostbusters, or else mounting an amateur production of *The Rocky Horror Picture Show*.

I was raised in the Unitarian Universalist Church of Amherst, which is a first ring suburb of Buffalo, where my mom was the assistant treasurer for a decade. A man named Ralph was our treasurer. It was the 1970s, and women were assistants. Putting women in charge was way too risky—one hormonal swing and they might blow the whole endowment on go-go boots, Jean Nate body splash, and Neil Diamond record albums. No, back then you only wanted to entrust women with the life and education of humans as mothers, nurses, and teachers. My mom didn't even have her own name on a credit card or the house deed. Heck, she didn't have her own middle initial anymore after getting married. She was Mrs. John A. Pedersen, and man oh man, did not having her name on the house deed (for which she made the down payment) ever come back to haunt her when Mr. John A. Pedersen filed for divorce.

Our church was a higgledy-piggledy edifice created by adding a chapel and a wing onto an old mansion with a carriage house. At a small church you do everything yourselves. If volunteering to serve coffee, you get up early, go to the store, *buy* the coffee and cream and sugar and napkins, *bring* it to church, *make* the coffee, put out all the mugs, spoons, and napkins, and then don an apron and *clean* the coffee pot and mugs and put everything away. When I first went to coffee hour at the Unitarian Church of All Souls in Manhattan, I couldn't wait to call my mom. "You won't believe it, someone gives you the coffee and tea and mugs, you stand there and pour it, and then just take off like a hit and run accident. It's insane!"

Similarly, being treasurer at our church didn't mean hiring bookkeepers and accountants. As assistant treasurer, my mom kept all the records. Ralph, God rest his soul, rode high in the saddle, steepled his fingers, and delivered reports. Mom typed the budget, tallied receivables, banked the money, reconciled statements, filed information returns with the government, and mailed out pledge cards and reminders. Starting at age five, that last part was my job—copying, folding, licking envelopes, stamping—this was before self-adhesive stamps and envelopes and meant incurring major tongue paper cuts.

Sometimes people at my Manhattan church say, "I have an idea, you could be on the board." Obviously they don't have any idea how many board meetings I sat through before I was legally able to drink. Hiring a babysitter was a luxury in recession-hammered Buffalo. I went along with Mom at an age when an hour felt like a year, and there were no iPads or video games. The grownups gave me a piece of string to play with, as if I were a cat.

My Protestant friends complained when they had to attend church twice a week. My Catholic friends whined because they had to go four times a week, though I'm not sure playing basketball and bingo and a spaghetti dinner count as church. With everything my parents were involved in plus youth group and church work parties most Saturdays, I was there five or six times a week. People thought we were so religious no one dared to curse around me. Hearing we were at church all the time caused other parents to hide the liquor when my family came over.

Then my parents divorced, and my mom went back to school to become a nurse, so it happened that at age ten, I became assistant to the assistant to the treasurer. What was in it for me? Times were tough, and if I wanted to belong to ski club, I had to be Uriah Heep and keep the church books for her. What did people think when they realized the treasurer was thirteen years old? They were delighted that I wasn't old enough to drive, and it was basically a hostage situation, so they also put me in charge of our auction. While my Catholic friends were having ashes applied to their foreheads, I was at the bank filling out forms so we could have our first credit card machine at the auction and used my library card as ID.

Since I've been a writer for several decades people are often surprised that I have a finance degree from New York University's Stern School of Business. But while the Baptist kids across the street were absorbing transfiguration and Paul's conversion on the road to Damascus, I was learning double-entry bookkeeping and how to file 501c3 forms for charitable organizations.

Accounting and business policy classes were not a problem after that.

Despite a general knowledge of business administration among UUs, the majority of our churches are on the brink of bankruptcy because all our money goes to stop sex trafficking and purchase fair trade coffee. As a result, we rent space to everyone and anyone. Usually it's for interdenominational weddings—the main aisle is wide enough that two families can sufficiently glare at each other without a scuffle. We're also in demand as a venue for funerals of people who long ago left their own church or temple, marriage of same-sex couples, and home-going ceremonies for beloved pets. Most UU churches rent space to preschools because we run on opposite sides of the clock and both favor the use of construction paper—protest signs for us and caterpillars for them. But if you want to throw a fiftieth birthday party for your parrot, we've got a hall. The church is busy every day and night of the week as we strive to keep the lights on. Recently a number of events were happening simultaneously—a community meeting, birthday party, Seder dinner, and several support groups. At least four people barged into the AA meeting with a bottle of champagne or Manischewitz and said, "Okay, let's get this party started!"

Nevertheless, we celebrate the two big Christian holidays along with hosting a Passover Seder. The Easter sermon tends to view the resurrection more through the lens of spring and battling greenhouse gasses. For Christmas we dance around scripture with a few qualifiers, for instance, "On this day it is widely conjectured that a Person of Interest going by The Virgin Mary gave birth to the infant Jesus, an alleged son of God who was visited by the proverbial Wise Men as attributed to Matthew in the creative nonfiction known as the Gospels and acquired under the Freedom of Information Act."

Church of the Free Refill

Church of the Free Refill

Unitarian Universalists are considered weak tea sisters to the Methodists, and the last step in organized religion before Ethical Culture or brunch. Although sometimes we're referred to as Noisy Quakers, since both groups are active in Washington promoting social justice and nuclear disarmament. Quakers and UUs both believe that The Kingdom can be realized here on Earth if we treat each other with respect, that the energy we put into war can be channeled into love, and that all our chains can come off; it's just that UUs add wine and cheese parties with a marimba band. Disorganized religion might be a better description for us, considering the internal dissent and propensity for over-sharing. But UUs have been ahead of the curve on every social justice movement from abolition to women's suffrage to tightening drunk driving laws, so it's a good place to be a humanist. The dress code is decidedly lax—wear a sweat suit or a three-piece suit, whatever speaks your truth.

Despite a coffee hour of signing petitions and letters to congresspeople, better known as cacophony hour, we manage to have our liberal fun. One minister had a Christian background and referred to the vestibule, or lobby, as the narthex. Whenever he was scheduled to preach, we'd organize a pool based on how many times the word "narthex" would appear in the service. Popular guesses were one and two, but zero or three could occasionally work. We'd record all the bets (winnings bound for the collection plate, of course) and begin counting. Whenever the word "narthex" was uttered there'd usually be a flutter on our side of the church and some people did start to wonder about it, including the minister. One Sunday we placed our bets and by the time the sermon was over not a single "narthex" had been heard so it appeared that the folk who chose "zero" were going to be the big winners. However, the worship assistant walked across the altar and whispered something to the minister. He returned to the microphone and said, "Information about Wednesday's Heart and Soul auction can be picked up in the narthex." It was the final word of the service. There was a collective gasp followed by muttering, "Did he say it?" Then a wave went across our side as everyone turned to the person in front or behind saying, "The Word–like a touchdown the final minute of the Super Bowl." You could go to church for another thirty years and never witness something like that again. It was truly historic, bordering on miraculous. This time the minister definitely noticed the brouhaha and following the service came over to us like the principal who knows something is up but lacks definitive proof. "Everything okay over here?" We confessed and told him about the decades-old Narthex pool. He thoughtfully stroked his chin. Instead of chastising us, he announced that next time he'd be joining the pool.

How do you tell if you might be a Unitarian Universalist? That's easy–if you feel no special event is really complete without a butterfly release to "We are a gentle, angry people and we are singing for our lives," accompanied by an Appalachian dulcimer while surrounded by patchouli meditation candles with accents of Canadian fir needle, Mysore sandalwood, and Aloha orchid.

UU HAIKU

Gratitude journal
filled with deep thoughts on life and
names of litterbugs.

Seasons of our lives,
naming, wedding, funeral.
Must choose Birkenstocks.

Church of the Free Refill

First snow of winter
Cold coffee, pamphlets blowing,
fewer protesters.

March on Washington.
Hand-painted signs with slogans.
Met some nice Quakers.

Prayers for those in need
seem to work that much better
when checks are attached.

Children grow and leave,
religion doesn't stick like
Jewish and Catholic.

The Goldman-Murphys
dressed in beads, robes, and sandals
back from Nepal trek.

Raised as a UU.
How to explain to school friends?
Thomas Jefferson.

Air-conditioning
is costly, but give money
and it's named for you.

UU funeral.
Deceased in best suit of clothes
with no place to go.

A Theory of Everything Else

Has everyone signed
my anti-nukes petition
to send to Congress?

What do you mean that
you didn't vote on Tuesday?
End of a friendship.

Holidays are here.
Card tables at coffee hour.
Buy Unicef cards.

No church in summer.
Vacations, sabbaticals.
Because God trusts us.

Not known for singing.
Too busy checking if we
agree with the words.

Coffee is UU
sacrament, so please join us.
Volunteers needed.

Gave all my money
to support MADD.
Now can't afford wine.

Living in a tree
confronting angry loggers.
Uh-oh! Lyme disease.

Church of the Free Refill

The child of my ex-
wife's son with her first husband
makes him what to me?

It's a holiday.
Martin, Abe, George, Christ, Cupid.
What about Susan?

Recycle body
by donating to science.
Tax deductible.

Five presidents and
over one hundred thousand
liberal arts majors.

MADD meets
in the same room as OA
right after AA.

Historic old church.
Flaming chalice/clog dancing.
Alert Fire Marshal.

Catholic Godparents
at Naming Ceremony.
Confused, overdressed.

Humanism, yes.
Transcendentalism, yes.
Armageddon, no.

Chipped ceramic mugs.
Rinse out after coffee hour.
No UU landfill.

What is the question
to which war is the answer?
Make bumper stickers.

No, you may not have
a BB gun to play with.
Parkland, Florida.

People like to say
"You can't stop war with folk songs,"
but we keep trying.

We can save the world
and bring peace among nations.
Start with a survey.

Success is the ability to move from failure
to failure without losing enthusiasm.
—often attributed to Abraham Lincoln

Chapter 15

Blue Collar Blues

"Dy-no-mite" and "Funkadelic," like "Stagflation" and "Collective Malaise," are words you don't often hear anymore. In the 1970s these meant persistent high inflation combined with high unemployment and stagnant demand. Another term for this is "flat broke." Anytime there was fifty dollars left after paying the rent and grocery bill, tough choices had to be made—repair the roof, replace bald tires on the car, or put it toward grandma's lifesaving operation. This led to a lot of day drinking, but because the days were so short, it didn't matter all that much. However, one great money-saver continues to be that when Buffalo sports teams reach the playoffs, police needn't grease sign poles since they're already covered with ice.

A non Jell-O dessert, such as cake and ice cream, was only for birthdays and special occasions, so it really felt like a treat. When guests joined us for a meal we borrowed extra chairs from church, and in the kitchen Mom whispered "FHB," which meant "Family

Hold Back" so the guests could have their fill. Without money for actual recreation, a popular pastime was seeing how many people could be crammed into a Volkswagen, so being underweight made you popular for that, while it could also help young men avoid being drafted for Vietnam. Mothers liked to say, "You won't die from wants and wishes." If that met with resistance, they followed up with, "There will be tears before bedtime."

Kids were generally shielded from despair by parents, but we could see the worried looks on weary faces. Whether a birthday was December 24th or in June, we were told that the present was for both occasions. Anyone who complained was reminded that the gifts brought to Jesus by the Three Wise Men were for his birthday and Christmas combined. Meantime, grownups were happy to tell us that "The best facelift is a smile" (because it was free). More than one kid in my class had lost a parent to suicide. There were so many jumpers that the Buffalo police carried cigarettes and a lighter even if they didn't smoke. Meantime, in nearby Niagara Falls, one family made its living off dragging suicides out of the river. The honeymoon brochures don't include the fact that twenty to forty people take their lives at the Falls every year. Add to that a 25 percent mortality rate for "daredevils," or "low IQ performance artists," as my mother calls them. Some psychiatrists say there's a hypnotic pull toward rushing water. Mom says that you may just need to use a restroom. Whereas many older people have a DNR in a file cabinet, my mom carries it in her purse.

When Buffalonians encounter one another in different parts of the country and even around the world, we appear to be part of a secret society, immediately launching into who we know and where we grew up. It usually takes only one school and a single large family name to produce dozens of friends in common, which could be considered unusual for an area with over a million inhabitants (including the surrounding suburbs). As a result, I'm regularly asked, "What is it with people from Buffalo? Why is it so special?" Why is someone a New York State resident based on tax returns but a Buffalonian by the grace of God? Why does a Buffalonian have more fun at a funeral than a San Franciscan does at a wedding?

Have you ever been through a group emergency—stuck in an airplane on a runway for six hours or in an office building during a storm? The hit Broadway musical *Come from Away* is about travelers stranded during the week following the 9/11 attacks after their planes had to land in Gander, Newfoundland, a town of eleven thousand inhabitants (when all the fishing boats are in for the night). A group of residents mobilized to care for seven thousand anxious and disoriented travelers. The show is a cathartic reminder of the capacity for human kindness in the face of adversity during a dark time, and the triumph of love over hate.

Buffalo lost half of its population between 1940 and 2010 while the poverty level sat at twice the national average. When I was growing up, it was a frigid vortex of entropy with a long soup season. Imagine a million people wrapped in heavy knitwear, trapped together in a permanently flatlined economy while suffering one newsworthy blizzard after another, which we tried not to take personally. My Catholic friends were taught that God the Father cared very much whether they lived or died, but apparently Mother Nature didn't, not one bit. Even the Keep on Truckin' mud flap crowd and Yosemite Sam conservatives were scouring the out-of-state want ads.

Most people didn't leave Buffalo because they were dissatisfied with the lifestyle or wanted more than their fair share. They were happy to remain in proximity to friends and family in "The City of Good Neighbors," with its extended ski season, terrific restaurants, cutting-edge music scene, aspirational sports teams, and a stop for all the big shows, concerts, and comedians. This propensity for pleasantness was confirmed when *Travel and Leisure* magazine ranked Buffalo as America's Friendliest City in 2017. In addition to major points for hospitality toward tourists, "neighborly love," manners, and politeness, locals were celebrated for their "warm dispositions," just like Irish setter puppies. But wet kisses weren't enough, and sky-high unemployment drove many of us in search of a living elsewhere. This was especially true for women, since they weren't deemed "breadwinners" and would never be considered first in line for a job at a time when that line already reached around the block.

The result was forced exile, which is unlike chasing your rainbow, but rather the difference between voluntary departure and being driven out by circumstances. European groups such as the Jews and the Irish also share a Diaspora mentality that complicates their relationship to what really is "home," a layered identity marked by suffering. Cue up "Danny Boy" and *Fiddler on the Roof.*

Another thing Buffalonians of a certain age have in common is the innate sense that *hot is good* and *cold is bad.* For instance, we'll put heat on any injury because that feels good to us. So do hot baths, hot showers, heated pools, and Jacuzzis. Likewise, electric blankets, heating pads, and heated seats. We prefer our soups and sandwiches hot and rarely pass up a flaming dessert. We like hot coffee, hot chocolate, chicken wings slathered with Frank's Red Hot Sauce, hot mustard, Weber's hot piccalilli relish, five-alarm chili, and hot roast beef on kimmelweck rolls. Given a choice between Heaven and Hell we'll go for the warm place. I don't think I ever heard the words, "It's too hot for a fire." In a Buffalo winter, we worried far more about Jesus' nudity than the blood pouring out of his hands and feet.

Providentially, conditions in Buffalo are much improved nowadays, including the weather, so don't send me letters saying I haven't been there recently—I wrote a book chronicling the start of the revival called *Buffalo Unbound* which is now considered positively prophetic. It transpired that our fortune was right in front of our faces the entire time in the form of exporting chicken wings around the globe. Over a decade ago I went so far as to designate Buffalo as a climate refuge and—tada!—real scientists have now designated it as the best place along with Duluth, Minnesota, to survive global warming. Western New York's "sources of energy production are stable, they have cooler climates and they have access to plenty of fresh water," according to climate adaptation expert Jesse Keenan. The area has attracted medical facilities and tech companies whose workers can enjoy a refurbished downtown along with a pulsating waterfront, a.k.a. The Buffalo Riviera. And while our story hasn't yet been made into a musical, yes, a secret society does indeed exist, and you can still purchase a Blizzard of '77 sweatshirt, board game, tote bag, or set of drinking glasses on eBay. Or you can become an official member by living there. Just be prepared to start your tomato plants in Dixie cups indoors and then replant them outside after Memorial Day.

I won't be impressed with technology
until I can download food.

–Unknown

Chapter 16

Speedy Delivery

Most things take less time than they did forty years ago. For instance, when I was growing up, if you wanted a photograph, it was a major investment of time which involved several planning stages. First of all, you had to locate your camera, since it was so much trouble to take pictures that we rarely used them. Or else you had to borrow one, since they weren't cheap. Next you had to purchase film (usually twelve pictures), and different cameras used different types of film. If you were going to be in anything except bright sunlight (a rare occasion in Buffalo), it was also necessary to purchase flash cubes, which usually had four flashes per cube. After putting in the film and advancing it and attaching the flash, you were ready to ask the group to pose and snap your photo, although more often than not the flash didn't go off, so it was necessary to try again. If the flash did go off, the subjects were blinded for several seconds as if they'd just stared directly into an eclipse. So now you had a photo, right? Ha, far from it! It was necessary to finish the role of film, because film was expensive, so you might wait several months or a year for a birthday party or wedding. Once all the pictures were taken, you brought the film to a small hut in the local plaza and in return they gave you a paper stub, like a dry cleaning ticket, and said to return in a week or so depending on how busy things were, since they in turn sent the film somewhere else for "processing."

No one dared take any pictures that weren't squeaky clean because the people developing the photos were going to see them, along with the person who worked in the booth and went to high school with your brother. Next, if you even remembered the photos had been dropped, and you could find the little paper stub, you picked up the envelope. It was with great anticipation we opened our prize, oftentimes a year in the making, only to reveal four photos that were indecipherable due to under- or overexposure, four blurry ones, two where most eyes were closed (in anticipation of the blinding flash), and two where most subjects had red eyes like startled guinea pigs or angry demons. So if you're young and see old framed photos in your grandparents' house, you now know why they're framed like prized possessions and will never be taken down or replaced. Just getting a single picture was a one in a million shot.

What orange polyester was to the 1970s, home delivery is to the 2020s. In Manhattan, large trucks bleep and belch smoke while backing up in front of my building from morning until night, seven days a week, sometimes to drop off a single pack of razor blades hermetically sealed in cardboard and plastic, then bubble wrapped and taped into a large brown box cushioned by Styrofoam popcorn. It's possible to receive books, pills, groceries, cigarettes, cosmetics, electronics, pets, plants, drugs, Spanx, gyroscopes, blowup dolls, and basically any product that exists.

You can push a button and have a single can of cat food or a dozen cars delivered.

The real question here is: How were my parents tricked into going to stores? Because back in my grandparents' day, they called the local grocer and a delivery boy on a bicycle brought the goods over in a box. This was oftentimes my dad, who attached crates to the front and back of his Schwinn bicycle. Similarly, my grandmother put her empty milk bottles out front, and they were replaced with fresh ones early in the morning. There were regular stops by the coal man and the ice man, which is why my dad was still calling the basement a "cellar" and the freezer an "icebox" fifty years down the track. UPS delivered everything from toys and underwear to appliances and furniture selected from the Sears and J.C. Penney catalogues. Better yet, Sears would deliver a mail-order home that you could build yourself or hire a contractor to assemble. If someone was sick, a doctor came by the house with his magic black bag of remedies, or else the drugstore sent over whatever he (and it was always a he) prescribed.

The *Courier-Express* landed on our doorstep each morning and the *Buffalo Evening News* in the afternoon courtesy of a local newspaper boy, and the mail arrived by human carrier six days a week. Every spring C.J. Krantz delivered a load of topsoil for the garden. It was deposited at the side of the driveway and had to be moved to the backyard using a rusty wheelbarrow. This job fell to me and was another reason everyone in the neighborhood wondered why my parents hadn't "gone for a boy." Any person with grass and trash knew that boys were a necessity for yard work and waste removal. Thus, I was the only singleton female child some people had ever seen and a bit of a local curiosity.

On weekends marauding gangs of teens sold Freddie's Doughnuts door-to-door in order to raise money for their sports teams, cheerleader squads, or class trips. They were the only ones who used the front door aside from the Jehovah's Witnesses, so it was necessary to peek out a window before answering and make sure you were going to get fresh glazed donuts and not pamphlets about the dangers of Satan.

When it comes to inventions, electronics, and gadgets, I'm what could be called a late adopter. Let's start with the fact that a number of innovations from when I was a kid turned out to be deadly—Agent Orange, asbestos, DDT, thalidomide, Red Dye #2 and the Ford Pinto come quickly to mind. Then there are the items that were just plain stupid such as pet rocks, spray shampoo, car alarms, fake dogs on a leash, and New Coke. Now factor in that all my money from age ten through forty went toward upgrading my music collection from vinyl 45s and LPs, to 8-track tapes, to cassette tapes, to CDs, and then to streaming music. Still, this doesn't take into account wasted time. I spent hours entering addresses into machines that promptly died (often upon falling into the bathtub). It took an entire Saturday to create a Myspace profile, and by Monday morning everyone had switched to Facebook. So now I want to know that something is going to be around for at least a decade before getting involved, even better if it's waterproof, although I still believe some old-fashioned items are best, such as photo albums, clock radios, toaster ovens, and handmade clothes brushes.

Nevertheless, I think we've officially gone overboard. Lion Air flight 610 crashed because the high-tech anti-stall system on the Boeing 737 Max kept forcing the plane down in reaction to incorrect flight data while the pilots desperately fought to right it. Unfortunately, the humans lost out to the Maneuvering Characteristics Augmentation System (MCAS), and 189 lives were lost. Not long afterward, another Boeing 737 Max crashed because the software was too complicated. This made me think of my brand new $4,000 shiny white Miele state-of-the-art stackable washer and dryer, which I'd very much like to launch into space, since it's so complicated that no one can work it. The dashboard looks like what I envision one finds inside a robotic minesweeper. I'm now on a first name basis with the repairman, Tim, whom the dogs love because he sits on the floor with them and finds lost plush toys behind the dryer and bones underneath the washer. Tim checks to see if the problem is with the machines or the idiots attempting to use them by connecting his computer to the façade of the washer and dryer with a cable that appears to have a stethoscope on one end. He monitors their vital signs on his flashing screens as they perform various feats and it looks like an appliance emergency room. Tim comes by regularly to give washer/dryer tutorials while everyone just stares in disbelief and says, "You've got to be kidding." There are three steps one must take before even starting to program for a load of laundry, just to deactivate all the systems you *won't* be using, such as the automatic detergent pump. I ask, "What if I'm out of the country and house guests arrive and want to throw in a load of wash?" He proceeds to (once again) go through the litany of directions I must explain to the guests before they can wash their T-shirts and jeans. I say, "Tim, I'm not here, I'm in another time zone, asleep." Tim is stumped.

Then the eighty-two-year-old in the house asks, "What if an eighty-two-year-old wants to use it?" Tim is silent because he knows that not even a seventy-two-year-old has any chance of working this Batmachine and will be lucky not to be swallowed up alive by it. I have an idea for appliance manufacturers: offer a "classic model" like the ones we had in the 1970s, with one big red button to start each machine, where the babysitter or even a burglar could walk in off the street and successfully wash and dry their clothes. So I've officially reverted to the Stone Age; it's just easier and less complicated to hand wash my clothes in the sink next to the $4,000 appliances and hang them up to dry. I do hope there's some irony in the fact that scientists are working hard to colonize the moon while I can't get a clothes dryer to work down here on Earth.

More recently, I was alarmed when a set of household machines cut me out of the loop entirely. My husband installed Amazon's Alexa in the bedroom and demonstrated all the wonderful things it can do. Call me when Alexa can walk, feed, bathe, and pill all these dogs. But she was small and kept out of my way so I forgot about her. That is until she started listening to the nearby television, where it transpires she can hear her name even in the *off* position. Suddenly, she starts playing sea shanties and trying to order takeout Korean barbecue. Around the same time, I read in the newspaper that Alexa is recording people and has been busy partnering with the local police in solving murders. Next my Samsung smartphone, which is by far smarter than I, also began communicating with the television, which appears to have become the star athlete of devices around here, with all the lesser contraptions competing for its attention. When I went to make a phone call, instead of the normal home screen I was faced with what appeared to be a television remote control. Only I already have a TV remote–actually I have four TV remotes–and the last thing I need is another one. Then I saw on a TV news program that your smartphone watches what you watch. So do my dogs, but they don't care, unless it's tennis, in which case every time the ball bounces off screen the Frenchie runs into the next room thinking he'll find it there. I tried to make the new screen go away, and it refused.

What did Alexa have to say about all this? She laughed, and

it wasn't a normal ha-ha laugh, but a decidedly eerie one. Finally, I went to the phone store where a young person attempted to make the TV remote on the home screen of my phone disappear but also failed. He informed me that because my TV was also a Samsung, this behind-the-scenes communication couldn't be avoided. So now I've entered into one of the scary sci-fi movies I used to watch as a kid. The phone and the television are plotting against me, and Alexa may be my only hope of recording what actually goes down so blame doesn't land on the dogs.

Granted, with any new technology there's a right way and a wrong way to use it. Fire comes to mind—cook food *or* burn down a forest. Automobiles—get people to a hospital quickly *or* drag race. Nuclear fission—cheap power *or* obliterate humanity. Facebook—stay in touch with your friends *or* rig elections and destroy democracy. Twitter—allow nonbinary kids to communicate with others experiencing similar challenges *or* help neo-Nazis organize a rally. Obviously, it's necessary to impose humanity on technology. Meantime, in New York City, which is famous for cramped apartments with paper-thin walls, and neighbors are privy to every argument, crying baby, and tuba recital, people can now take advantage of ordering from Amazon on the Alexa next door. Just be sure to intercept your packages.

Up through the 1990s, before the world became "wired," going on vacation was like visiting another galaxy since you had no contact with your friends and neighbors while away, aside from mailing postcards which arrived ten days after your return. Before leaving, we stopped the newspapers for the week so they wouldn't pile up out front and alert burglars to our absence. We asked a neighbor to take in the mail so any checks wouldn't be stolen and hired a kid to water the plants and feed the pets. Still, shit happened. People returned after a week of being devoured by mosquitoes in the Adirondacks and their entire house had burned down or beloved Fido was dead and Lucky was missing. Neighbors had babies and new cars while others had moved away and left no forwarding address. Your own backyard, including a swing set, was swallowed up by a giant sinkhole, but no one had been able to reach you. Worst of all, a new cement sidewalk had been installed, and every kid but you had carved their initials and made handprints that would last for two decades directly in front of *your* house.

This was before you could see pictures and videos of any-place in the world on the Internet, so people took photographs and made them into slides to show the neighbors. A stained white sheet was hung in the living room while everyone was given their fill of Sangria and Brandy Alexanders along with meatballs slathered in grape jelly, Lipton onion soup dip on Ritz crackers, and celery stuffed with cream cheese and sliced cherry tomatoes. Then came seven hundred shots of blurry squirrels in the Grand Canyon and washed out sunsets at Gettysburg. This resulted in rampant alcoholism.

In the 1970s, my friend's grandmother insisted that the door-bell was spying on her. The family decided she was getting senile and widely curtailed her independence. In hindsight, she now appears prophetic.

One of the great joys of living in a city used to be browsing in secondhand bookshops, which was second only to not having to cook. For twenty years I kept a list of books I wanted that had gone out of print. I wasn't searching for particular editions or signed copies, just any old version with dog-eared pages, pen marks, or warped pages from being dropped in the bathtub. On my wish list was everything from obscure volumes of poetry and long forgotten "coffee table" art books, to translations of foreign novels and biographies of robber barons. One by one, I checked off books as I discovered them in dusty corners, to my extreme delight, and added new ones as they were referenced in other things that I read. Then in the late 1990s, a sales clerk at my nearby bookstore told me that Ernest Hemingway's *A Moveable Feast* was out of print and suggested I look for it on a computer. I did, and in the space of about thirty minutes, I'd ordered every book on my list, a few of which I didn't even want anymore, but it seemed so amazing that I could have them by pressing a button, I bought them anyway.

At first there was a tremendous sense of excitement and accomplishment, like in the book (and marvelous movie version) *84, Charing Cross Road*, where a Manhattan reader discovers she can fulfill her dream list of obscure classics through an antiquarian book dealer in London in the mid-twentieth century. However, this was quickly followed by a sinking feeling of disappointment and loss. The greatest treasure hunt of my life had abruptly and unexpectedly come to a halt, along with the thrill of entering secondhand bookshops famous for their overstuffed, musty aisles and cranky proprietors (one wondered if they truly desired to sell a single volume), never knowing what lurked on the shelves just waiting to be discovered, rescued, and given a good home.

My mom is a big reader, basically a book a day, so I happily reported this new book-finding technology. Mom has her master's degree in geriatrics and informed me that recent studies said scavenger hunts were found to be the number one activity used in assisted living facilities to help residents maintain their mental and physical agility. So now we can easily locate all these books which supposedly make us smarter, but we're actually losing ground since we no longer need to search for them. There has to be a book in that.

I grew up in a very large family in a very small house.
I never slept alone until after I was married.

−Lewis Grizzard

Chapter 17

Hurly-Burly

Growing up before computers, Internet, cell phones, video games, and laser tag, my main source of entertainment was my friend Mary's large and adventurous family. Entering the five-bedroom house—which held eleven people, two dogs, and a cat—was like boarding a pirate ship. Despite never having had a lesson, they invented Riverdancing in the upstairs hallway. Every weekday morning starting at five o'clock, a line would form to use the bathroom. Eventually the sound of running water would cause those waiting outside to start hopping up and down. If someone remained in the shower more than their allotted three minutes, one of her brothers went downstairs and switched off the hot water until he heard shrieking.

Whereas most older siblings don't want to hang around younger ones, Mary's brothers and sisters were happy to let us join the fun since more often than not we *were* the fun. If they weren't tricking us into waiting for the school bus at seven thirty in a blizzard after school had been canceled, they liked to sit on the paper box with one of us inside, or encourage us to fly off the roof holding an umbrella. It was excellent training in creative fiction since we had to explain our bumps and bruises to our mothers without implicating anyone; kids operated under the mob credo that "snitches get stitches."

When Mary's older brother David returned from several years in the Army, he remarked to us that their parents looked old. I'm still not sure if that was just an observation about the passing of time or he believed we had a direct hand in their premature aging, because Mary's brothers and sisters were more than intrepid; they were downright inspired. When Barbara continued using Melinda's shampoo (while insisting that she wasn't), Melinda replaced the shampoo with Wesson oil.

Meantime, Mary's brothers were capable of rerouting trains by altering the switch at the edge of our neighborhood. They also created an innovative system for ice fishing with M-80s, but it was abandoned before devastating the fish or human population. Too bad, since fishing and fireworks just feel like they belong together. As that master of the miraculous, Pope John Paul II, who survived not one but two assassination attempts, said, "Stupidity is also a gift of God, but one mustn't misuse it."

Most famously, Mary's brothers played Robin Hood every June by providing the neighborhood kids with ice cream sandwiches on the first warm day of summer. These came compliments of our local public school; therefore, it wasn't stealing since our parents paid the taxes which supported the institution. In the center of the building was a glass-enclosed atrium, and because it was surrounded on all four sides by brick walls, there wasn't any need to lock the glass doors leading outside—you could only pass through them if already inside the building. At least that was true unless you used the outdoor athletic equipment lockers next to the gymnasium to hoist yourself onto the rooftop, climb across, drop into the atrium, enter the school, and then leave through a back door that only locked from the outside (so it wasn't a fire hazard). However, before exiting, they'd breeze through the kitchen to pick up a few dozen ice cream sandwiches. And that marked the official start of summer.

As it happened, one day I returned late from a field trip to Toronto where my class had visited the Ontario Science Centre. After being delayed several hours on the way home due to an accident on the Queen Elizabeth Way, we arrived back tired, hungry, and locked out of the school. Not only did we need our books and homework assignments, but this was before cell phones, and it was necessary to call our parents so they could come fetch us. In those days the school was in the middle of nowhere, or Upper Rubber Boot as some teachers called it, while we students preferred Moose Crotch. My science teacher was a delightful, kind man who let us kids call him by his first name, joke around, and was a dad himself. I went over and whispered, "I know how to get into the school." We went around back to the storage lockers, he boosted me up, and I crawled across the roof like a cat burglar, dropped down into the atrium, walked through the dimly lit school, and opened the front door. I can't say that it helped my grade any, but he was definitely impressed. "I'm not going to ask how you know about this," he said with a wink. "I can get everyone ice cream if you want," I replied.

The education system changed drastically between the 1940s and the 1970s. My parents both went through the New York State public school system from age five through eighteen, just as I would three decades later. However, they never employed a pronoun incorrectly or ended a sentence with a preposition, they used "who" and "whom" properly, knew where Europe could be found on a map, understood that South Africa was a country and not a continent, and had full knowledge of how local and federal government worked thanks to civics class. Those were all necessary for graduation, just as I had to perform a trampoline routine in order to receive my diploma. Based on the current crop of low-information voters, one has to wonder if there was a conspiracy along the way, most likely a result of the Vietnam War and simultaneous youthquake, to remove young people from the political process by dumbing them down with regard to how government operates. Nowadays, it seems like we only find out where a country is located after it experiences a horrendous natural disaster or some kids explore a cave and forget to bring snorkels. Then there was my tour of George Washington's Mount Vernon, during which several planes flew overhead at a low altitude, and one young person asked the guide why our first president had built his plantation so close to the airport.

My suspicions were confirmed when a group of Rhode Island students recently filed a class action suit alleging that their state provided such a substandard civics education that it violated their constitutional rights to be capable voters and jurors. Indeed, studies show that nationwide students have a 23 percent proficiency in the workings of government, which is slightly lower than the number of Nirvana fans who think Kurt Cobain is still alive.

I was even more encouraged that civics hasn't been left for dead after overhearing a conversation between two eight-year-olds:

Boy to Girl: Shut up!
Girl to Boy: I can talk as much as I want—it's a free country.
Boy to Girl: If it was a free country you'd be dead.

Hurly-Burly

In the final analysis, the joke is on the department of education. The Trump administration has been the best civics lesson in the history of our democracy, and now gas station attendants, assistant wrestling coaches, and Ayurveda yoga instructors are fully conversant in political terms such as the 25th Amendment, gerrymandering, emoluments, judicial activism, suborning perjury, and unhinged. Furthermore, Donald Trump saved urbanites a fortune in gym memberships, as they became extremely active painting signs and marching every weekend.

Adventure is worthwhile in itself.
−Amelia Earhart

Chapter 18

Tips for Rebel Girls

During the summer months—or, since it was Buffalo, I should say "month" —Mary and I would pitch a canvas tent in my backyard. Our parents thought it was cute that we liked going "backyard camping" well into our teens. What they didn't realize was that sneaking in and out of a tent after midnight was much easier than sneaking into our respective homes, especially with the cow bells on my front door, which necessitated storing a ladder in the bushes beneath my bedroom window. This ladder did not go unnoticed by my mother, Eagle Eye Ellen, but I told her it was for fire safety without explaining how, in the event of a fire, I was planning to lean ten feet out my window in order to hoist the ladder up and then climb back down to safety. At Mary's house we faced a long, squeaky staircase, and even if we circumvented that by climbing atop the low-slung enclosed porch up to the second story roof and in through a window, she shared the room with two older sisters who were robust blackmailers: i.e. I'll keep your secret if you make my bed for a month.

Despite not having much disposable income aside from a little babysitting money, we always found fun things to do which did not involve adult supervision. In those days there were Catholic Churches and bars on every corner, and most of us were aware that while Southern Baptists and Methodists abstained from alcohol, booze was part and parcel of the Catholic faith. (Not to name names, but another popular faith was commonly referred to as Whiskopalian and worshipped at the Church of the Very Well Dressed.) Many of our young male friends volunteered as altar boys and freely admitted they were just in it for the sacramental wine. It transpired that the clergy left the wine to the novices and preferred more intoxicating spirits. Indeed, the route from St. Leo's rectory on Sweet Home Road to the Scotch 'n Sirloin restaurant and lounge on Maple Road was well-traveled, and I'd go so far as to say that several priests' cars knew the way even before GPS. A fun craft project for us was to create JUST MARRIED signs with magic markers and flowers made from tissues and affix them to whatever end of the priests' cars faced the curb so the placards couldn't be spotted prior to driving off. There was also a van for transporting housebound and elderly parishioners to and from church which was enjoyable to decorate with signs saying PRISON TRANSFER.

I often feel sorry for later generations of youth with their high rate of accountability. A cell phone is like a parole ankle bracelet or perhaps a security chip implanted in your shoulder. Parents know where kids are and presumably what they're doing. If you don't acknowledge the calls or texts, they want to know why or assume the worst. There's no more being off the grid, which was where we had our most memorable times. Meantime, caller ID has completely ruined the art of the prank phone call, and no more lonely homebodies will experience the thrill of winning thousands of dollars or a new refrigerator on our fake quiz shows, even if the money and appliances never arrived. Worst of all, you can't tell someone that you've been trying to get in touch with them for weeks but they must not have been home, even though you didn't call once. The phone was a regular throw of the dice back then—it could be your best friend or it could be a lady from church asking you to bake a hundred snickerdoodles for an interfaith fair with a Faster Pastor car race and Christmakkuh Dunking Booth.

When the phone rang, it was like a volleyball game with everyone shouting, "I'll get it." A frisson of excitement raced through the household—it could be *anyone*, you had no way of knowing. "Who is it?" When was the last time you heard that? And if you were mad you could say, "The next sound you're going to hear is plastic hitting plastic," and slam down the phone. Although sometimes we wouldn't get a call for days. If my parents were the type to be conscious of social status, they would have been nervous they'd committed a horrendous faux pas, but in fact were so indifferent to the opinions of neighbors that our outside Christmas lights remained up well into August. No calls for a long stretch usually indicated that the cat had knocked the receiver off the white Princess phone on my mother's night table, which was hidden under a pile of paperback mysteries from the library. Interrupting phone service was one of the cat's favorite tricks, along with scooping an unsuspecting guppy out of the fish tank, coughing up a hairball on my pillow, and depositing live chipmunks in the laundry basket, as apparently he loved mysteries, too.

I'm not even sure why kids need cell phones nowadays when every sport has its own assemblage of safety equipment and playgrounds are built atop rubber mats. If parents sent a child off to a pre-1980s playground today they'd be arrested for reckless endangerment. Every single piece of equipment was a deathtrap, starting with steel slides and metal monkey bars that had been baking in the hot sun and were set upon dirt packed so hard it felt no different than landing on concrete. My friend Shannon broke one arm and sprained the other when a Japanese dismount went wrong and had to walk home before going to the hospital. Then there was the weather-beaten, wooden teeter-totter that left toothpick-sized splinters in your butt. And the Cape Canaveral merry-go-round, where the strong gleefully launched the weak into space like projectiles destined to crash land.

Still, it wasn't as if parents were completely absent from our lives. When boys wanted to date Mary's older sisters, they first had to go inside the house and meet her father Eugene. And I don't mean shake hands and say "Hello," but an actual sit-down cross-examination as if the young man were applying for top secret security clearance at the White House. Eugene was a detective with the Drug Enforcement Agency and not to be trifled with. As the youngest children in the brood, we were careful to stay way under his radar, which was easy because he was six foot eight and hard of hearing after operating radar during WWII bombing raids. Nicknamed "Huge Euge" by us kids, Mary's dad was so large that initially he'd been turned down for military service because they didn't have any clothes, boots, or cots large enough for him. He went anyway, ordering his clothing from a store in Philadelphia that custom made officers' uniforms, and building his own bed. It wasn't a good idea to complain about going to bed around him unless you wanted to hear how he had built his own bed and maybe we'd enjoy doing the same or else sleeping on the floor.

As potential dates pulled into the driveway at Mary's house, her father noted their license plate number. He claimed it was in case there was an accident. We assumed he was going to run the plates through the system at work the next day, checking for priors and DUIs. He shook hands with the young man at the door, not hiding his scowl upon seeing long hair (anything that wasn't a brush cut) and the two sat down facing each other in the living room, at which point Mary's father took out his badge and placed it face up on the coffee table. That was our cue to leave, but I assume they had a delightful chat and became best of friends. However, in the hopes of making a favorable impression, one ambitious suitor had told Mary's sister that he worked for the FBI, even though he didn't. That ended badly.

I only mention this bygone ritual because, with the advent of the #MeToo movement, I'm sensing that we may have come full circle, and instead of finding a guy online and meeting at a bar or apartment, potential dates might soon be heading back to living rooms around the country to squirm through uncomfortable interviews with ill-tempered fathers asking about "intentions" and leveling threats, slightly veiled or otherwise. Plus, I hear that you can now purchase real badges and polygraph machines on eBay to set up a high-quality home interrogation station.

There was indeed a certain amount of vigilante justice surrounding sexual harassment when I was growing up. If a girl arrived home from a fraught date, there were no 911 calls or parental summits. Whatever the hour might be, some combination of her brothers, brothers-in-law, and male cousins immediately tossed baseball bats into the trunk and drove over to the gentlemen caller's place to discuss the matter in person. There weren't any repeat offenders, at least not in her case.

Old people are often asked what thing they are most proud of. Sometimes it's military service, the achievements of a child, or housetraining a Yorkie. I'm most proud of not having used a plastic straw in over four decades and protecting the environment from that calamity. However, my motives back in 1978 weren't exactly driven by too much landfill and saving our oceans. When Mary and I would sneak into bars, she instructed me never to use a straw, even with club soda, because it makes you look thirteen years old, which in fact we were. So I've never used a straw. Now it's almost a half century later, and getting off the straws is an environmental priority right up there with dumpster diving for meals and banning plastic bags. It's a fantastic feeling when life catches up with you.

Give strong drink unto him that is ready to perish,
and wine unto those that be of heavy hearts.

—Proverbs 31:6 (NIV)

Chapter 19

Omnibibulous

Within the last decade Buffalo miraculously shot from every list of Worst Cities to almost every list of Best Cities in which to live. Not that hometown pride wavered for even a second during the six-decade slump, but it's nice when the rest of the world finally appreciates your value; when they don't just come for the skiing and stay because they can't find their cars. Nevertheless, Buffalo is now number sixteen on the list of America's Drunkest Cities. Though I prefer to think we're intoxicated by success.

Buffalo is no stranger to cocktail culture. There's a thriving craft beer, wine, and specialty cocktail business that crosses age and socioeconomic lines. As students, we knew how to spell words like "foreigner" because of Professor Irwin Corey's rule, "Remember, 'I' before 'E' except in Budweiser." Sociologists immediately point to the blue-collar roots, a plethora of colleges, low cost of living, cold winters, and let's just say you wouldn't want hockey season to be any longer. Go Sabres! During Prohibition, the city enjoyed the benefit of being a short rowboat ride across the Niagara River to Canada. The majority Catholic population also had the foresight to make wine a sacrament and an obligatory part of most church rituals, thereby skirting the alcohol ban.

Additionally, Western New York has a large Irish population. During the Potato Famine, the inhabitants of Ireland gathered round their maps to find a place overcast more than fifty percent of the year with bars and churches on every corner and a super-short growing season. Buffalo! As a result, everyone in Western New York knows there are two types of rehab (aside from rich people's and poor people's). One only takes you if you're sober, and so it's necessary to dry out before evaluation and check-in. Oddly, the other kind only admits you if you're drunk.

Recently, a good friend finally landed her brother a spot in the drunk rehab and poured him into the waiting room, but there was a problem with transferring his hospital paperwork. Admittance was delayed, so he began sobering up. Since it was Sunday morning the liquor stores were closed, and so it became necessary to summon friends to bring over whatever booze was on hand. Then she had the delightful task of re-inebriating him in order to maintain his eligibility. He was a big-boned fellow with a high tolerance, so quite a few volunteers were pressed into service. Fortunately, the admissions glitch was finally sorted out just before it became necessary to go door-to-door in the neighborhood with a plastic cup in hand.

I don't drink alcohol. For the past several generations, the family has been too close to the grape, as Aunt Sue likes to say, and occasionally engaged in an ambivalent relationship with orderly living. It was noted about one gone-but-not-forgotten member of the family, "Never walk a mile in his shoes or you'll end up lost, incoherent, and searching for your shoes." That said, my grandfather Watson was in downtown Buffalo one busy Saturday night when it was burgeoning with shoppers. While a mother stopped to look in a window, her three-year-old daughter strayed into the street. Running north at top speed was a Grant Street trolley. A dozen sober onlookers saw the child standing directly in front of the lead car, motionless and terror-stricken, in the middle of the track. There was a clanging of the bell followed by a screeching of brakes, but the car barreled directly toward the small child. Grandpa Watson dropped the chess set under his arm and dashed into the street, sweeping up the child as he ran. He leaped to clear the track but the car struck his shoulder, spinning him around and tossing him out of its path. The child was unharmed, her dress unspotted and as white as the motorman's face, who brought the trolley to a stop and ran back to the scene. By that time over a hundred locals had gathered around to see what all the excitement was about. A frantic mother clutched the child in her arms. "How can I ever thank you?" she asked as onlookers lined up to shake the rescuer's hand.

"Forget it," Grandpa said and gathered up his chessmen. He refused to give his name to the motorman and headed north on Grant Street. He'd be the first to tell you that a few cocktails help prevent one from overthinking important decisions, and a few more cocktails help one forget about any shoulder pain.

I'm not coming down on one side or the other with regard to alcohol. After all, Douglas Adams thought up his bestselling *Hitchhiker's Guide to the Galaxy* while lying drunk in a field, Jackson Pollack turned dipsomania into an art form, and Charlie Parker once vomited onto his microphone during a live performance. In 1968 the rock band Iron Butterfly released their first album, *Heavy*, but it floundered, and drummer Ron Bushy was supporting them by making pizza. Ron returned from work one night to find primary composer Doug Ingle sloppy drunk after consuming an entire bottle of Red Mountain wine so that when he played his new song "In the Garden of Eden" it came out "In-A-Gadda-Da-Vida." The rechristened seventeen-minute song and eponymous album *In-A-Gadda-Da-Vida* went on to sell over 30 million copies, earning enough money for Ron Bush to quit his pizza-making job.

However, in Buffalo it's not just the people who love a good party. Come autumn, birds have been known to overdo it on fermented berries and crash into car windshields and buildings. In fact, cedar waxwings have a reputation for excessive revelry right up there with Buffalo Bills fans. When driving toward Letchworth State Park, a.k.a. "the Grand Canyon of the East," to enjoy fall foliage, you may think you've entered the video game *Angry Birds*. A farmer friend picked up what he believed was a dead owl lying next to the driveway. However, its eyelids weren't closed so much as droopy, and it transpired that after a wild night of crabapple-tinis, he just needed to sleep off a mighty hangover. My friend lined a box with a towel, placed Mr. Owl inside, and softly played "Gravity of the Situation" by Hootie and the Blowfish. Had my friend been a Catholic instead of a Quaker, he could have claimed bringing the bird back to life as a first miracle on the road to sainthood.

I can't speak for birds, but certainly the best thing about being Irish Catholic is that you can be late and inebriated for every occasion throughout your entire adult life, yet the moment you're gone, they immediately elevate you to sainthood, and all the good stories you provided will be appreciated for generations to come.

*The most remarkable thing about my mother is that
for thirty years she served the family nothing but leftovers.
The original meal has never been found.*

—Calvin Trillin

Chapter 20

Come Hell or High Heels

As many moms do, mine adores telling the story of the day I was born. People like to say that a story belongs to the person who tells it best, but she rather owns this one since my dad was off chain-smoking somewhere. Mom is a little less clear on why she had her tubes tied five minutes after my birth, especially since in 1965 Buffalo, if your first child was a girl, it was just assumed that you'd keep trying for a boy. The highlights of the tale of my birth include one of the worst thunderstorms in Buffalo history and a head of hair that required the first blow dryer in a maternity wing. Truth be told, everyone in my family could have fronted a 1980s hair band. Mom always concludes by saying that she never had hemorrhoids before my birth, and she'd been a solid sleeper right up until the day before I arrived.

I only knew Mom as an ill-tempered light sleeper. She used

various sound machines on high volume, or else Mary and I would never have been able to sneak in and out of the house. On the flip side, rather than sleep, Dad and I went into more of a hibernation mode, eventually waking up starved, searching for a calendar to check the date and asking who was president.

This innate capacity to self-anesthetize never failed to irritate Mom, who would appear at the breakfast table in a bathrobe, haggard with dark circles under her eyes, and complaining, "That electrical storm last night was one for the record books." Dad and I were dressed, ready for work and school, and just looked at each other with the same puzzled expression. Storm? No, she must be mistaken. Perhaps it was the TV. "You didn't hear it?" she crowed with disbelief. We stuck with our story—we really didn't believe there'd been a storm. Then she pointed out the window at a telephone pole lying in the road and tree limbs scattered across the yard.

It was the same when we went on vacation. Somehow we always stayed near a busy railroad track. Well, that's not exactly a mystery when you consider we only ever went to Long Island to visit my grandfather, and the place is a long, narrow sandbar with trains constantly running from end to end. Once again, Dad and I were in our bathing suits and ready for the beach every morning when Mom dragged herself to the breakfast table and said, "I think a train must have gone through the backyard once every half hour. How could anyone sleep a wink?" Dad and I hadn't heard any trains. Nor did we hear alarm clocks, ringing phones, sirens, barking dogs, or people shouting directly into our faces while slumbering. It was before smoke alarms, so I guess we should have been more appreciative of the fact that Mom most likely would have saved us in a fire. However, she despised us for our rested selves and rosy glow, and I suppose

A Theory of Everything Else

she could have murdered us in our sleep if she'd had a mind to, as we certainly wouldn't have known about it.

Mom spent many years working in rehab centers and mental hospitals. It could be awkward when schoolmates went to visit their relatives in the psych ward, and there was my mom. "I saw your friend Betsy today!" she'd announce at dinner. When I visited Mom at work, I noticed they had plenty of crafts but no sports. I assumed that they didn't want people with mental issues to have bats and racquets, but Mom said it was more about people not being allowed shoelaces to hang themselves and so they couldn't wear sneakers.

Mom ran the household budget, and because food prices were rising by the hour we weren't allowed to waste anything. We ate leftovers of our leftovers and then put those leftovers into a Crock-Pot for a miscellaneous mélange, the recession version of that hobo camp staple, Mulligan stew. When I pointed out the *actual mold* growing on a certain food item, Mom replied that mold is good for you—it's how they make penicillin. Regarding the dented cans we purchased for half price and the chicken a week past its sell-by date I asked, "What about botulism and salmonella?" She scoffed, saying cooking in the oven at 350 degrees or boiling on the stove would kill all the deadly bacteria. What was I so worried about?

Mom has been retired from nursing for over two decades, but she is still considered a potent force in public health—just try lighting a cigarette in front of a school. She picks up hastily abandoned dog poop using a Kleenex tucked in her sleeve, follows the owner home, dumps the poop on their lawn, and triumphantly proclaims, "You dropped something." I've also been told that people hide all their medication before she arrives to avoid certain lines of inquiry and advice. Sort of like teachers

130

who go around correcting grammar for the rest of their lives, nurses can't help but remain vigilant.

A few years ago, Mom moved into a retirement community in the suburb where I was raised. As a nurse, with specialties in psychiatry and geriatrics, Mom has developed a theory on home decorating schemes. For instance, your bedroom should be a soothing tone such as a cream or pastel color and not dark or dreary. Similarly, she insists that common areas be cheerful, just short of vibrant, and if she enters a home with a predominantly blue interior, she immediately assumes you're an alcoholic. She made one exception with regard to blue for a friend, who was indeed a functioning alcoholic, but also experienced mania and "needed the blue to calm her down."

Mom's color scheme philosophy has provided substantial amusement for me and my friends over the years, although no one has dared to paint a room blue, or even green, and definitely not gray. One friend's spouse surprised her with an electric blue bathroom, and a divorce quickly followed. Mom's interior design ideas have likewise created a splash at her retirement community. Whenever the administration wishes to show a prospective resident how an actual apartment looks when furnished and decorated, they use Mom's as the model, and as a result of more than a dash of obsessive-compulsive disorder, it's always display-ready. To thank her (perhaps they're under the mistaken impression that she was inconvenienced by having to tidy up at the last minute), they give Mom free meal passes to use in the dining room. The dining room is like eating at a four-star restaurant, everything from soup to steaks and ice cream sundaes with terrific service and plenty of smiles, and Mom now has so many meal tickets that she can throw dinner parties every night if she wants.

I provide this model apartment pay-per-play only as a contrast to the fact that Mom receives absolutely no compensation for saving lives in her community, not so much as a free dessert. Because her place isn't classified as assisted living, the workers aren't permitted to touch any of the residents. If one falls, sustains an injury, or stops breathing, employees can only call 911 and/or a priest to give last rites. However, under New York's Good Samaritan Law, which protects health care professionals who voluntarily render medical assistance, Mom is allowed to jump into the medical fray, and does she ever, the bloodier the better. To date she's unclogged two diners using the Heimlich maneuver, resuscitated one stroke victim, and changed multiple bandages on burns and various suppurating wounds. When one friend didn't show up for dinner, mom went into tracking mode and discovered her bleeding profusely after having fallen in her apartment.

For acting as nurse-in-residence, Mom gets nothing but appreciation, which is fine. However, one diner, unfamiliar with the Good Samaritan Law, complained, "You can't touch people here!" when Mom *brought someone back to life* before the paramedics could arrive. In fact, by the time the emergency workers appeared, Mom's patient was sitting up and able to recite her list of medications. The resident who protested had better hope that if she chokes or loses consciousness, Mom doesn't suddenly decide to finish dinner in her apartment.

That said, being on the OCD side, I don't think Mom could ever bypass an opportunity to jumpstart someone. I've found that living with OCD people has its ups and downs. On the minus side, they tend to want to review and update lists and plans while you're in the shower or on the toilet. And they enjoy giving organizational tutorials. I often find myself the student of TED-like talks on how to properly load the dishwasher and pick up dog poop. But my question is, why does it matter how we load it since no one has ever seen this dishwasher even half full before it's run? On the plus side, when visitors unexpectedly arrive, you don't have to yell, "We've been robbed," because rather than falling into disarray, the house remains hospital clean. By cohabitating with an OCD-er, if you weren't a neat freak beforehand, you eventually discover that clean-as-you-go really does make life easier and more pleasant. You rarely find yourself in the bathroom or kitchen without any type of paper products on hand. Bills are paid the day they arrive and so the power doesn't get turned off the night before Thanksgiving or at any other inopportune time. Nor does a car suddenly disappear from the driveway.

One benefit for Mom is that she knows exactly how she left the house—from hand towel placement to soap and toilet paper levels—and can tell when someone has been inside. And that's how she caught the apartment manager at her old place using her Mom cave as a love nest while she was in Florida. However, when a person is this fastidious, it raises suspicions more quickly when things are out of place. And this led to an eldercare catch-22. After Mom battled a vicious infection that was treated with several different antibiotics over a period of months, I determined that she was having memory difficulties. For instance, she asked about my sister, and I reminded her that I'm an only child, to which she replied, "Then I guess that's that." The following week was the opening night party for a play I'd written and she went around telling the cast and crew that I'd tricked her into moving into a retirement community (after she'd selected the place herself).

The Internet said it was common for individuals to take

up to a year to completely recover from this type of situation, especially seniors. Still, I mentioned to Mom's physician that I thought she'd experienced a cognitive setback, and he gave her a test that determines if people have all their marbles. Only, unbeknownst to me, it was a take-home test. So Mom phoned me, and I became the unwitting accomplice in answering all the questions she didn't know. A week later the doctor called me and reported that Mom's memory and knowledge base are actually remarkable for her age. This system must be from the same medical school where my gynecologist learned the best way to record the weight of female patients is to just ask them and not confirm by using a scale. His is without a doubt the thinnest practice on the East Coast. You can shed five pounds just by walking through the door.

I regularly remind myself I'm not the only one with a parent who keeps me on my toes. The following week, my friend's seventy-nine-year-old mom did up her hair and makeup before a hip operation and told the hospital she was only sixty-two. Her reward was a bill for $13,500, since Medicare doesn't cover operations for people under age sixty-five.

More than for saving lives, Mom is going to be remembered for her holiday exhortations, at least among my friends. One Thanksgiving a large casserole dish crashed to the floor in the kitchen, and all the guests in the dining room immediately dove under their chairs. Everyone in Buffalo grew up doing duck-and-cover drills as part of our doomsday scenario planning. You'd think this would have involved crawling through tunnels and descending into a fully stocked bunker ten feet below ground, but no, we were ordered to crouch beneath a desk or face a wall with our eyes tightly closed, waiting for the world to end. In Catholic school you were allowed to sing, "Jesus Wants Me for a

Sunbeam." We were told the Soviets' first target was nearby Niagara Falls because of the major power plant and chemical industry located there. Of course, Pittsburgh, Chicago, and Youngstown insisted they'd be first because of the steel industry, and Detroit because of the automobile assembly lines. Fact of the matter is, we would have been offended had we not been first. These drills ended the week I graduated from high school.

Such as it was, when the casserole crashed to the floor, Mom announced, "Happy Fucking Thanksgiving!" My people are of Black Irish and Scandinavian descent, so holidays are an unpredictable cocktail of abnormal psych class, hostage crisis, and *Survivor* finale where it's best to hunker down with a bottle of Bailey's and pray for daylight. As people of Celtic and Nordic ancestry well know, the holidays can be a particularly stressful time, and my house was no exception. We're like a Navy Seal team expedition. The overarching objective is to have the same number of people who began the mission at the end of November still with us once we've reached the first of January. From a young age, I'd help Mom make the necessary holiday preparations—a reluctant cook paired with a hyperactive child and a house full of animals—already a recipe for disaster. As things inevitably went wrong, I'd regularly hear Merry Fucking Christmas, Happy Fucking Birthday, Happy Fucking Easter, Happy Fucking New Year, and . . . well, you get the idea. As a result, five decades later it's impossible to pass a holiday, especially my birthday, without having these sentiments texted, phoned, or included in greeting cards from all my friends—a very special family legacy indeed.

Only get-well cards are missing our favorite expletive. Once Mom was bitten by her cat, and I can't tell you the number of people who asked me if the cat died. If Mom ever does get honored for saving all those lives, I hope it's called The Damn Good Samaritan Award. And I hope I've inherited a bit of her medical jujitsu. When my husband was hacking and wheezing for six weeks with no sign of improvement and still wouldn't see a doctor, I told him, "I'm only going to say one thing–at your age, if you have pneumonia, you'll die." He flew out the door to a walk-in medical storefront open on Sunday and was prescribed antibiotics.

Elsewhere the sky is the roof of the world;
but here the earth was the floor of the sky.
−Willa Cather

Chapter 21

Smokey John's

Most neighborhood moms had "collections" when I was growing up. There were display cases featuring Hummel figures in muted colors, snow globes with slow leaks, ceramic salt and pepper shakers, or at the very least an apostle spoon collection. Dads regularly collected stamps, sports memorabilia, or tools. Interestingly, no one in my family collected anything. No seashells, record albums, cookie jars, comic books, or dolls for us. Not even shot glasses or Pez dispensers. We were ready to bail out at a moment's notice. I think everyone in my house knew early on that this particular living situation had an expiration date, and those who travel light travel fastest.

Whenever a judge asked who I wanted to live with during my parents' divorce, the right answer was Dad. Whenever the school wished to speak to someone about why I was at the Fort Erie Race Track instead of trigonometry class, the right answer was Dad. Whenever I needed twenty dollars for a poster of dogs playing poker or a kitten hanging from a tree branch and promising that Friday was coming, it was to Dad I turned. Because Dad was operating in a parallel universe and didn't ask any dumb questions the way Mom did.

For instance, if my teen friends and I were leaving the house with flashlights and ski masks at midnight, Dad never asked, "What are you doing?" or "Why do you need ski masks in the middle of summer?" If he asked, "When will you be back?" and we said, "Around 3 AM," he'd say, "Then I guess I'll see you in the morning." If I climbed a ladder and cut a hole in my bedroom ceiling for a skylight, Dad would ask, "Do you want anything from the store?" I could request a blowtorch or a gallon of liquid fertilizer, and he'd add it to his list. Then he'd say, "So I guess we'll eat dinner around five." He loved having dinner at five o'clock, and even though we had dinner at five o'clock every day, he always raised the prospect as if it was the first time this had ever been considered.

It's hard to imagine anyone wanting to leave sunny Buffalo, but Dad lived out his retirement in Truth or Consequences, New Mexico, which was cleverly abbreviated to T or C. It's an odd name for a town, or what's now billed as "a spa city," even by the standards of someone who grew up in a state that's home to places named Lackawanna, Chili, Mechanicville, Killawog, Throop, Truthville, Coxsackie, Java, Horseheads, Wawayanda, South Schroon, Schaghticoke, and Neversink. Dad's retirement mecca was once known as Hot Springs, like dozens of other places around the US. However, in 1950 the radio quiz show *Truth or Consequences,* which is perhaps best remembered for giving a contestant a Turkey dinner in the form of sending him to the country of Turkey to eat dinner, offered to hold a tenth anniversary program in the first town that changed its name to that of the show. This was only supposed to last for a year, but the residents ended up liking the name so much they kept it—a happily ever after story if there ever was one. Maybe marriages should have a one-year trial period.

New Mexico is rich in natural beauty and has mesmerized artists from all over the world including Georgia O'Keeffe, Judy Chicago, Reynaldo "Sonny" Rivera, Peter Hurd, and Henriette Wyeth. Painters in particular are attracted by the magical light, mystical scenery, complex history, aura of enchantment, and welcoming communities. For an artistic know-nothing like me, New Mexico was delightful to visit because 1) While the desert looks dead from afar, the closer you get the more you find it's actually teeming with life. 2) People are incredibly friendly. 3) It completely dried up my sinuses. It's also a magnet for skilled UFO spotters, where patriotism can meet full-blown paranoia.

Truth or Consequences is in the desert, 150 miles south of Albuquerque and 120 miles north of El Paso. In addition to having amazing geothermal mineral water, it's home to a variety of plants and animals that want to stick you, prick you, sting you, bite you, snag you, stab you, and kill you. While residing there, it's necessary to shake your shoes for scorpions and keep small household pets safe from coyotes prowling the fence line. Spiders out of science fiction movies lurk in shadowy corners, and residents hope that the venomous "recluse spider" remains reclusive. Snakes regularly nap in the space between the screen door and the outside door, and Dad became especially talented at removing them from the pool. I wouldn't have guessed snakes to be such accomplished swimmers—do they also enjoy skiing?

Once Dad was no longer required to wear a suit and tie for work, he adopted a more casual look of sweat pants cut off at the knees (by him) and a Colonel Schultz T-shirt (*I know nothing,*

I hear nothing, I see nothing) from his favorite old TV show, *Hogan's Heroes*. At any given moment, it was hard to tell if Dad was having his first coffee and cigarette of the morning or his last coffee and cigarette from the night before. The Southwest was a good place for Dad because most cafes served "cowboy brew" coffee for people who had lost all their taste buds due to one adventure or another, and there were rarely any dress codes. Prior to heading into town, Dad would switch from his sweats or plaid pajama bottoms into a pair of faded blue jeans. With his wild gray hair and holes in all his shirts and pants from hot cigarette ash, you still couldn't be sure whether he'd spent the night in a house or an alleyway.

Dad's best friend, Alvin, who lived across the street, regularly informed me that Dad needed a haircut, cataract surgery, and a hearing aid. In my opinion, those were the least of our problems when it came to lifestyle choices. For one thing, I was highly allergic to cigarette smoke, and Dad was a chain smoker. Second, Dad's glasses were so grimy that even if he did have cataract surgery, what difference would it make? As for hearing aids, after having worked on the incredibly loud trading floor of the stock exchange, I needed those too, so it was fine by me that we blasted the TV and shouted at each other.

Constantly playing in the background during our pool marathons (shooting, not swimming) was Dad's favorite TV show, *Pawn Stars*, which chronicled haggling over artifacts brought into a family-owned shop two miles from the Las Vegas strip. At mealtimes Dad liked to discuss the ins and outs of the latest wheelings and dealings, including conflicts among the staff, especially when the intelligence and judgment of the young was brought into question by more seasoned pros. We ate all our meals at local restaurants, and I could see that people were listening to our conversations. Dad had a clear, resonant bass voice as if he were a radio announcer, and we were both accustomed to talking loudly. Still, I never knew if we had an audience because they were also interested in the show or because Dad's New York City accent made *Pawn Stars* sound exactly like *Porn Stars*.

Even more diners began eavesdropping when *Hardcore Pawn*, or "Hardcore Porn" in Dad's vernacular, debuted in 2010, and he never tired of telling people that the owner's real name was Les Gold. However, the new TV series was about a pawn shop in Detroit, Michigan, and there was a great deal of focus on the sad stories that had forced customers to part with their cherished possessions. Having lived and struggled in a declining Rust Belt city his entire working life, Dad found it depressing and therefore wasn't crushed to see *Hardcore Pawn* canceled after four years. He much preferred watching hotshot youngsters getting schooled by the "old man" on his beloved *Pawn Stars*.

When visiting Dad, I always brought along my Tibetan spaniel, Roxy, mostly because no one at home would deal with her mischievous antics. For one thing, Tibetan spaniels are small dogs, but they love high places and insist on perching atop the tallest furnishing in a room, even if it's a lamp. And she loved Dad since he fed her bologna four times a day. In fact, I stopped bringing dog food because why eat that slop when Grandpa was pan frying bologna so it was hot and crispy? We got to the point where I didn't even need a flashlight to clean up the yard at night. Her turds glowed in the moonlight as if encrusted with diamonds and took no more time to locate at eleven at night than in broad daylight. The only downfall was when she started scratching on Dad's door earlier and earlier saying, "Bologna Man! Wake up! Get out here—you have a customer!"

Similarly, Roxy was fixated on Alvin and his wife Connie's

house across the street. One Christmas Roxy ate roast beef there, and ten years later she was still straining at the leash every time we walked past since she knew it was where they kept the free roast beef. Dad was what we liked to call an "outdoor guest" because he smoked so much people entertained him in the yard, and that was fine by him. Even then it was best to have a raging bonfire that not only deterred the kamikaze mosquitoes but also covered the smell of Dad's cigarettes. However, once a year he was allowed inside Alvin and Connie's house for an hour to have Christmas dinner. They are devout Lutherans and as much as they loved Dad, I'm certain they felt if they just prayed hard enough it would be possible to make him an "indoor guest." But Dad had been presentable in his youth and working years out of necessity, and was now happy drinking, puffing, dressing like a hobo, and listening to the sound of standards dropping to the ground (upon which he stood in ratty white deck shoes bound up by black electric tape) with *Pawn Stars* blaring in the background. In fact, if you said "John, you look like a bum," he'd happily reply, "I resemble that remark!"

Toto, I've got a feeling we're not in Kansas anymore.
—Dorothy Gale, *The Wizard of Oz*

Chapter 22

The Tin Man

My dream upon high school graduation was to attend the University of Pennsylvania's Wharton School of Finance, which offered one of the only entrepreneurship programs in the country during the early 1980s. When I received a thin envelope in response to my application (and not the one with registration forms, housing options, and orientation times) I headed off to the University of Michigan with my longtime friend Debbie, since she had a normal family, and I knew I could hitch a ride. It turns out that major life decisions shouldn't be based on available carpool options. The first week in Ann Arbor, I called the stock exchange in New York City and asked for an entry-level job. A woman replied that I needed to have a high school diploma and be at least sixteen years old. Check and check.

At the end of 1983, having recently turned eighteen, I found myself in dystopian, fight-or-flight Manhattan, working on Wall Street. These misadventures are discussed in *Play Money* and *Life in New York: How I Learned to Love Squeegee Men, Token Suckers,*

Trash Twisters, and Subway Sharks. However, I was recently at a stock exchange reunion where we were swinging the lamp and reminiscing about the days of yore, back when we used pencils to record trades, our brains to do math, and hand signals to communicate above the din, and was reminded of a favorite story. First, to set the scene, a typical practical joke on the stock exchange was to send mice back and forth through the pneumatic tube system. I'll let you decide whether it was worse to receive a live or dead rodent.

Not only was our work environment absent computers and cell phones back in the day, but footwear options weren't so great, either. Thus people who stood on their feet all day tended to wear sneakers if they were under forty, and what can only be described as a Frankenstein's monster shoe, which resembled a black orthopedic brick, if they were over forty. Whereas millions of Manhattan employees arrived at the office every morning and put on their good shoes while stowing their bad shoes for the work day, we did just the opposite.

When not busy trading, the guys specialized in elaborate practical jokes, played mostly on newcomers. Everyone had their specialties, just like some people love limericks over puns while others enjoy wrestling more than cage fighting. A popular place for mischief was the trading pit where I worked, as a large crowd stood shoulder to shoulder with their attention focused upward, intently scrutinizing rows of screens blipping with market information.

There was a clerk stationed across from my index option trading pit who particularly enjoyed thwacking people atop the sneaker using a pencil with a big, hard eraser on the end of it. By the time a guy looked down, The Thwacker was of course gone. One morning The Thwacker homed in on fresh prey—a young trader who'd just started working for a large financial firm. It was The Rookie's job to maintain his place in the hub-bub all day and swiftly execute orders issued by his firm. After the opening bell, it appeared to be a slow day, so The Thwacker went to work using his pencil eraser to wallop the top of The Rookie's canvas sneaker and then disappear into the crowd and out of the trading pit. The problem with getting the top of your left sneaker thwacked is that you immediately look down at your foot and not over your shoulder. The Rookie was also unaware that highly-paid professionals who owned expensive seats on the stock exchange and were tasked with safeguarding the capitalist system spent a large part of their days pranking each another.

The trading pits are piled high with machinery that flashes and hums, along with thick cords snaking every which way, so The Rookie decided he was receiving electrical shocks, which was not an outlandish assumption. He went over to my friend Andy, who was a floor official and supposed to know how to deal with such issues, to report that he was receiving electrical jolts. Andy was all too familiar with The Thwacker, who is not to be confused with the guy who inserts fake lottery tickets with winning numbers into people's drawers, or the trickster who goes around every half hour with a pocket knife cutting a half inch off the bottom of canes used by brokers who are injured, or the guy who replaces traders' hats in the cloakroom with different sizes until they think they have a brain tumor and check into a hospital. Andy assures The Rookie that he'll take care of the problem immediately and heads off in search of Joe the maintenance guy, his pal of twenty years, so they can determine how to build on the joke since it's only ten o'clock, slow, and everyone is bored.

Joe usually wears a tool belt, but for this occasion he does himself up more like a Ghostbuster and charges over to the trading pit. He takes lots of measurements and then places his jumper cables on The Rookie and makes an attached dial react wildly. Joe proclaims, "Wow! I assume you've been struck by lightning at least three or four times." The Rookie is dumbfounded—he's *never* been hit by lightning. Joe looks as if he finds this hard to believe. "I've never seen anyone conduct electricity like this before." The Rookie is concerned. Joe sweeps his hand across the pit and reassures him, "Look, I'll rip all this out after trading today. In the meantime, just be sure to stand on the frames of the floor tiles and don't let your feet touch the middle of any squares."

The Rookie is unsure about all this, goes to his boss, and says that he needs to leave work for the day. His boss tells him to get the hell back in the pit, pronto. Andy then goes to The Rookie's boss, who is known for being a hard ass with no sense of humor, and explains the prank. Boss Man finds nothing funny about the whole enterprise, especially since any mistakes made trading can cost the firm a fortune. When The Rookie leaves the floor to grab a sandwich for lunch, he walks past the other posts by traveling at right angles, only touching the frames of the floor tiles, the opposite of "step on a crack and break your mother's back." By now everyone is in on the joke, all 1,800 of us. The Rookie right-angles his way back across the trading floor to the pit with a sandwich and resumes his place. The Thwacker goes back to work and lands four good ones spaced about fifteen minutes apart. The Rookie reports to Andy that he is receiving *more* high-voltage shocks. Andy promises to remedy the situation immediately.

A few minutes later, maintenance man Joe heads into the pit with a ridiculous-looking hat fashioned out of tinfoil and assures The Rookie it will insulate him against further shocks. But The

Rookie doesn't want to put it on. He returns to his boss and says he needs to go home and come back tomorrow when the floor has been fixed. Boss man sees the ridiculous tinfoil hat and asks, "What's *that?*" The Rookie explains how the hat will keep him from getting shocked. Boss Man orders him to put on the hat and resume his position in the trading pit. The Rookie does so, and even the hardhearted boss has to laugh. People begin to crowd the balcony in order to get a look at The Rookie in his tinfoil hat. But the joke is on them because the tinfoil hat works—The Rookie is never shocked again. However, a guy who starts a few weeks later will experience a similar problem. . . .

No one should come to New York to live
unless he is willing to be lucky.
—E. B. White

Chapter 23

The Big Apple Blossom

When I first moved to New York City, the cost to be unlisted in the phone book was $25. That's right, one had to pay *not* to be in the phone book. However, a friend informed me of a simple workaround—there was no charge to list any name that came to mind instead of your own. That's how Goa Way became a Manhattanite for several decades and eventually landed on every telemarketer's list. When a call came for Ms. Way I sadly reported that she'd recently gone to glory, sometimes quietly in her sleep, but more often than not a casualty of a tragic public transportation mishap, such as falling between the cars of the Q subway train while trying to rescue an escaped African ringneck parrot. Goa still receives a call every month or so, and I remember her fondly, especially when giving a technologically updated account of her untimely demise, usually involving a drone strike, a self-driving taxi, or a fugitive Burmese python.

A city changes faster than the human heart according to

French poet Charles Baudelaire. Times Square was an open-air sex shop when I first arrived, and now it's been sanitized to the point of censorship. I went to the M&M store on Broadway and custom-ordered holiday M&Ms with the initials of my friend Heather Osgood to be printed on them. However, the letters H.O. offended their delicate sensibilities and also those of the M&M master computer. It was necessary to call headquarters and request permission to print such a scandalous M&M on the sacred ground of a block that had been home to a dozen peep shows and porn shops just two decades earlier.

As much as I try to be a booster for New York City—and I wrote a book about all the positive changes since the grim 1970s and '80s—transportation has actually gone downhill over the past few years. In fact, New York is currently one of the most prosperous cities in the world, yet subway delays have become so prevalent that straphangers now share a credo with Unitarian Universalists: *Your guess is as good as mine.* In some stations debris rains down on platforms, while others are swamped following every storm, and passengers post videos of swimming rats on YouTube. Overnight Internet sensation Pizza Rat of 2015 was replaced by Flood Rat in 2018. In addition to rodents and trash are rust-colored veins from water damage, flaking paint, dirty wall tiles, dingy concrete floors, life-threatening icicles, broken escalators, and bad smells. Few stops have elevators or escalators, and you risk your life trying to access one with a cane, suitcase, or baby carriage. Nevertheless, the subway remains a popular haven for proselytizers and straphanger messiahs who loudly insist they "have a message from God." The question then becomes whether to move closer or farther away.

The roads are also in horrendous shape, average driving speed has slowed, and congestion is up dramatically. That doesn't even take into account traffic on the Tinder app, since New York may be best known as the City That Never Sleeps Alone. Whereas taxi drivers were regularly robbed and even murdered in the bad old days, now they have a high suicide rate. Cabbies can barely make ends meet as the city is flooded with for-hire cars. I'd compare our infrastructure to that of a third-world country, but I'd be insulting places where the trains, buses, and roads are better and more reliable. How bad is it? After 106 pedestrians were killed by motor vehicles and more than 10,700 injured in 2017, the busiest intersections have been assigned crossing guards for grownups, complete with glow-in-the-dark jackets, who will even take your arm and usher you to safety upon request. Meantime, doctors have been suggesting that patients Uber to the nearest hospital, even if they have to share.

Our airports (JFK, LGA, and Newark) consistently make every list of the country's worst, with LaGuardia dependably ranked number one. LaGuardia is a category killer with abysmal marks for long lines, outdated facilities, bad service, and "other problems," which include infectious diseases and a variety of wildlife. I suppose one could argue it's doing tourists a favor by preparing them for the subway. Still, when it comes to bad airports, you really have to work hard to beat out Chicago's O'Hare. When New York residents protested Amazon's new multimillion-dollar Queens headquarters with its promise of at least 25,000 jobs in 2019, all the company needed to do was announce they were going to help improve the subways and nearby LaGuardia airport. We would have hailed them as conquering heroes and put the Amazon arrow logo on MetroCards, briefcases, windbreakers, caps, and backpacks, and it would have shot to the most popular tattoo overnight. There's only one way to survive the New York City airports: you must continuously imagine the number of days or weeks the same trip would take by horse and buggy, relish the time saved, and don't for a second allow yourself to fantasize about the teleportation machine used in *Star Trek*.

The best thing to be said about apocalyptic Pennsylvania Station is that a new one is supposedly under construction. Otherwise, the enlivening human announcer who called out, "All Aboard!" has been replaced by electronic updates that fill the air like humming cicadas. However, there's some new entertainment in the form of an Amtrak employee jollying up tired, grouchy, and occasionally bewildered passengers on the eight thirty to Boston with a comedy routine delivered in basso profundo that includes the line, "If you're not a Morning Person you shouldn't have taken a Morning Job!" and "It all sounded better in the PowerPoint presentation, didn't it?"

Two other quality-of-life issues are also making one look back fondly at the days of drugging and mugging. New York City is considerably louder with the nonstop caravan of trucks (complete with backup alarms) delivering everything apartment dwellers desire, including gallons of water that are in some cases no better than what comes out of their faucets, and in many instances much worse. Restaurant delivery now operates via motorized bicycles and buzzing scooters. Laws have banned smokers from office buildings, restaurants, all transportation, and even public parks; as a result, the sidewalks have become one large smoking section. Subway entrances normally blocked by gaggles of tourists huddled over maps and teens checking their sext messages now share space with stalled smokers firing up cigarettes. If you still haven't had your fill of carcinogens, cars and trucks idle everywhere while heavily air-conditioned stores leave their front doors wide open in ninety-degree heat.

That said, some things haven't changed much at all. When people move out of an apartment in New York, they just dump everything that's no longer wanted on the street, and in the ensuing five minutes, it's all re-homed by passersby. The downside is that if you leave your new chair or lamp unattended while opening a door, it will disappear quickly, not because people are stealing, but because they believe they're performing a community service.

Whereas a bathroom debate recently began on the national level, in New York we were forced to reach certain tacit accommodations decades ago. Because if women didn't use men's restrooms, they'd never see the second half of a Broadway show or enjoy dinner while the food is still warm. New York women "identify" with whatever bathroom has the shortest line. Just try and get the gals out of the men's room when *Hamilton* is about to start. To be ladylike, we give the gents a warning that the urinals are about to be stormed, such as, "Close your eyes because we're coming in."

Along similar lines, the difference between the East Side and the West Side of New York hasn't changed much over the past century. Any mover can tell you that Westies have more books than clothes and Easties have more clothes than books. It's on the East Side that people own designer "rain coats" without hoods—apparently they stay dry by traveling under a canopy of umbrellas held aloft by doormen and drivers.

New Yorkers still have more dogs than any other city dwellers. They say this is because Manhattan is a lonely city. They also say it's because if you're a single guy, the best way to meet women is to take a puppy to the park. A study reports that 90 percent of New Yorkers refer to themselves as Mom or Dad when speaking to their pets. Hopefully all the dogs don't send away for DNA tests and log onto ancestry.com, or there's going to be a lot of explaining to do. The most popular names for dogs in New York are King and Prince. Meantime, the most popular names for dogs in London are Donald and Trump.

For Manhattan dogs with digestive problems, vets instruct their owners to order chicken with white rice off the diet menu of the nearest Chinese restaurant. Many people say it's cruel to have a dog in the city—that it's inhumane to confine a living creature to a tiny, airless, windowless apartment with little access to sunlight, fresh air, grass, or space to exercise. And it's true that New Yorkers tend to work long hours, travel, socialize, and are rarely home. However, I'd just like to point out that the same people find these conditions suitable for raising children.

When I first moved to Manhattan, the closest thing people had to snow angels were the police chalk outlines decorating the streets and sidewalks, and a cocaine dealer in Washington Square Park who went by the name Snow Angel. After umpteen robberies, the KFC on 125th Street installed bulletproof glass to protect its workers, as if they were guarding gold bullion at Fort Knox rather than fried chicken, mashed potatoes, and sides of slaw. While it took six months to have a Jennifer convertible couch delivered and eight weeks to get a land line installed, it took less than an hour to buy a gun on the street. It's been said that everyone has some skeletons in their closet, but when it came to New Yorkers' closets, they were often real. While in most parts of the country, a friend is defined as someone who will help you move, in New York it was someone who would help you move a dead body.

After being labeled the Murder Capital of the Country following a record high of 2,262 homicides in 1990, crime is now at a record low. This can be attributed to living in a relatively cashless society, sex and drugs having moved onto the Internet and out of sight, and since the TV series *Blue Bloods*, no one wants to land in the crosshairs of detective Danny Reagan. These days New York is often called the country's Safest Big City. However, we still struggle with more than our share of mental health issues. Fewer people are bitten by sharks worldwide on an annual basis than are bitten by other people in New York City.

The arts are thriving, with more concerts and shows every day than one could attend in a lifetime. However, whereas in the old days you had only to police your row for people snoring and unwrapping candies, there are regular brawls about cell phone usage. It usually starts as theatergoer-on-theatergoer violence, but often escalates to involve ushers, managers, and even law enforcement. Meantime, performers are publicly shaming patrons by halting shows and receiving bigger applause than after the finale.

So text at your own risk. Not long ago I went to see *Girl from the North Country*, a musical based on Bob Dylan songs, which is set in Duluth, Minnesota. Before the show was supposed to start, an usher walked up the aisle requesting that audience members turn their cell phones not just to vibrate but completely *off*. Despite it being show time, the stage remained dark, so patrons continued sexting potential partners and researching their symptoms on WebMD. The usher went down the aisle with the same request to turn *off* phones with the same result. Then she adopted a threatening tone which caused one person to complain, "You said the show was going to start but it didn't." The usher insisted that it was going to start. Everyone looked at the dark stage and returned to their screens. Clearly the audience members weren't from Minnesota. The usher ordered everyone to turn their phones off *now*. It was fifteen minutes after the official start time, and one patron loudly remarked that in London shows begin at two minutes past the hour. Another added that in Germany shows begin exactly on time, and the audience isn't punished for punctuality. The usher said that if the phones weren't switched off, people would be removed from the theater. A (white) patron told the (black) usher that the manager should be called as this had become a racial incident and she felt "unsafe." At that moment the actual show started. I enjoyed both productions enormously.

While watching a performance of *The Ferryman* on Broadway, a woman's watch phone went off *six times*. Granted, the show was three hours and twenty minutes long, but how is that even possible–since after the fourth time wouldn't you have fled to the bedside of whomever was dying or alternatively crushed the device with your shoe? Especially after having noticed that Tony Award-winning actor Matthew Broderick was sitting in our row. It's safe to say that most of the audience was against the death penalty in principle but were willing to give it serious consideration for this situation.

In dating news, the number of eligible women remains higher than the bachelor pool. As proof I offer the man at the corner of 5th Avenue and 80th Street (in front of the Metropolitan Museum of Art) holding a large sign that says WILL MARRY FOR FOOD. Theories as to this accepted imbalance include women being too picky, New York City's abundance of gay men, and dating apps that make settling down less appealing.

Otherwise, there are more restaurants than ever before, overflowing with food from all corners of the globe. Just don't ask your waiter for a "smidgen" since you've just ordered a small pigeon. And every autumn you may wonder if your mom is hiding in Manhattan kitchens when upscale restaurants attempt to gourmetize turnips and parsnips by slathering them with olive oil, sea salt, and oregano and pass them off as food.

No one complains about culture-hopping here. Be white with dreadlocks or African-American with a beehive hairdo. Speak like you work in a jazz dive or went to finishing school. Everyone appreciates some conversational Yiddish, and therefore anyone can qualify as "Jewish-adjacent," meaning you've learned to properly use *putz* and *schmutz* in a sentence. It's similar to the Jews who live "Christian-adjacent" in the Midwest and know that as much as it may pain them, they have to put out butter and jam with bagels at brunch. In fact, my Ohio friends are fascinated by the "bagel bar" near my apartment, presided over by the "Schmearmonger," who bears an uncanny resemblance to *Seinfeld*'s "Soup Nazi."

It's no coincidence that fictional superheroes live in New York City; Batman's Gotham and Superman's Metropolis were modeled on Manhattan, which was gritty, exciting, and real. The Avengers' Beaux-Arts Mansion was based on the Frick Museum. Dr. Strangelove's Sanctum Sanctorum has a real address in Greenwich Village. And Peter Parker, a.k.a. Spiderman, hailed from Ingram Street in Queens. The Yancy Street Gang, a recurring antagonist of The Thing, was named after Delancey Street on the Lower East Side.

In fact, fearlessly stopping automated closing doors with just our bodies is the superpower of all New Yorkers. After years of training on the subway, we're not only reckless, but determined, and even when those metal doors begin crushing our intestines and squeezing our spleens, we hold our ground so the doors either open or we're flattened trying. So, if you're a longtime New Yorker out traveling in the rest of America and want to create some excitement, the best way is not to say, "I told you so" about Donald Trump, but rather to hurl yourself into the jaws of a closing elevator. This will elicit shrieks and gasps all around. Comic book heroes are about outcasts making good, and New York is still the best city for differently-abled dreamers.

No man does it all by himself.
Y.M.C.A. by The Village People

Chapter 24

The Chicken Dance

Ten years ago I decided I was ready to start a family. Since I was no longer in peak childbearing years, I looked on the Internet to adopt. In a small village outside of Gulu in Northern Uganda, I found the perfect little girl and began sending fifty dollars a month to help Eunice, her family, and her village improve their lives. At the time there weren't any secular outfits willing to match sponsors with a specific child, so I worked through a Christian evangelical outfit called World Vision International. As a result, my child always writes that she's praying for me and thanks God for the clothes, soap, cooking oil, and livestock that are purchased with the money I send. Every month I mail Eunice and her many siblings a box of school supplies along with some educational toys. At Christmastime there are dolls, bikes, and lollipops. Since I began assisting the family, in addition to Eunice and two older brothers, her mother has had eight more children.

Eunice writes every few months, keeping me up to date on

her schoolwork and livestock. She was born and raised in a farming village and, like any good rural conversationalist, she always inquires as to the health of my crops. Living in an urban high-rise, I don't have any crops per se, but I give her weather updates along with a report on the Bonsai tree that was a gift from someone who doesn't know I can't keep a cactus alive.

After several years of sponsorship, I found myself working in Southern Africa and arranged to visit my sponsor child on the way home. From Johannesburg I took a flight to Kampala, Uganda, and then caught a ride in a construction worker's jalopy for the five-hour trip to Gulu over potholed dirt roads. The countryside was a vibrant explosion of color and commerce that Edward Hopper would have no interest in painting. It was possible to buy food and fresh honey in towns along the way from rough-and-ready carts and blankets spread upon the ground. However, for restrooms we used the "bush toilet." Upon stopping by the side of the road I would head one way while the male driver went in the opposite direction. I was advised to watch out for snakes, specifically cobras, puff adders, mambas and the Gaboon viper. Regrettably, there weren't any photos or trading cards so I could know exactly what I was watching out for.

In the small city of Gulu, I connected with an aid worker and asked if there was a chart containing pictures of the snakes I needed to avoid. She informed me that it would be wise to spend more time on the lookout for land mines. The following morning we drove into the countryside where Eunice lives with her family on a small patch of dirt among several neighboring subsistence farmers. They grow corn, beans, greens, and plenty of cassava, which is the potato of tropical countries. The main difference is that when preparing cassava you need to be careful to remove traces of cyanide from the flesh. They also kept some livestock.

Over the years I'd given them chickens and most recently a goat. I drew the line at guinea pigs because I feared those were headed straight for the pot, and I've always been fond of guinea pigs, especially the ones with hair going every which way, just as mine tends to do.

It transpired that the family was worried about my visit, and indeed I sensed a certain foreboding upon arrival. After so many cheerful, loving letters, Eunice kept her distance, which at first I put down to shyness. Then the aid worker said Eunice wished to speak with me privately, so we went inside a grass and mud hut but needed a translator since the locals speak Luo, and even though Eunice was learning English in school, she was eight years old and not yet up to speed. My Luo is even worse, although I know that "diel" is a female goat. It transpired that the goat I'd provided for the family had met with some kind of terrible fate but I couldn't make out exactly what happened. It appeared that people were trying to throw each other under the bus with regard to who had shirked his or her goat responsibilities.

I told Eunice not to worry about it anymore and that we'd get another goat, but she was not to be consoled. The fact is that Eunice had loved livestock from the time she was a toddler. I'd mail her what I thought were terrific sandals, T-shirts, games, and coloring books, but she always looked sad in the photos. Even when I gave Eunice and her brother new bicycles to make it easier for them to fetch water and attend school, she merely nodded. But when I sent money earmarked for livestock, you never saw a happier child, beaming and grinning from ear to ear. It soon became apparent that Eunice was extremely entrepreneurial with regard to increasing her chickens, profiting off the eggs, raising a cow while her many siblings benefited from the milk, and then trading it for several baby goats. But at this early stage, I wasn't aware of her animal husbandry dreams, so mixed in with her shame of squandering a gift was also the sense of loss regarding her future plans for this particular goat.

We left the hut, and it was time for the children to return to class after lunch, so I headed off to see where Eunice attended school and the place I'd been sending books and pencils. It was a primitive setup and looked more like a picnic shelter at a local park. About sixty children sat on the dirt floor facing a blackboard. That said, the students all wore uniforms, were for the most part smiling and cheerful, looked healthy, and without exception were well-behaved. The teacher told them my name, that I was from America, and how happy he was that I'd be giving the lesson that afternoon. Lesson? Lesson in what? The only full sentence I knew in Luo was "*Mbura ni ne ongegi iwe*" ("The cat did not have a tail").

The students were aged five through fourteen. My desperate gaze landed on a boom box in the corner, and I quickly looked through the cassette pile. There it was: "Y.M.C.A." by the Village People. Growing up in Buffalo, every wedding featured the hokey pokey, the chicken dance, and "Y.M.C.A." Whereas the hokey pokey involved full body movement and the Chicken Dance was arm flapping and preening, Y.M.C.A. merely required your basic cheerleader arm formations to match the letters as they appeared in the lyrics. I told the children our English lesson would involve four letters and pointed to anything in the room that began with a Y, M, C, or A, and then showed them how to make the letters with their arms. I started the song and we had a wonderful time singing and dancing. Furthermore, the locals had no idea "Y.M.C.A." is about gay cruising, and therefore it was a nice subversive protest to the anti-homosexuality laws in

Uganda that criminalized same-sex relationships and punished gay people with life in prison or the death penalty.

When we returned to Eunice's hut, the sun was setting through the trees, and it was time for me to leave. In much of Africa it's traditional to present a visitor with a gift, and so Eunice's family gave me a live chicken, which was incredibly generous since they had next to nothing. Still, there were several issues with this gift–I'm a vegetarian, it wasn't allowed on the plane, and I'd given them the chicken in the first place so it was rather redundant. After profuse thanks and a thorough appreciation of the chicken, my interpreter explained that I couldn't travel to America with a chicken and would they be so kind as to continue to care for it and send me progress reports. In the meantime, were they interested in learning the Chicken Dance?

The wisest are the most annoyed
at the loss of time.
–Dante Alighieri

Chapter 25

Senior Central

Millennials are currently discovering what Irish ne'er-do-well children have known for decades–that if you live at home long enough, your parents will eventually start to need you. The critical phase is twenty-five to thirty-five, where you must make yourself useful by mowing the lawn, changing light bulbs, walking the dog, and taking out trash. Always say thank you for cooked meals and fresh laundry. Most important, do not leave the gas tank empty.

I'm the only child of an only child of an only child on my dad's side. Meantime, my mother's brother and sister did not procreate. As a result, since childhood I've had an inverted elder-care pyramid poking me in the eyeball. I'm afraid to pick up the phone, since every time I do, someone has another engraved silver tea set they'd like to pass on to me. Even when ancestors left the Old World with not much more than the clothes on their back, it would appear that they all managed to fit a silver tea set into their pockets. I have five so far with more on the way—when was the last time anyone had a tea party?

Now that I'm in my fifties and the senior circus is eighty and beyond, I've come to some important conclusions. The first is that when you're married and have only one child, you should not be allowed to file for divorce. If couples do get divorced, they should not be permitted to move more than ten miles apart from each other. If I thought going to two different houses in one city for holidays was difficult, traveling to different sides of the country is just about impossible.

Otherwise, I've noticed a number of parallels between raising kids and corralling seniors.

Age zero to five: Most of your attention goes to juice boxes, medical issues, and safety. There's a lot of talk about being careful and what they should or shouldn't do. A large part of the day is spent looking for a bathroom. There needs to be a schedule or one ends up angry while the other ends up in tears.

And. . . .

Age sixty to seventy: Are you drinking too much? Did you get a flu shot? Should we get that hip checked? A large part of the day is spent looking for a bathroom. They do *not* care what other people think, obviously.

Age five to ten: You worry less about every sniffle and fall. "Range of motion" refers to allowing kids to walk to a friend's house or playground without adult supervision. However, you feel better if they carry some form of ID or have memorized their address and an emergency phone number. Questions about what they should or should not do become rhetorical and annoying. "Punishment" feels more like it punishes you. There's a whispered conversation about an "accident," and they're covered in Band-Aids.

And. . . .

Age seventy to eighty: You have the tenth conversation about why it's not a good idea to drive at night. You bring up getting a Life Alert for the tenth time. "Range of motion" refers to how high an arm can be raised or an elbow bent and is a box that needs to be checked on physical therapy forms and home health care requests. If they leave the house independently, you want them tagged like wildlife with identification and an emergency phone number. There's a whispered conversation about an "accident," and they're covered in Band-Aids.

Age ten through fifteen: The question "Where are you going?" regularly arises. They're looking to make friends with someone who has a car. Your lectures about drinking, drugs, and unprotected sex fall on deaf ears. Then you let them do what they want to a point, since you really can't stop them.

And. . . .

Age eighty to eighty-five: They're looking to make friends with someone who has a car. You sigh a lot and say, "I'm not going to fight about this anymore." Then you do.

Age fifteen to twenty: There are troubling test results and disappearances. When the authorities call, it's not *really* your fault anymore. You did the best you could. You tell the police about all the lectures.

And. . . .

Age eighty-five to ninety: There are troubling test results and disappearances. You tell the police about the lectures and inform everyone else, "I said this would happen. Do you remember? This is exactly what I said would happen!"

Age twenty to thirty: Do whatever you want. You'll do it anyway. We have different last names now, so it really doesn't matter.

And. . . .

Age ninety and over: Do whatever you want. No one can possibly blame me for any of this. Plus, everyone knows how hard I tried.

Meantime, I'm becoming more like my parents and older people in general every single day. I no longer care what the neighbors or really anyone thinks anymore, for the most part. I also find that, whereas my schedule as a younger person was jam-packed morning, noon, and night, I now prefer to do one thing a day. If a friend calls and asks about dinner I'll say sorry, I have a haircut at eleven o'clock, and if she's also older, she'll reply, "Call me when things calm down." However, this "one thing" is different than the "one thing" mothers like to rant about, "I gave you *one thing* to do" (i.e. unpacking the dishwasher), which was just one of many things in your day and the one you purposely skipped or completely forgot about.

I've made plenty of mistakes in my life, including setting the kitchen on fire and cracking my head open five times, so I'm the last person who should be giving advice or saying, "Trust my judgment," but let me share one thought. People who grew up before mass markets and plastic everything were indoctrinated in scarcity and reusability. They remember privation from the Great Depression, the Dust Bowl, and World War II. Many walked or biked everywhere because food and gas was either rationed or unaffordable. Tomato plants crowded windowsills or victory gardens were planted in backyards. Their kitchen drawers are filled with sugar packets from restaurants, and they'd have taken the ice cubes if there were a way to keep them from melting in a purse lined with a plastic bag.

My mom vividly remembers how her mother scrimped and saved enough sugar to make their father a birthday cake.

However, the three sweet-starved kids ate all the frosting off the cake before Dad arrived home from work. Their mother cried. They felt terrible, but still, since there were three of them, each blamed the other two.

Dad loved recalling wartime reminders by radio announcers about everything from turning off lights at night to scrap metal drives. As a way of helping produce the glycerin needed by the military, housewives were tasked with collecting kitchen waste in metal coffee cans. This consisted mostly of used cooking oil and lard. Dad would imitate one disc jockey who enjoyed saying, "All you housewives need to get your fat cans down to the depot."

Deprivation in Western New York has always meant eating more than our share of apples, since they're cheap, hardy, and prevalent. A bushel you picked yourself would last the entire winter in our frigid basements and garages. Ironically, during World War II, Americans were in the best physical condition of any time during the twentieth century as a result of getting plenty of exercise by walking and cycling everywhere, and consuming little red meat and sugar but lots of fresh fruit and vegetables. Ration books equaled portion control. Meantime, no one was on a diet, hitting the gym, taking buttrobics, or signing up for Zumba.

In retrospect, my friends and I were lucky to have parents who had grown up during the Great Depression (though I'm not sure what was so Great about it, much like the Great War) and World War II. They'd experienced privation and couldn't help but raise us to be aware of waste while appreciating what we had, even when it wasn't much. Every child was told how the starving children in Europe would love nothing more than the Brussels sprouts sitting bereft on their plate, and every wiseacre child suggested we mail said unloved vegetables to Europe. Our parents used every bit of soap including the sliver. You know that cotton wad in aspirin bottles? They saved it and many still do. Clothes were mended until they became material for remaking clothes (origin of the "shabby chic" movement), then quilts, rags, and finally rag rugs. Even during the worst years of the 1970s recession, when it came to improvising, we were rank amateurs compared to our parents, many of whom had lined the inside of their shoes with newspapers, used newspapers as wallpaper, and even wrapped themselves in newspaper to stay warm (a.k.a. "Hoover blankets"). Fire logs were made out of old newspaper. Our parents had so many uses for newspaper that they pioneered origami in America. They were also accustomed to having extended families including out-of-work relatives, parents, adult children, and grandchildren cramped under one roof and sharing a single bathroom. Most living room couches doubled as someone's bed, and bureau drawers served as baby cribs.

One thing poverty-stricken countries have in common is they produce little to no garbage as everything is reused or repurposed. Those of us growing up in the 1970s were trained to save paper cups and plates, lightly used napkins, envelopes from greeting cards, pieces of used tape with some stickiness left, half-burned birthday candles, and even bloody butcher string. Sandwich bags were washed out and reused, not to save the planet but to save money. Paper bags were employed as book covers and gift wrap. Teabags and coffee grounds were never thrown away after one pot. A quarter of an uneaten potato or carrot was put in the fridge. Leftovers became stews, soups, and sauces. Women had nifty tricks for preserving pantyhose, such as using clear nail polish to stop runs, and if one leg was ruined it was cut off, and the surviving side was matched with the good leg of another half-ruined pair. Cardboard boxes were considered anything but garbage, and corrugated ones were eagerly hunted. These could be used for moving, storage, mailing, animal homes and beds, garden kneelers, toy boxes, signage (especially those hung around the neighborhood for garage sales), car mats, blocking vents, and covering holes. However, to get any box it was necessary to fight off a mob of kids, since we desperately needed them for castles, forts, spaceships, tunnels, and armor.

As a result, today's crop of senior citizens are tough customers. They managed to live without cell phones or Internet for fifty years! Doctors were usually only summoned in the event of broken bones and dismembered limbs. Otherwise, everyone knew to lie down and rest for a headache or fever, gargle with salt water to cure a sore throat, and wrap duct tape around your warts. Tea made from chicken gizzards cured diarrhea, tobacco smoke fixed an earache, a spoonful of baking soda was taken for indigestion, and a clove was placed on a sore tooth. For all other aches and pains, you offered the anguish up to the Lord, and He'd take a view on whether to heal you or not. "Redemptive suffering" was an economical favorite of parents, priests, nuns, and gym teachers everywhere.

So . . . don't get frustrated when old people are moving to a smaller place and resist throwing things away. Don't bother explaining that organizations will no longer accept items with upholstery, ticking, or fabric due to bedbugs (or because your grandparents were chain-smokers). Save your breath on arguing how the deviled egg trays (in three different colors), dress shields, and metal ice cube trays won't find eager buyers at the flea market, or that cookie jars, crocheted tea cozies, and dolphin salt and pepper shakers are no longer the hot ticket must-have items they once were. Forget trying to make them understand that even though a bedroom set has been in the family for three generations, it's not revered as an "antique," and young people want to pick their own stuff from Pottery Barn, IKEA, Restoration Hardware, and Wayfair. You'll probably find yourself explaining there's no rummage sale at church, since all the women who washed, sorted, and labeled everything went back to work decades ago. It's not worth your trouble to point out that stored high chairs, cribs, car seats, swings, and even toys aren't considered safe anymore. Plus, the old strollers don't have cup holders, hand warmers, smartphone pouches, aromatherapy, or Wi-Fi.

Just say that it's all going to "charity"– every last worn dish towel, mismatched sock, button collection, and latch hook rug will be used and appreciated by a needy family and hospital thrift shop. Get your seniors out of the house, maybe to a nice all-you-can-eat-buffet, and then *make it all go away*. One more thing: those T-shirts with the funny slogans you gave your parents and they never wore? You're getting those back, and I expect to see you in them.

I go to seek a Great Perhaps.
—François Rabelais

Chapter 26

All Dads Go to Heaven

When it came to childrearing, my dad never established any rules. Bedtime was wide open. Want to use the electric drill, go wild. Snack whenever and wherever you want. Swim while you're eating. Jump hurdles and chew gum at the same time. He wasn't interested in controlling people and operated as a free spirit within most of society's parameters. Live and let live, learn from experience. A self-described humanist, he wouldn't cross picket lines, ignored any wildlife discovered indoors (or re-homed it when people were shrieking), and always picked up hitchhikers. By the 1970s, the era of killer cults and crime sprees, stopping for hitchhikers was considered a bad idea so Dad would always say, "Don't tell your mother," just like when his lit cigarettes landed in my crotch after he tossed them out the car window and they blew back inside. I never bothered to ask why he picked up hitchhikers, since it was something he'd always done. I imagine it was because he liked to think that on balance people were good, and perhaps growing up in the

Depression without much money he'd done some hitchhiking.

Another thing Dad didn't bother about was seeing doctors, despite having Grade A Cadillac health insurance from New York State after all those years working as a Supreme Court reporter. All we knew was that he'd passed a draft physical back in 1949 and been sent to fight in the Korean War. In 2011, when Dad was eighty, I enjoyed hassling him about the fact that the Korean War wasn't officially over. Every time we passed an Old Navy store, I suggested he go inside and re-up to finish the job.

Dad's medical philosophy was that if you had something, it would get better or else it wouldn't, so why bother with doctors. When people asked how he was doing, the choice was simple—vertical or horizontal. That said, as a chain-smoking, power-drinking, pastrami-and-potato-chip-loving, black-coffee-swilling octogenarian, when he turned eighty-one with no visible health problems, others were encouraged to resume their bad habits and also start some new ones.

However, a year later Dad was having trouble walking. Of course he wouldn't use a cane, and there was no chance he'd seek medical advice, since they might find something wrong. He was always a fan of telling me where all the keys were to everything in preparation for his eventual demise, but that Christmas I stayed an extra week, and he made additional references to the "bucket file," a cabinet with the house deed and his will. I could tell he was just hoping to go to sleep. He was a solid sleeper, so a few times I thought he'd succeeded until the smell of frying bacon and freshly brewed coffee brought him back.

When Dad turned eighty-one, my mother the nurse declared, "You know he'll never see a doctor. You're going to have to shoot him like an old horse." Typical of Mom, she didn't trust me to do it and announced that she'd fly out to New Mexico and euthanize Dad in her self-appointed role as a public-spirited health official. My sense was she had the barbiturate cocktail they used at the nursing home where she used to work in mind. Once again, I thought best to decline her generous offer. Even as a "mercy killing" in the Wild West, I didn't think it would play well with the sheriff, she being the ex-wife following an acrimonious divorce and all.

Meantime, Dad and I spent most of our time in what I called the Bad Habits Lounge, a renovated boat house adjacent to the main dwelling with a large television, overstuffed couches, and a regulation pool table. With air so dry it created sparks when I brushed my hair, a permanent haze from Dad's cigarettes, lightning that flashed through large windows during storms in the mountains, and *Pawn Stars* blaring in the background, I imagined it was like an Apache vision quest with a tribal elder. Roxy the Bologna Queen was our spirit animal, and instead of peyote we ate Wise potato chips.

When we parted in January, I knew it might be the last time I saw Dad, yet with his lifestyle choices, I'd been assuming that since he was in his forties and I was ten. From wherever I was, I'd call him every afternoon at five o'clock. I enjoyed talking to him, but he wouldn't use a Life Alert, so it was also a good way to determine that he wasn't lying on the floor with a broken hip. This February day I happened to be working in Minnesota, and it was so cold outside that I drove to the Mall of America to stretch my legs since walking outside was unpleasant at best. Dad and I had our usual phone conversation about favorite TV shows, the weather, and what his neighbors Connie and Alvin were up to. His kitchen window faced their driveway, and he kept track of their comings and goings like Gladys Kravitz on *Bewitched*. There was absolutely nothing odd about our conversation.

The following day I called at the appointed hour but the phone rang and rang. Dad didn't have an answering machine, just like he didn't own a computer or wear a seat belt. Sometimes he didn't replace the telephone receiver properly, and I got a busy signal, or occasionally he was out front chatting with Alvin or in the back talking to Tino the pool guy. Trips to town normally occurred in the morning, but he may have run out of cashews. If I didn't reach him on the first attempt, I would try back in thirty minutes and then an hour. If there was still no answer, I'd call Alvin and he'd go over to check on things. However, Connie and Alvin were on their way back from Las Cruces where Connie had undergone a hip replacement. I left a final message for Alvin saying that if they couldn't get back to me in thirty minutes, I'd have to call the police because something was wrong.

Alvin phoned twenty minutes later and said that Dad was gone. It's always a shock to hear that someone has died, but I couldn't say that I was entirely surprised. He'd taken his own life. Connie and Alvin are Lutheran, so Alvin was probably more stunned than I, unaware that this option had been on the table all along. I figured Dad owned a pistol, but I made a point never to look for it. In New Mexico it isn't necessary to have a license to buy or keep a handgun (but it's a petty misdemeanor to sing the state or national anthem incorrectly in public). Furthermore, despite being a pacifist, as a result of the Korean War Dad knew his way around a gun. As a kid, whenever we were at an arcade with a shooting gallery, and I wanted to win something, he'd do his crotchety act of, "Oh fine, if I have to," hand me his lit cigarette or move it to the side of his mouth, pick up a rifle, and perfectly clear a bunch of targets until I was happy with my prize.

Dad had typed up some lovely farewell letters for Alvin and me. His eyesight was shot by then, and he refused to have cataract surgery, so occasionally he went off the home keys, but it was all comprehensible. In the kitchen he'd left his notes underneath his wedding ring, and then gone out to the garage with his pistol. I can picture his look of "here goes nothing" while he put the gun to his temple and pulled the trigger, making a clean shot and dropping dead instantly, bleeding out on the cement floor, which he knew would be easier to clean than the cream-colored linoleum in the kitchen.

I made travel arrangements to fly out the next morning. Poor Alvin. He was Dad's best friend, but also the chosen one—Dad planned for Alvin to find him. More than once Dad had told me that because Alvin was a farmer, he knew how to deal with everything. And it was true, Alvin knew a lot about most things and a little bit about all the rest, from setting up power lines, to checking water tables. Dad had left Alvin a detailed letter explaining his thinking and even the timing—it transpired that he'd been trying to find a good day for weeks but a production of one of my plays in Manhattan and Connie's hip replacement in Las Cruces had delayed his plans.

Through the local funeral home, Alvin engaged a man to wash Dad's blood out of the garage. I arrived just as he was finishing, which spooked him, because I guess he worried I might go berserk. Since it's the desert, the ground is mostly different shades of beige, so when buckets of blood are thrown onto the lawn everything turns red. Oddly, I didn't mind having Dad around in liquid form. He'd always been a terrific card player, so I told him he'd played that last hand very well.

Whenever there's an unattended death, the police are required to do an investigation to ascertain that no foul play occurred. They'd already confiscated his pistol and the notes, but left us photocopies. Still, the police had plenty of questions for me. They'd turned over the entire house, including the Bad Habits Lounge, and found no medications. How was it that someone almost eighty-two who claimed he was "very ill" in these letters had no medication? "Did you check the garage?" I asked. There were three solid rows of Corona beer, several bottles of crème de cacao, and a half dozen cans of Chock full o' Nuts coffee.

However, the police were in search of pill bottles in order to get the name of Dad's primary care physician. There weren't any. These seasoned officers had seen pretty much everything, but were impressed that an octogenarian with full medical coverage didn't have a doctor. Because of the letters, there didn't seem to be any real question as to what had happened. The officer who'd read the letters looked at me and said, "He sure loved you a lot." Yes, he had. I was a lucky girl. On the other hand, when you're an only child, parents don't have much choice.

I went to Dad's "bucket file" where he'd organized his birth certificate, Army discharge papers, and Social Security card. He'd gone through and put funny post-it notes on everything. The first instructed me to give the pistol to Alvin since I'd be arrested for taking it across state lines. Another said "I requested a copy of my death certificate, but they said I had to wait. Damn bureaucrats." At the end of the instructions he wrote his traditional sign off: "Other than that, the future is bright."

His letter specified that he be cremated. He'd departed in his favorite outfit—Sergeant Schultz T-shirt under the shorty pink bathrobe belonging to his deceased wife (which he wore as a smoking jacket), red and black plaid pajama pants, and taped up, slip-on canvas shoes. I didn't request any wardrobe changes but I did suggest they cordon off a several block radius as I couldn't guarantee what the secondhand smoke situation would be like.

In his obituary I listed the cause of death as "heart failure" after concluding that, when you shoot yourself in the head, your heart fails to proceed. Dad had also specified in his letters that an autopsy would "make no sense," but New Mexico law requires one for an unattended death. The coroner's report, which I'd always assumed would list his cause of death as "pastrami" said, "gunshot wound of head." However, it did *not* say it was self-inflicted, and in fact sounded rather like Dad died in a gunfight at the O.K. Corral or a drive-by shooting. He definitely would have enjoyed that. A month later I received a letter from the chief medical investigator offering me a free appointment at the Grief Services Program in Albuquerque. Well, that was nice! But probably not worth flying out from New York.

In addition to the pistol, the wall of Corona beer was Alvin's legacy, so Dad would be happy it didn't go to waste. The house was sold to a family with children who were excited to swim in the pool and ride bikes in the neighborhood. Dad would be thrilled by that outcome, since he loved it when kids were having fun. The family who purchased the house is religious, and if I could tell Dad one thing it would be that the Bad Habits Lounge has been transformed into a prayer center. If the new occupants see a lingering cloud of smoke, I wonder if they'll think it's the Holy Ghost. I'm also tempted to ask if the room smells like Lucky Strikes, or Corona, or perhaps sulfur. . . .

Here's the strange thing—I've had to bring Dad back to life. I'm not like Norman Bates in *Psycho*, it's not that I haven't accepted he's gone—I know for a fact he's gone because my hair and clothes no longer smell like cigarettes and potato chips. He was such great material that I've always included stories about Dad in my talks, like how he was trying to prepare a healthy diet for my stepmother during an illness and went right past aisles of wonderful-looking fresh food to the canned meats and vegetables. "Why don't you use fresh food?" I asked.

"It doesn't come with any directions," he replied.

After he died, I continued including him in my work but mentioned that he'd passed away. Only that took all the fun out of it, and people felt bad, including me. So I've resurrected him for artistic purposes, and I know he'd be fine with that because he was a natural entertainer.

My earliest memories are of Dad standing in front of an audience singing with nothing but an acoustic guitar, not even an amplifier. He was blessed with a rich bass voice, perfect pitch, and had easily taught himself to play guitar. Whether crooning American classics such as "Scarlet Ribbons" and "Tom Dooley" or protest songs like "Where Have All the Flowers Gone?" and "Which Side Are You On?" his shows always drew a big crowd. Dad knew hundreds of tunes, including all the humorous ditties by Allan Sherman ("Hullo Muddah, Hello Fadduh") and Tom Lehrer ("Poisoning Pigeons in the Park") along with camp songs such as "Goober Peas," "John Jacob Jingle Heimer Schmidt" and "The Cat Came Back." He was wonderful at leading people in a round, which was an actual form of entertainment before cable television. People engaged when he performed. He possessed a magic power to make humans happy, and I wanted nothing else than to do the same. I learned the guitar at age five, but when Fortuna spun her wheel, the Pedersen musical gifts were not passed on. However, on special occasions, such as parties for anniversaries, retirements, and bon voyages, I'd write funny lyrics to a popular tune, and Dad would sing them to the assembled revelers.

I didn't need to be the one on stage so long as words could be used to make people smile.

It seems unfortunate that such a gentle soul had to die in such a violent manner, and perhaps that's something our society needs to consider remedying. It would have been better if we could have spent his last hours together telling jokes and eating cashews with *Pawn Stars* blaring in the background—though maybe not holding hands since we are Scandinavian after all—rather than him having to go into the garage all alone and slaughter himself like a broken-down race horse. The former scenario would by far have made for the better memory of his final hours.

I still talk to Dad every day. I know he isn't there, but I subconsciously prepare my script consisting of notes on TV shows and movies I've seen or read about, and updates on friends, coworkers, neighbors, or UU pals he'd remember. I don't believe he can actually hear me, nor do I believe in ghosts, unlike everyone on Mom's Irish side of the family, who are constantly being visited by spirits and tapped on the shoulder by deceased relatives.

Still, the people in my life regularly pop up in dreams, usually playing themselves, and act in character. For instance, I'll be trying hide something from my mother, or I'll be stuck inside a volcano with Mary. They'll both have lots of dialogue. Mom asks probing questions, while Mary has an idea that involves an impossible-sounding adventure.

However, I've only encountered Dad in a dream once, and he didn't identify himself until it was almost over. My car broke down on a highway in the middle of the night. Trucks barreled past at breakneck speed every few minutes, but hitching a ride or soliciting help wasn't possible—dreams always seem to have inexplicable constraints just like TV game shows, candlepin bowling, and being Amish. A man in faded jeans and a navy hoodie appeared out of the darkness and strode alongside me so he was closest to the traffic. We walked in silence until we reached an off ramp and the glow of a gas station. No words were exchanged. I turned toward the exit ramp, but he continued down the highway. I glanced back, and the flame of a lighter illuminated his face as he lit a cigarette.

That was always my big concern about Dad going to heaven—do they have a smoking section? Alternatively, he's wandering the highways of the Southwest for all eternity, possibly because he always liked hitchhikers. Or else the afterlife is like the inside of Connie and Alvin's Lutheran home and not a good fit for people like Dad, so he prefers being outdoors, and the clouds above us are actually cigarette smoke.

Section 3

ESTROGEN-
AMERICANS

Chapter 27

Working Girl

G rowing up in the 1970s and going to work in the '80s felt like passing through the vortex of the Women's Movement. My friends and I, without exception, had mothers who stayed home to cook and clean, while most knew how to sew and knit, and oftentimes quilt and crochet. They had come of age during a time when it was cheaper to make their own clothes, and food was prepared mostly from scratch.

Many moms were accomplished at shorthand and typing, as they'd taken the secretarial track then offered in public high schools, which was intended to supply basic skills to support young women while husband-hunting. My mother knew how to do all these things in addition to gardening, canning, painting, and wallpapering. She sewed her own clothes and mine until I was eight and made the bedspreads and curtains for our home. When I was ten, she went back to school for nursing, earned a master's degree, and began working, at which point all house-wife activities came to an abrupt halt.

However, I still needed skirts hemmed, a prom dress ironed, cookies for the bake sale, and term papers typed. My mother broached a secret covenant which I did not understand at the time. She offered to teach me how to cook, sew, iron, and touch type so long as I promised never to tell anyone I knew how to do these things. It sounded as if they were dangerous weapons, like Wonder Women's projectile tiara, lasso of truth, invisible jet, and bracelets of submission. As we ironed at night in the basement, I wondered why I needed to hide the exact same attributes which were supposed to be put on display to catch husbands and whispered, "Why does it have to be a secret?"

She said, "Because if people find out, you'll be doing it for the rest of your life for free. Trust me."

As a teenager I worked as a paper girl, dog groomer, dishwasher, and children's birthday party magician. I was also popular as a house sitter, especially for families with lots of animals. I'm flattered that other pet companions view me as a responsible caretaker, just like I've always been flattered to be mistaken for a prostitute. I mean, how many hookers or even showgirls wear a double-A bra?

The first time this happened, I was twenty and working on the trading floor of the stock exchange. Management would sometimes ask one of us to visit investment firms around the country that traded our index options to field questions. Thus it happened that I trundled off to Seattle and Vancouver with one of the marketers to spread the joys of trading the Major Market Index (20 blue-chip stocks of US corporations). Thirty-something Jay and I rented a car with the intention of driving from Seattle to Vancouver and with no concerns aside from whether to go whale watching or visit Butchart Gardens in Victoria in our spare time.

Having grown up only a bike ride away from Canada, I'd crossed the border weekly and never had a problem, not even when smuggling fireworks, Bauer Turbo plastic hockey skates with hinged ankles, and several pounds of Canadian bacon in the form of an enormous sandwich. However, this time we were immediately pulled over and I had no idea why, unless mild-mannered Jay was actually the Green River Killer, and the last five years on Wall Street had just been an elaborate cover story.

It transpired that the I-5 North was a popular route for men transporting American girls for the purpose of becoming sex slaves. I was eventually able to convince the border security agents that working in a trading pit had left me with the ability to solve math problems quickly in my head, so I had no need for the added income of a street walker, nor the time to earn it since I was taking night classes toward a finance degree at New York University. But it was certainly flattering to be considered a candidate for white slavery! In truth, I was hardly asked out on any dates, even as one of just a few women traders working in a city-block-sized room containing thousands of men, many of whom had substance abuse issues and shouldn't have been all that picky.

My next brush with sex tourism was similarly an international incident, but this time at the southern border. Following my adventures on Wall Street, I worked on *The Joan Rivers Show* which taped in midtown Manhattan. However, several times a year we decamped to Los Angeles for a week of shows to access a fresh group of movie stars, celebrities, and popular chefs. With a day off before heading back to Manhattan, a group of us gals decided to pop over the Mexican border to Tijuana. The others went shopping for tequila shot glasses and folk bags, while I decided to try my hand at chess against the locals in a neighborhood park. Afterward, I arrived at the designated corner to meet up for lunch and was about twenty minutes early, since I'm always early (New York buses and subways demand leaving extra time, and it becomes a habit) and stood waiting in shorts, a T-shirt, and sandals. Two police officers approached and in fairly proficient English told me I was under arrest for solicitation. They took me to the police station and offered three choices. First, I could be put in a jail cell and await the judge. It was Saturday and he'd be back on Monday. No, that definitely wasn't happening. Second, I could pay a $200 fine. Ah, the good old tourist shakedown. Now we were in business. But what could possibly be behind door number three? The final option was that I could purchase a prostitution license for $25. We had a winner. I am officially a licensed prostitute in Tijuana.

The next stop on my harlotry trail is Louisiana, where I was scheduled to address the New Orleans Chamber of Commerce following the publication of my book *Play Money*. As is the case with most speaking events, I was told to meet my contact person in the hotel lobby. However, it was Friday night, a wedding reception was gearing up, and so the spacious Marriott lobby brimmed with people in dress clothes, especially men in suits. Not knowing what my guy looked like, I began approaching middle-aged men standing by themselves and asking if they were from the Chamber of Commerce. In hindsight, I can imagine how this appeared to the undercover cops working the hotel. Upon asking the fifth gentleman if he was there to pick me up, and being smiled at politely while he shook his head to indicate no, two burly plainclothesmen escorted me to a back office and explained that solicitation was illegal. Despite the temptation to inform them that I am indeed a *licensed prostitute*, I showed them the paper containing the name of my Speakers' Bureau, event, schedule, and contact person. Honestly, I think they were even more skeptical that a twenty-five-year-old blonde female was addressing the New Orleans Chamber of Commerce back in 1991.

Great writers were so obviously
supposed to be male, and not anyone's aunt.

–Lucy Worsley

Chapter 28

The Pen Is Mightier Than the Broom

Not long ago I went to the 92nd Street Y in Manhattan to hear the insightful *Washington Post* media columnist Margaret Sullivan interview Alexander B. Heffner about the revised edition of his 640-page book *A Documentary History of the United States.* An audience member asked why there wasn't a single sentence by a woman in the entire tome. The author replied that American history was written by men. True as that may be, I was sad that room couldn't have been made for Sojourner Truth's "Ain't I a Woman?" speech, Elizabeth Cady Stanton's "Declaration of Sentiments," and Eleanor Roosevelt's "Universal Declaration of Human Rights." Surely half a page could have been given over for "The New Colossus" by Emma Lazarus, which was cast in bronze at the Statue of Liberty, and essentially reinvented the monument's purpose from celebrating triumph to welcoming immigrants.

Growing up, I adored Huck Finn and Tom Sawyer, but it sunk into my consciousness that girls weren't given much to do in those stories, while boys had all the fun. When playacting, I certainly never imagined myself as Becky Thatcher, which Cliffs Notes describes as "not a well-developed character." Even when women were the cause of the drama, like Helen of Troy, men got all the action. As I began writing novels, I wanted females to take the lead and have adventures, wind up in scrapes, and acquire the learning that comes with both failure and success. After all, experience comes from having experiences, and good judgment is usually a result of bad judgment. In most of my books and plays, females encounter obstacles and search for answers. In the children's and young adult stories, I sought to allow the youths to discover or create their own resolutions, rather than have them decided by a parent or teacher. That's not to say they can't receive feedback, support, or ideas from those arenas, but problem-solving is driven by the protagonists.

Women's writing has an altogether separate history than that of men's. From the start, it's been a struggle for women to tell their stories. In *The Odyssey,* Telemachus informs his mother, Penelope, that "speech will be the business of men" and sends her upstairs to her weaving. Of all the writers who flourished in what historians define as the Old English period, the Middle Ages, and the Renaissance, from *Beowulf* through *The Canterbury Tales* and Shakespeare, few were women.

In most cases, no one put a formal ban on women's writing, but it was suppressed using the same tactics by which it was suppressed in slave societies. Strategies, some more subtle than others, were employed to ignore, condemn, disparage, or doom artistic works. Methodology included informal embargoes, inaccessibility of training and materials, asserting that the content represented the author's bad character, or simply ignoring the work by not letting it be reviewed or even sold.

The following was written by Anne Finch, Countess of Winchilsea, in 1713: *To write, or read, or think, or to inquire would cloud our beauty, and exhaust our time, and interrupt the conquests of our prime, whilst the dull manage of a servile house is held by some our utmost art and use.* Hamlet famously told Ophelia, "Get thee to a nunnery, why wouldst though be a breeder of sinners?" Ironically, the convent often served as the best place for a female to gain an education and even become a writer.

There's a slim history of women's writing until the eighteenth century, which culminated in the American and French revolutions. In addition to being denied the necessary education and promotion, laws and customs prevented women from succeeding as authors. For one thing, they were not voters. Second, they were permitted to be wage-earners only in narrow capacities, as it was considered unseemly for well-bred women to enter professions. Furthermore, in England it was perfectly legal for men to imprison wives in their homes until 1891. That could make research a little difficult.

Surprisingly, the first collection of original poems produced in America in 1650 was written by a woman, Massachusetts resident Anne Bradstreet. However, the circumstances of its publication reveal much about the condition of a female author during the seventeenth century. In the prologue, Bradstreet acknowledged that many of her contemporaries thought a needle fitted her hand better than a pen. She could not have expressed herself had her father not given her an education superior to that of most women, or her husband not supported such intellectual pursuits.

Finally, her poems were printed because a brother-in-law took them, without her knowledge, to a publisher in England.

In an effort to remedy inferior treatment, women frequently employed male names, initials, or pseudonyms. "Why were most big things unladylike?" E.M. Forster wrote in *A Room with a View* (1908). "It was not that ladies were inferior to men; it was that they were different. Their mission was to inspire others to achievement rather than to achieve themselves. Indirectly, by means of tact and a spotless name, a lady could accomplish much. But if she rushed into the fray herself she would be first censured, then despised, and finally ignored. Poems had been written to illustrate this point."

The Brontë sisters often wrote under the male pseudonyms Currer, Ellis, and Acton Bell. George Eliot, author of seven novels and a leading writer of the Victorian era, was born Mary Anne Evans. Jane Austen published *Sense and Sensibility* as "A Lady" in 1811, while Mary Shelley released *Frankenstein* anonymously in 1818, and Pamela Lyndon Travers of Mary Poppins fame wrote as P.L. Travers. More recently, Pulitzer Prize winner Annie Proulx was made to publish outdoor stories under E.A. Proulx because editors said men wouldn't read them if it were known they had been written by a woman.

Things took a turn between the War of 1812 and the Civil War, when close to half the literature published in America was produced by women. The popular press openly encouraged female authors to submit, and they outsold names like Herman Melville and Nathaniel Hawthorne. These women were well-suited to the task, since it was possible to write from home while tending to their many other responsibilities. However, this publication bonanza was built on the understanding that women function in a separate sphere from men—one that didn't include politics, current events, worldly success, and competition. Authoresses were to promote domestic values of love, sympathy, morality, and family ties.

Charlotte Brontë wrote to then poet laureate Robert Southey in 1837 asking his opinion of her verse. Southey said it showed talent but advised her to give up thoughts of becoming a poet, since literature cannot be the business of a woman's life and ought not to be. It was a time when men wrote all the published poems *about* women—women who were beautiful and susceptible to the loss of beauty and youth, or beautiful and unattainable, or beautiful but destined to die young like William Wordsworth's Lucy and Edgar Allan Poe's Lenore.

Louisa May Alcott of *Little Women* fame was writing stories under the name A.M. Barnard in the mid-1860s. When she shared an essay about a stint as a governess called "How I Went Out to Service" with publisher James T. Fields, he rejected her work and advised, "Stick to your teaching, Miss Alcott. You can't write."

What women were able to accomplish depended on their responsibilities at home and whether there were servants. It's telling that of the four great female English novelists—Jane Austen, Emily Brontë, Charlotte Brontë, and George Eliot—not one had a child, and two were unmarried. Being Brits, they all had dogs and gave many of their characters dogs. In America, Emily Dickinson, Harper Lee, Flannery O'Connor, Louisa May Alcott, and Eudora Welty come to mind—all unmarried, all childless. (However, Flannery O'Connor had peacocks and a chicken that could walk backwards.) Many more women with writerly aspirations who followed would share such solitary circumstances. Harriet Beecher Stowe, abolitionist and author of twenty books including *Uncle Tom's Cabin*, is the exception, having given birth to eight children. One legend has it that, upon meeting Stowe in November of 1862, President Abraham Lincoln said, "So you are the little woman who wrote the book that started this great war." Apocryphal or not, from breast feeding to warmongering, Stowe was the original multitasker.

Still, men questioned whether wielding a pen was healthy for women. American writer Charlotte Perkins published a short story called "The Yellow Wallpaper" in 1892 about a woman prohibited from writing so she can recover from her "nervous depression." Virginia Woolf argued in her 1929 extended essay *A Room of One's Own* that both literal and figurative space be made available to women writers in a literary environment dominated by patriarchy. Woolf said that the obstacles faced by women writers are "immensely powerful" yet "difficult to define." One that wasn't hard to define was how the modernist Virginia Woolf was denied access to the library at Cambridge because she was not a "fellow" (a word which has no female equivalent). A male guardianship system in Saudi Arabia similarly prevents women from embarking upon certain fact-finding missions.

The imbalance continues to be hard to define. Men are more often considered to be writers of "literary fiction" while women write "popular fiction" or "chick lit." More books by men are reviewed than books by women. More book reviews are by men than by women. Some who study the issue say it's about persistence—that if a woman presents an idea but is told "this isn't quite right for us, try again," she doesn't return the following week with three new ideas, whereas a man does. She hears "this isn't quite right" while the man hears "try again." And maybe it's just a fluke, but bookstores, unlike supermarkets, tend to be unfriendly to baby carriages.

Joanne Rowling's publisher asked that she use initials when

publishing her first Harry Potter story in the 1990s because "young boys may not want to read a book by a woman." I wonder if Lewis Carroll was asked to disguise his male identity when putting out *Alice's Adventures in Wonderland* for fear of scaring off little girls, or if Roald Dahl was asked to use only his initials on *Matilda*.

For a long time in newspaper and TV journalism, it remained the case that legions of men would cover hard news while a few women were allowed to report on soft domestic issues. When Barbara Walters started out in the 1950s as a journalist, she was only allowed to cover the four Fs: food, family, fashion, and furnishings. As for column fodder, there were the goings-on of high society and advice to the lovelorn. By the time Wellesley College graduate Diane Sawyer entered the field in the 1960s, pretty faces were hired as "weather girls." Fortunately, both women were ambitious and decided a female could also interview world leaders and address political issues. When I was a child in the 1970s, there was a bra commercial presented by a man whose untweezed eyebrows and nose hair suggested he wasn't a cross-dresser. Not only that, it was an eighteen-hour bra, so the question arose: If you put it on at six in the morning and were out somewhere at midnight, did it fall apart, or worse, explode?

In the words of Virginia Woolf, women were "bitter and angry" by the time they finally took a seat—or rather a stool—at the table. Since then we've seen courage and determination in surmounting opposition and letting talent speak for itself. Just as people of different origins and classes often hold different values and perspectives, people of different sexes can have different values, concerns, and opinions that they need to share—in the quest for common ground and respect, and oftentimes change.

Does someone have to be a "woman writer" or can you be a writer who also happens to be a woman? Do you have to be a woman to write great female characters? Should men write only about men's concerns? In *Beowulf,* the oldest English epic poem, women are objects of exchanges, servants to men, monsters, and mothers of monsters. However, the roles were suddenly reversed in 1818 with Mary Shelley's *Frankenstein* when a grotesque male creature is produced in an unorthodox experiment, and is often considered to be the first science fiction story.

William Shakespeare, the greatest writer in the English language, didn't create inspirational roles for women, which isn't surprising when considering that he was at work between 1589 and 1613. In Shakespeare's plays, women were usually marrying down class-wise or intellectually as a result of being swept off their feet by men, stripped of their independence, and then submitting to a husband's power. The bard declared that to "end well" a woman must, like Viola in *Twelfth Night,* become her lord's "mistress and his fancy's queen." Meantime, his Joan of Arc (*Henry VI Part I*) begins wonderfully courageous, ready to lead men into fierce battle, yet just a few scenes later is a witch to be feared and destroyed. Cleopatra (*Antony and Cleopatra*) and Tamora (*Titus Andronicus*) are beautiful, brilliant, and ambitious to rule. Both have affairs and, perhaps in a nod to the reality of the times, both die tragically. The ruthless Lady Macbeth goads her husband into committing regicide, and after she's crowned, commits suicide; perhaps even worse, she dies offstage. The literate, lovely, and brave Juliet along with the ethereal, dutiful, stressed-out Ophelia likewise end up as suicides, alas and alack.

William Thackeray brought to life a rather complex character in Becky Sharp, a cynical social climber who employs her wiles to seduce upper class men. John Updike, on the other hand, was accused of writing two-dimensional women, while Norman Mailer was often an outspoken opponent of equal rights for women. Meantime, I'm not certain that F. Scott Fitzgerald ever wrote a likable female character.

What about creating romantic idols? Many people think Emily Brontë's Heathcliff is a passionate hero, while others believe him to be an enormous lout. In my opinion, the best character in literature is Scheherazade. She stopped a systematic female genocide while her stories taught the king how to be a better and more benevolent ruler. Interestingly, we don't know who created this character because the Arabian Nights tales were oral stories passed down for hundreds of years before finally hitting the page.

Even more than women authors, women dramatists have had a difficult time. Off the top of your head, can you name five women who've had their plays produced on Broadway? Similarly, few women have directed Broadway shows, or been producers, conductors, composers, lyricists, stage managers, or light and set designers.

Women's stories are important because everyone's stories are important. Aristotle says in *Poetics* that storytelling is what gives us a shareable world. We tell stories to heal and support one another in groups such as Alcoholics Anonymous because hearing about the hopes and challenges faced by others—to walk in their shoes or high heels or hiking boots, whatever the case may be—helps us to better understand and address our own problems, concerns, and fears.

*Seize the moment. Remember all those women on
the Titanic who waved off the dessert cart.*

—Erma Bombeck

Chapter 29

A Woman's Right to Joke

In 2007, scorched-earth journalist Christopher Hitchens, already famous for excoriating Mother Teresa, wrote a biting article for *Vanity Fair* magazine insisting that women aren't funny. However, this wasn't anything new. Hitchens was one in a long line of comedienne bashers that included funnyman Jerry Lewis, who consistently dressed up as a woman to get laughs. On *Saturday Night Live*, my favorite show as a teenager, comedy icon John Belushi would only act in sketches if he was told they'd been written by men, and regularly asked for the women to be fired because "chicks weren't funny." I was always told that Jews, despite comprising just one percent of the population, dominated comedy because it's all about experiencing oppression and marginalization. Yet, based on that theory, women should have been running the comedic universe, since they were created from Adam's rib as the original leftover.

Every year we see more females soaring ahead in occupations

previously considered male-only preserves. There are women surgeons, CEOs, presidential candidates, and fighter pilots, none of whom existed when I was growing up. We even have women suicide bombers and serial killers. Until recently, women weren't allowed to be firefighters or go into combat. Nowadays, women are being paid almost as much as men for playing tennis and are allowed to join previously restricted clubs. We're able to wear pants to work. My husband recently bought phlebitis stockings and complained how uncomfortable they are. He should try them with control top pantyhose and a pair of shoes that causes corns and bunions. The famous line that Ginger Rogers did everything Fred Astaire did except in high heels and backward is funny because it's true.

When I was growing up, it was fine for men to wear shirts open to the waist with gold medallions, a gunfighter's mustache, and tango dancer boots. Add gold hoop earrings, and he was a swashbuckling pirate or wish-granting genie. But God forbid, if a girl so much as pierced her ears, she was labeled a prostitute. And if she had two holes in each ear, she would probably grow up to be an *actress*. Pretty bows were attached to the heads, fronts, backs, and shoes of school girls, making them appear hastily regifted. I constantly hear how men over forty are "single" (happy) while women over forty are "alone" (sad). On the plus side, when a man talks dirty to a woman it's sexual harassment, but when a woman talks dirty to a man it's approximately four dollars per minute.

When I began doing stand-up, there were few women onstage, and comedy club bookers weren't exactly welcoming. However, for me this was a step up, since I'd previously had a seat on the stock exchange. In a comedy club I used the same bathroom as the men, or else the facilities were similar and side-by-side. At the stock exchange, women had only recently been allowed to become members, so the men enjoyed a palatial marble lavatory on the main floor with an attendant, conveniently located a few yards from the trading floor entrance. Meantime, the gals had to descend a flight of stairs to the basement where there was a setup just like in elementary school—three narrow stalls with thin metal dividers covered in peeling tangerine paint. I always expected a hall monitor to poke her head in and shout, "Are you girls smoking in there?"

Wall Street featured plenty of "locker room talk," propositioning, and inappropriate touching. One learned how to respond with a cutting remark or quick jab. Jackets with shoulder pads the size of couch cushions were in style, and this was fitting sartorial symbolism for the rough and tumble environment. Most firms were public about the fact that they wouldn't hire women to be brokers. However, as a trader, the field was somewhat leveled because at the end of the day, your success or failure is measured almost solely by profit or loss. Thus, if you were any good, it might be possible to rise to the top using your own abilities and earn a substantial salary plus bonus.

This wasn't true as a stand-up comedian. Women had difficulty securing equal time in clubs and exposure on TV shows, yet these sought-after slots were the launching pads for stand-up specials, sitcom deals, and jobs as late-night talk show hosts. The decision-makers were men, and they took a dim view of women performing stand-up. The managers and agents, who were predominantly men, while seeking new acts, and bookers scouting talent for the late-night shows, rarely chose women.

Comedy clubs were also the perfect storm for bad interactions with the opposite sex, as dozens of men drank at the bar while waiting to perform and often stuck around to fraternize with their cohorts. Clearly the best way to create opportunities would have been to make myself available to the men who ruled. One even followed me home and slept on the mat outside my apartment door.

It didn't take long to decide that the world of stand-up comedy clubs and TV bookers wasn't a place I wanted to work or felt I could succeed on my own terms. I left to be a humor writer and took a job at *The Joan Rivers Show*. After years of guest-hosting Johnny Carson's *The Tonight Show* to great acclaim, it had been made clear to Joan that she wouldn't inherit his throne (which indeed went to a man), so she launched her own late-night talk show in 1986. Carson (the hero of every male comic) immediately blackballed Joan throughout the industry for having the nerve to proceed without his explicit permission, and her show failed. However, Joan went on to land a daytime television talk show for which she quickly won an Emmy Award.

Joan continued doing club dates, and I watched as male comics regularly got angry when she received more laughs, and many bookers continued to abide by Carson's fatwa against her. She was passed over to win the Mark Twain Prize for American Humor again and again for sixteen years, and she died at age eighty-one in 2014 without ever having received it. Joan was not only a comedy writer and performer, but a producer and director. In addition to the Daytime Emmy Award for outstanding talk show host, she won a Tony Award for her tour de force performance on Broadway as Lenny Bruce's mother in *Sally Marr . . . and Her Escorts*, and a (posthumous) Grammy Award for Best Spoken Word Album for her book *Diary of a Mad Diva*. What more should she have done? Several recipients of the Mark Twain Award were merely comic actors and didn't even write.

Joan Rivers was friends with comedian Phyllis Diller, who died at age ninety-five in 2012 after a career that spanned seventy years. Diller took great pains to make herself ugly by wearing fright wigs and hideous makeup when performing. Funnily enough, in real life Diller was pretty and had a fantastic figure that she hid underneath clownish costumes that obscured her shapeliness so she could joke about how unappealing and unattractive she was to men. In addition to being a groundbreaking stand-up comic, she performed in more than forty films. Phyllis Diller was never awarded the Mark Twain Prize for American Humor either. Bill Cosby won in 2009 only to have it rescinded in 2018 after his conviction for sexual assault.

Despite the jokes, both women knew better than anyone how looks mattered when it came to getting ahead in show business and underwent multiple plastic surgeries as they aged. Their "love of plastic surgery" was featured in both their obituaries, and how they'd gamely joked about it. People often say it's hard to define humor. It's not. Humor may vary from person to person, but it's whatever makes you laugh—Lucy and Ethel stuffing their faces with chocolates speeding off a conveyor belt, Carol Burnett as Scarlett O'Hara wearing curtains still on the rod, the exceptional wit in Margaret Edsen's Pulitzer Prize-winning play *Wit*, or the musings of Dorothy Parker, who said "I'd rather have a bottle in front of me than a frontal lobotomy."

The way I see it, we have two choices. 1) Keep demonstrating in print, on screen, and on stage that women have a voice, unique perspective, and are, indeed, funny, because laughter is a form of liberation. Or 2) As my favorite camp counselor Dee Dee liked to say, "Cry all you want. You'll have to pee less."

Let us choose for ourselves our path in life,
and let us try to strew that path with flowers.
—Émilie du Châtelet

Chapter 30

Lady Scientists

In the old days one often heard the words "Ladies and Gentlemen." But I guess that's not politically correct anymore and it's safer just to say "Chains of Atoms." When discussing Women and STEM—by women I mean over 50 percent of the population and by STEM I mean science, technology, engineering, and math—the fact is that women make up less than 25 percent of people who work in STEM.

The reasons spring from societal and cultural norms and expectations. One overriding factor has been that, until recently, restrictions on women's educations were common, and in much of the world still are. If women did write they weren't supposed to publish, if they painted they weren't supposed to exhibit, and if they were talented musically or theatrically they weren't supposed to perform outside the drawing room. The same was true in science where they weren't supposed to work in labs or publish scientific papers.

Leading male academics have proclaimed that women, in addition to not being funny, aren't as smart as men, and more specifically, aren't as good at math as men. Yet it took mother and columnist Erma Bombeck to make the groundbreaking mathematical discovery that you should never have more children than you have car windows. As for the social sciences, Rita Rudner has successfully tackled psychology. She says, "When I meet a man I ask myself, is this the man I want my children to spend their weekends with?" and advises looking for a man with a pierced ear since they're better prepared for marriage because they've experienced pain and bought jewelry.

When women finally gained wider access to higher education there was usually a catch—often they'd be given no space to work, no funding, and no recognition. Lise Meitner wasn't allowed to enter the university building because of her gender and undertook her radiochemistry experiments in a dank basement. As a result, we have nuclear fission and nuclear reactors to generate electricity. Without funding for a lab, Marie Curie handled dangerous radioactive elements in a tiny, dusty shed, yet she pioneered research on radioactivity and was the first woman to win a Nobel Prize. After making one of the most important discoveries in the history of astronomy, Cecilia Payne-Gaposchkin received little recognition and for decades was limited to work as a technical assistant.

If you read the book or saw the movie *Hidden Figures* about black female mathematicians working at NASA during the space race, it was clear that creativity, persistence, and love of discovery were the greatest tools these women had. It would be nice if young people were taught that Rosalind Franklin made an enormous contribution to the discovery of the double helix structure of DNA by James Watson and Francis Crick; that we have Grace

Hopper to thank for creating modern computer programming; and that famous film actress Hedy Lamarr pioneered the technology that made smartphones possible.

One can rightly argue that we want diversity in *every* field because different problems and experiences bring a variety of approaches and solutions. Elizabeth Blackwell was the first woman in America to receive a medical degree, from Hobart College in 1849. She was voted in as a practical joke but showed up anyway. Blackwell became a pioneer in treating and promoting women in medicine and an early advocate of hand-washing when very little was known about communicable diseases.

Silicon Valley in California embodies the idea that advances are made through proximity. Likewise, the web of medical research, technology, and treatment facilities that have grown up in Buffalo, NY, where mass industry similarly rose a century earlier, highlights the advantages of synergy. Women also need proximity to contribute.

We must encourage girls when it comes to the sciences, but we also need to stress that because they may not be especially good in math or physics or biology it doesn't mean there isn't a place for them. Because that just isn't true. Talented musicians aren't necessarily able to play every instrument, sing, conduct, write, and teach music. In fact, almost every woman can tell you that someone who cooks fantastic entrees won't necessarily bake a good cake. And everyone who bakes will tell you that most cakes either look bad and taste good or conversely look good and taste bad, because the creators tend to excel in one arena over the other.

Then there is the circular argument that because more men occupy the highest levels of STEM, they have a natural predilection for such disciplines, and this makes the rise easier for them.

Ironically, research demonstrates that boys and girls have, on average, similar abilities in math, but girls are consistently better in reading and writing. So even though her math skills are as good as those of the boys, she feels that she's better in language arts, and she's right. Feeling that you're bad at something is the quickest path to disliking it. Not wanting to devote attention to math class and homework soon turns an aversion into an actual weakness. Math is like playing a musical instrument in that the learning is cumulative and practice is obligatory. Unfortunately, doing math is not always agreeable, the same way practicing an instrument isn't always fun, while reading a book for an English or history class is normally engaging.

The good news in the US is that the obstacles which have left women with a 25 percent representation in STEM (while they make up 52 percent of the population) are cultural and psychological rather than legal or institutional. And these can be changed as awareness is raised and accomplishment noted. If women were really biologically incapable of performing well in science and math we'd have to give up the fantasy of increasing their numbers, but that's just not the case. We don't need to elevate young women's IQs, only their confidence. One way is to provide images of female scientists and toys that nurture. Another is by encouraging girls to take AP calculus, and change the problems in their textbooks so they don't presume an interest in football or war. It would be nice if girls could appreciate the joys of designing a computer game that doesn't involve blowing off people's heads, while working in spaces that feel more like classrooms, offices, and laboratories rather than a fraternity house gone bad.

We can fight the anti-intellectualism that pervades our culture and equates nerdy females with unpopularity. This prejudice strikes most cruelly at adolescent girls, precisely at a time when exaggerated concerns about social status dovetail with important academic choices. It would be delightful to see more creative Halloween costumes and fewer slutty (fill in the blank). If all else fails, one can rest assured the real advantage of being a woman in STEM fields is that there's never a line for the restroom.

The way I see it, we have two choices. 1) Keep demonstrating in print, on screen, through inventions, innovations, patents, and academic excellence that women have a voice, a unique perspective, and the talent to solve problems, heal people, and help cure society's ills. Or 2) As my favorite camp counselor Dee Dee liked to say, "If you don't like the way something is then tie-dye it."

Christian culture has too often offered women a push toward
contentment that can numb us to our own desires,
without offering the tools to discern whether those desires
could be good or Holy Spirit-inspired.

–Katelyn Beaty

Chapter 31

Does God Have a Woman Problem?

Whether you believe that man invented God or God invented man, religion is a manmade institution, literally. At the end of a prayer we say Ahh-men, not Ahh-women. Having male leaders wear dresses and shawls is not fooling anyone.

Most religions were created by men, who then gave themselves power over women. Women were supposed to follow the religion but not study it too closely or, God forbid, lead it. The majority of the world's religions have no female leaders and have treated women as second-class citizens, from Orthodox Judaism and Islam, through fundamentalist Christianity and Catholicism, with men controlling women's marital and reproductive rights along with numerous restrictions on their behavior, education, and life choices. Unitarian suffragette Elizabeth Cady Stanton said, "You may go over the world and you will find that every form of religion which has breathed upon this earth has degraded woman."

In Judaism there's a morning blessing by men which praises God "who has not made me a woman." The New Testament says, "But I suffer not a woman to teach, nor to usurp authority over the man, but to be in silence." The Koran stipulates that a woman shall inherit less than a man, and that a woman's testimony counts for half of a man's. Even if she's bigger than he is. When I was growing up in heavily Catholic Buffalo, girls who became pregnant in high school were said to have mononucleosis and shipped off to an aunt in Rochester or Cleveland to recover. The babies were taken from them and put up for adoption while they "went on" with their lives, always knowing that a child was somewhere out in the world, hopefully succeeding, but perhaps suffering.

Isabella Baumfree was born into slavery in upstate New York in 1797. Yes, there was slavery in New York State until 1827. She escaped with her infant daughter, sued for custody of her son, and became the first black woman to win such a case against a white man. At the 1851 Women's Convention in Akron, Ohio, she, by then known as Sojourner Truth, delivered a speech called "Ain't I a Woman?" which contains the lines, "Then that little man in black there, he says women can't have as much rights as men, cause Christ wasn't a woman! Where did your Christ come from? From God and a woman! Man had nothing to do with Him."

Evangelical Christians in this country have by and large aligned themselves with an administration that attacks women's healthcare and reproductive rights, thereby threatening their opportunities, ability to work, freedom, happiness, and of course their very lives. Rev. Paige Patterson, formerly of the Southwestern Baptist Theological Seminary, made this clever comment about women: "I think everybody should own at least one." Meantime, every Congressional chaplain since 1774 has been a white male Christian. Half a million of your tax dollars go to supporting that office each year even if you're a Frisbeetarian.

Tony Perkins, head of the Conservative Family Research Council, gave the Sexual Harasser in Chief "a mulligan," or do-over, after President Trump paid hush money to a sex worker with whom he had an extramarital dalliance—a single blemish on an otherwise spotless record. All are shenanigans they find unforgivably sinful when committed by a Democrat.

It seems almost counterintuitive, but women have always been central to the functioning of religion. One reason is that women most often deal with the important but everyday issues of life and survival, including birth, childrearing, cooking, housekeeping, and caring for the sick and dying. And when men can't find their keys and kids can't locate their shoes and the dog wants to be fed, do they ask God for help? Do they ask Jesus? No, they usually ask women.

So I think we can agree that women are good for religion, but is religion good for women? Some of us are old enough to remember when churches hollowed out in the 1970s and '80s, not because people suddenly became uninterested, but as a direct result of women going back to work. The women who supplied and organized the craft bazaar, potluck supper, ice cream social, auction, and white elephant sale were suddenly no longer giving away their time and talent for free. Back then every woman had a signature dish or famous baked good, while I just can't recall any Cory's Coffee Toffee Bars or Pete's Pecan Sandies. Laws controlling women's work had begun to change. When my mom first entered the labor force, laws written by men determined the number of hours she could work while marriage and pregnancy meant a pink slip. Additionally, the help wanted ads were divided into "men's work" and "women's work," and the "women's work" usually involved typing and filing the "men's work."

I grew up in a world run by men—they were my doctors, dentist, town councilmen, mayor, governor, senators, vice president, and president. They were airline pilots, ship captains, taxi drivers, disc jockeys, lawyers, judges, presidents of every large company and neighboring countries. They were the principals of my schools, where I learned about the founding *fathers*, and my newscasters who reported on the men fighting in Vietnam and the men who sent them to fight. They were my police officers, rock stars, disc jockeys, artists on view at the Albright-Knox Gallery, and statues in parks. Only men had cheerleaders leaping about at their sporting events. Only men had national holidays named in their honor. When my pockets contained money, it was coins and bills with engravings of men. In fact, it was announced in 2016 that abolitionist and suffragette Harriet Tubman would be the first woman to appear on paper money—and now the Treasury has no firm plans to go forward with that.

Men were my ministers as they were my friends' priests and rabbis. In our heavily Catholic neighborhood, the trajectory for girls and boys interested in theology was crystal clear. Girls became nuns. Males were altar boys, elders, priests, chaplains, deacons, lectors, abbots, prelates, bishops, archbishops, cardinals, and popes. A class field trip took us to hear the Vienna Boys Choir perform at the 3700-seat Shea's Theatre, and the Boys of

King's College singing at a Christmas Eve service was broadcast around the world. Where was the girls' choir? Women baked, taught Sunday School, sewed costumes for plays, and laundered the choir robes and tablecloths.

How do we know women's work was undervalued? The "laundry room" was always the smallest, ugliest, coldest, darkest, dampest room in the house, more often the basement. And there are "washerwomen" but no "washermen"—check your spell check right now. There were "men of letters" but no "women of letters." Imagine my surprise to learn in school that scientists believe women have actually been on the planet as long as men! And based on that, I've deduced they're probably here to stay, at least as long as men are around.

Then there were the invisible men: the Father, the Son, and the Holy Ghost or Spirit of Man, to whom one prayed and asked forgiveness. And let's not forget that old Devil. Come to think of it, Santa Claus and God have an amazing amount in common—old, super white guys with white beards, both all-knowing and extremely judgmental.

Women have Eve, who is singlehandedly responsible for the fall of mankind. In the New Testament's First Epistle to Timothy it says, "For Adam was formed first, then Eve. And Adam was not the one deceived; it was the woman who was deceived and became a sinner." Although sometimes I think we bury the lede in this story—it was a sin to acquire knowledge.

Speaking of wicked women, the ratio of women to men accused of witchcraft throughout history is about one thousand to one. Like other minorities, the witch has been blamed for social ills such as the Great Plague and the Hundred Years' War between England and France. Also for weather-related issues such as crop failures, the death of livestock, or houses burning down. It's nice to know that witches were at least given credit for being multitaskers.

These supernaturally empowered females were believed to undermine the authority of locally male-run governments and churches. Estimates of women tortured and executed for witchcraft are in the millions. Between 1560 and 1700 there were numerous witch trials in America, with hundreds of women executed by hanging, drowning, and burning. Women were easy targets because they had no political, judicial, or religious agency, and were being executed by male theocrats. Many accusations carried sexual undercurrents, and also political motivations, as coincidentally some of the women were property owners and involved in altercations over land and grazing rights. A number of girls were killed and also a few men. Two dogs were hanged for witchcraft but records don't indicate whether they were male or female.

In evolution there's an advantage to be had from our sense of revulsion since it creates avoidance, whether steering clear of unclean drinking water, spoiled meat, infection, or poisonous snakes. But through religion this feeling has been metaphorically transferred to disgust for the human body. And since sexual desire is part of the body's primary function, it must be controlled, which in traditional religions means controlled from the male point of view. By definition the Virgin Birth declares sexuality sinful and promotes the idea that the untouched female body is the best body.

In the Bible, the book of Deuteronomy states that if a woman does not bleed on her wedding night, "the men of her town shall stone her to death." Mohammad said, "I have left behind no temptation more harmful to men than women." Females are the focus of desire, so their bodies must be covered, hidden away, and undergo ritual cleansings. Their behavior must be monitored and limited, whether it means adult women having chaperones or being slut-shamed for dating in America. Then there's genital mutilation, being forced into marriage as a child, or having to carry a baby to term after being raped. In most countries, including this one, mostly male religious leaders, politicians, and judges decide women's health care and reproductive rights.

Women have been cast as temptresses and seductresses again and again, and therefore modesty in women is considered a primary virtue, certainly in the three Abrahamic faiths. Even a woman's voice is considered seductive and won't be heard in an Orthodox temple or mosque. As a girl I was regularly informed that smoking, swearing, and gum-chewing in public were fine for men but not for women. Many women have attempted to turn perceived shame and lack of agency into their own form of spirituality, such as with goddess-based religions. But I think you're working with a bad hand when forced to worship against something rather than toward something.

We're currently in the midst of a religious power struggle. Anglican women in Britain want to be priests and bishops. Catholic nuns want leadership roles. Buddhist women want equal status as monks. Some are calling for the next Dali Lama to be a Dali Mama. In Islamic countries, educated women are studying the Koran and demanding change. Dozens of women who've left the Mormon religion in America have written books about living in a sometimes polygamous faith where women must yield to male authority on Earth *and* in Heaven.

Then we come to religion as overt abuse—warlords in Congo cite Scripture to justify mass rapes. Brides are burned in India if the wife's family won't provide an additional dowry. A Muslim man can have four wives, but a Muslim woman can have one husband and good luck leaving if he beats her; she needs permission from her husband or religious authorities to file for divorce. Meantime, Jihadists throw acid in the faces of girls who attempt to go to school.

Beyond flat-out gender inequality, most religions haven't had much place or purpose for women who are not wives and mothers. They are continuously honored, but mostly for playing nurturing roles, much as Mary is celebrated for being the mother of Jesus. In Catholicism women may be martyrs and saints but are rarely involved in policymaking or governance. Religions derive their power and popularity in large part from the ethical compass they offer in a morally challenging world, so why do many continue to uphold what most of us regard as profoundly unethical: the oppression of women.

In 1776, when America was fighting for independence, future First Lady Abigail Adams said "remember the ladies." How perfect for a commemorative tea towel or needlepoint pillow. But here's what she actually said: "I desire you would Remember the Ladies, and be more generous and favourable to them than your ancestors. Do not put such unlimited power into the hands of the Husbands. Remember all Men would be tyrants if they could. If perticuliar care and attention is not paid to the Ladies we are determined to foment a Rebelion, and will not hold ourselves bound by any Laws in which we have no voice, or Representation."

There's a fault line going through religion at present—within Judaism, Christianity, Islam, and also Mormonism, the fastest growing faith in the US. Restrictive policies are damaging for women, while progressive faiths hold open the possibility of being beneficial because they allow for equal participation, cooperation, and thereby transformation of ourselves, our communities, and our world.

It makes sense that we all want to partake in the quest to understand why we are here and to imbue our lives with purpose. We *all* want the opportunity to explore a meaningful relationship with the divine and a moral relationship with each other. We *all* want to consider our moral compass and seek inspiration, a window onto our psyche, ways to create community, and have a place to share our joys and sorrows. Terrific! The only problem is that fundamentalists reproduce at least twice as fast.

So the answer is to have more babies. Not really. I mean, you can if you want. I suggest we employ the same forces used against slavery. Judaism, Christianity, and Islam all approved of slavery and most employed religion to justify it. Muhammad owned slaves, St. Paul condoned slavery, and twelve US presidents were slaveholders, including the author of the Declaration of Independence, Thomas Jefferson. And he didn't release them upon his death, unless we count his own four children by Sally Hemings, who was Jefferson's slave. I won't employ the term "slave mistress," since I'm not sure how much consent was involved in an institution where women were regularly raped and children sold from their families. And I don't use the word mistress since there's no male equivalent. It appears Jefferson first impregnated Ms. Hemings when she was sixteen. Sally Hemings was the daughter of slave Betty Hemings and Jefferson's first wife's father. So that made Sally the half-sister of Jefferson's first wife Martha, *and* Jefferson's sister-in-law. How's that for one degree of separation?

People of faith worked nonstop against other people of faith to end this oppressive institution. In 1833 social justice activist Lydia Maria Child wrote a book titled *An Appeal in Favor of That Class of Americans Called Africans* demanding the immediate cessation of slavery. Her work greatly influenced Unitarian theologian

Theodore Parker, who said in an 1853 sermon, "I do not pretend to understand the moral universe. The arc is a long one. My eye reaches but little ways. I cannot calculate the curve and complete the figure by experience of sight. I can divine it by conscience. And from what I see I am sure it bends toward justice." This was ingeniously paraphrased by Dr. Rev. Martin Luther King Jr. during the Civil Rights Movement a century later.

Little Women author Louisa May Alcott's childhood home was an Underground Railroad stop, and she grew to be a fierce abolitionist, in addition to an advocate for women's rights and African American rights, or human rights as they're better known. Charles Darwin finally published *On the Origin of Species* in November of 1859 in the UK and January of 1860 in the US. It emphasized the physical over the spiritual, saying that we all—black, brown, yellow, red, white—came from the same beginning or source, or well, Origin. This, as much as anything, rendered slavery impossible. The Civil War began fifteen months later.

Such changes, no matter how obvious they seem now, don't happen overnight. Elizabeth Cady Stanton and Susan B. Anthony didn't live to see women finally granted the right to vote in 1920. Martin Luther King Jr. didn't live to see passage of the Civil Rights Act in 1968. Movements are attempts at rebalancing. A hundred years after Abolition, we had Civil Rights, and fifty years after that Black Lives Matter. A hundred years after the Suffragettes came Women's Liberation, and fifty years later the #MeToo Movement. In 1924 the Society for Human Rights in Chicago became the first gay rights organization in the US. Fifty-five years later, the Log Cabin Republicans formed to effect change from within that party. What they all have in common is the objective of achieving full personhood.

I'm delighted to count myself a supporter of Black Lives Matter. But it does occur to me that a black man has been president of the United States and Secretary-General of the United Nations and governor of New York State and mayor of New York City, but there's never been a woman in any of those roles. Still, there are signs of hope all around us: Women in Saudi Arabia are permitted to drive. Women in Iran are removing their veils. Women in the US are running for elected office in droves, and winning, along with occupying more spaces in college and university STEM programs.

Is this bad for men? Quite the contrary. An equal world is a better world. Bangladesh was starving until women were given opportunity and agency. Just look at a list of the world's poorest countries—it's where the gender gap is largest. Conversely, men are able to explore work options formerly considered female, such as nursing and librarianship, without shame or stigma. They're getting manicures and waxing and dying their hair. Has anyone seen Tom Selleck lately, the septuagenarian actor and NRA spokesman? Do you think his mustache is really that black? There's a young man working at the East 86th Street MAC cosmetics store, and if that's not his dream job he should be an actor, since I can only fantasize about getting so excited over moisturizer. But seriously, no one is laughing at him or rolling their eyes. No one is shaming or shunning him, and most important, no one is blocking the path to pursue his passion.

A friend recently traveled to India and blogged about the trip. He said we should consider the benefits of arranged marriage because the divorce rate there is much lower. I said, did you ask the women what happens with their status, finances, kids, opportunities, and chances for remarriage if they get divorced? No, he did not. I remember people here bemoaning the divorce rate rising in the swinging sixties and saying how terrible that was. Prior to that the stigma was so great that people in terrible marriages were afraid to divorce—women in particular, because they sometimes lost custody of their children and ended up in low paying jobs and poverty by old age.

When I was young my parents stayed in a miserable marriage because of the disgrace attached to divorce. They used different entrances to the house, drove separate cars to church, and had me say, "Mom, Dad wants you to pass the salt and remember to put on the snow tires." It was not a happy household. Even the cat tried not to be home much. Reading *The Scarlet Letter* in school resonated with me as Hester Prynne and Rev. Arthur Dimmesdale's lives were in upheaval due to shame, guilt, and punishment, while daughter Pearl became increasingly rambunctious. My only complaint about the book was that all the good parts happened before it began.

When society places limitations on people, like preventing gays from marrying and thwarting blacks from living in certain neighborhoods and stopping minorities from voting, it inevitably results in a loss of freedom and dignity, with plenty of collateral damage, which can include the health and well-being of children. In addition to loss of opportunity, it also results in reduced circumstances, despair, and even suicide. If indeed every time a bell rings, an angel gets its wings, then every time a person is prevented from fulfilling his or her or their potential because of some made-up rules, there's a hole punched in the universe.

Abolitionist Lydia Maria Child said, "But men never violate the laws of God without suffering the consequences sooner or later." What might those consequences look like? Women leaving religion altogether and taking children with them? The question is, can we continue to make progressive religion appealing when there's such gender inequality in the world of faith? I believe we can if we continue to champion women and girls in our homes, schools, workplaces, houses of worship, government, and most important, in our lives, while encouraging others to do the same. How are we doing this? With social justice programs, sex education classes, support of pay parity, harassment-free environments, sports opportunities, and the fight against sex trafficking.

There will *always* be differences between men and women and those who define themselves otherwise, and that equilibrium is a blessing, as poet John O'Donohue explains in *To Bless the Space Between Us.* The greater our integrity and awareness, the more positive and creative our time together will become. As we see more women surgeons, astronauts, physicists, police sergeants, ministers, rabbis, imams, priests, popes, governors, senators, judges, and even presidents, that's the irrefutable science, and then there's no turning back.

Personally, I'd like to get to where we no longer need a Women's History Month; I hope I'm not reading too much into the fact that March is the crappiest month of the year, like one giant hangover. Finally, to paraphrase Dr. Martin Luther King Jr., and I feel fine doing that since Dr. King paraphrased Unitarian Minister Theodore Parker:

Well I don't know what will happen now. We've got some difficult days ahead. But it really doesn't matter with me now, because I've been to Wall Street. And Random House. And *The New York Times.* And I've looked over. And I've seen the Promised Land. I may not get there with you. But I want you to know that we, as a people, will get to the Promised Land. So I'm happy, today. I'm not worried about anything. I'm not fearing any man. For mine eyes have seen the glory of the coming of the girls.

Section 4

HUMAN KIND

People don't look like people anymore after they've
fallen from over a hundred floors above the ground.
–Rebecca McNutt

Chapter 32

9/11

I n 2001 I was hosting a television show where I interviewed politicians, celebrities, and businesspeople. On September 10, 2001 I flew to Dallas, Texas, to interview Colleen Barrett, the accomplished president of Southwest Airlines. However, I awoke to see the Twin Towers collapsing, just three blocks from where I used to work on the American Stock Exchange. Oddly, at first glance, the air was reminiscent of a tickertape parade, with millions of tiny slips of paper floating to the ground like snowflakes. The TV segment was not only canceled, but I wanted to get home as soon as possible. Having left Wall Street just a few years earlier, I knew over a thousand people who worked in and around the World Trade Center, including many good friends and old flames.

All planes were grounded, and it appeared the nation's airports would be closed for days, if not longer. Likewise, trains and buses were on hold when it came to routes destined for the tri-state area. I grabbed a piece of shirt cardboard and wrote NYC on it with the intention of hitchhiking if worse came to worst. I knew that food, especially dairy and produce, would still be heading north, and I could catch a ride with a trucker. Before hitting the highway, I stopped at a rental car agency only to be told that they'd just signed out the last vehicle—most travelers had the same idea once their airline tickets were rendered useless.

On my way out, I spotted four guys walking toward the parking lot of cars for hire who looked like they operated an accounting firm in Midtown and asked if they were heading for Manhattan. Sol, Len, Barry, and Nate were indeed stranded in Texas after a business meeting and intent on driving two days straight in order to return home. I could tell they weren't happy about the prospect and would much prefer to be in a business class cabin enjoying scotch and warm nuts, starting to read *The Wall Street Journal,* and then dozing off. Moreover, they looked at me as if I were a side dish they hadn't ordered. Still, I showed them my driver's license and said I could help drive if need be and pay for gas if they'd let me join them. They talked among themselves and acquiesced but said they were leaving *right now.* That was fine by me.

Suddenly I was worried about how many rest stops there'd be, with women's bladders being notoriously weaker than men's, especially on long car trips. Sol asked if I wanted anything from the coffee shop and I declined, instead deciding to use my five minutes to ensure I was starting out on a completely empty bladder, and secretly vowing not to drink a drop of anything for the next 1,600 miles. I then hurried to the parking lot, afraid they might leave without me. However, I was relieved when they all showed up carrying what must have been gallon mugs of coffee.

9/11

I was thirty-five at the time, and in the bright sunlight they all appeared to be in their mid-fifties. Out of the four, I estimated that at least one had to have prostrate trouble. Not even an hour into the trip we stopped at a rest area, and I purchased a (small) bottle of water.

It was an emotionally jarring time, and everyone was talking about what had happened and what it meant. The only reference point was the surprise attack on Pearl Harbor by the Japanese sixty years earlier when 2,403 people were killed, although the majority were military personnel. The terrorist attacks on the morning of September 11, 2001 involved four airplanes hijacked by Islamic terrorists and primarily targeted civilians. Two flew into the 110-story World Trade Center Complex in Lower Manhattan, causing most of it to collapse. One smashed into the Pentagon and partially destroyed the building's west side. The fourth plane was flown toward Washington, DC, but crashed in Pennsylvania after several brave passengers thwarted the hijackers.

However, we knew and understood very little at the time, other than that our country was under attack. We had no idea whether it was over, or if more aircraft had been commandeered and bombs were going to start raining down on us. The radio played the news nonstop, and we heard crazy reports, like that the people flying planes into the World Trade Center were suicide bombers who believed they'd be met in Paradise by seventy-two virgins (not a popular female fantasy, I couldn't help noting). The death toll was unknown but we were told to brace ourselves for how high it was going to be. I fretted over the number of friends I'd lost on Wall Street. Merrill Lynch had their morning meeting on a high floor of the World Trade Center, and almost everyone used the transportation center underneath to commute from

Long Island, Connecticut, New Jersey, Pennsylvania, Westchester, other parts of Manhattan, Queens, Brooklyn, and The Bronx.

I offered to drive, but the guys politely declined. At midnight they were still talking, and I recalled slumber parties from my youth where everyone stayed up half the night only to be nonfunctional the following day. We were gliding through Arkansas on I-40 East, heading toward Memphis, where Martin Luther King was shot dead fighting for his country at age thirty-nine and Elvis succumbed to the Rock 'n' Roll lifestyle at age forty-two. Only a few trucks remained on the road. I crawled into the way back and took a nap. When I awoke it was quiet, still dark outside, and road signs indicated that we were deep in the heart of Tennessee. I saw an exit for Murfreesboro and recalled speaking at a school there in my twenties, with the campus blanketed in wildflowers, and how friendly the people were. I'd had some extra time before the event, driven through McDonald's, and ordered a large French fry. This reminded me of the day that famous chef and doyenne of French cuisine Julia Child appeared on *The Joan Rivers Show* and shocked everyone by saying that she loved McDonald's French fries. I'd visited Cannonsburgh Village, a reproduction of pioneer life with grist mill, school house, and general store. Usually there wasn't time to do anything fun while traveling, so the experience stood out.

Barry was now at the wheel, and the rest of the guys were sound asleep. I felt the car lurch to the right and then straighten out. A few minutes later we jerked to the left, toward oncoming traffic. I whispered to Barry that I'd just awoken from a good nap and asked if he wanted me to drive. I sensed this wasn't his first choice. I've never had an accident, my license was clean (meaning a few speeding tickets had cleared off), and didn't even wear glasses, though I've been stopped by police for DWB–Driving

While Blonde. Or maybe his reluctance was a result of the millions of dumb blonde jokes that circulate on the Internet (and people regularly send me). Otherwise, I don't exactly exude authority. The one time I was on a cruise ship, the other passengers continuously asked me to fetch them cocktails and make up their rooms. When I'm shopping in clothing stores, other customers regularly touch my arm and ask if there might be a size medium of the sweater they're holding somewhere in the back.

Eventually Barry said it was time to stop for gas and we'd switch places. In Cookeville, Tennessee, I took the wheel and drove through Monterey, Crossville, Crab Orchard, and Rockwood, heading toward Knoxville. The news had become an endless loop of grimness. It was hard to escape as I quietly spun the dial in search of an oldies rock station, forgetting I was in the South, where country music dominated the airwaves. Finally, an eclectic musical mix rose up from the dashboard that included "Just Another Day in Paradise," "Prayin' for Daylight," and "Achy Breaky Heart." Along the highway were billboards for Elvis' home Graceland ("Enter the Blingdom"), Dial-A-Prayer, and the popular TV show *Baywatch* ("Frost Bites. Summer Is Coming!").

When dawn slowly broke, I was in the Blue Ridge Mountains and thought of Francis Scott Key awakening to see that our flag was still there. The veneer of civilization had cracked, but America's heart continued to beat. The guys began waking up and made noises about bathrooms and coffee. We were heading northeast on 81 and had just crossed into Virginia, which is where I relinquished the wheel for good. At eight o'clock that night, my new friends dropped me on the Manhattan side of the George Washington Bridge and wished me well before continuing on to Scarsdale. From there I could catch the A train and then a crosstown bus. Standing on my Upper East Side terrace,

I would see the smoking remains of the World Trade Center in lower Manhattan. When the large complex of seven buildings was completed in 1973, critics hailed it as an architectural disaster, and most New Yorkers agreed. Now the iconic skyline looked as if a big bully had knocked out its two front teeth. After almost four decades of life together, we'd become accustomed to one another and even grown on each other. As when any member of the family meets a bad end, bygones were bygones, neighbors and even strangers banded together and lamented everything we'd lost.

It transpired that a dozen friends and colleagues were murdered on that fateful day. Most had been at meetings on the hundredth floor or above. Some died trying to help others. One leapt from a window of the fiery North Tower, and for that reason I've never been able to watch TV footage of the jumpers. I was told that one woman held her skirt before leaping to her death. Two people held hands and jumped together. A doomed employee emailed a pal, "Thank you for being such a great friend." 9/11 was the single deadliest attack on the history of the United States, resulting in 2,996 people killed and over 6,000 injured. They were of all nationalities, including Arabs and Jews, and trod every walk of life, from janitors to billionaires. The multimillionaire head of one company, who was rather renowned for being an asshole (which many on Wall Street viewed as a compliment or badge of honor), was told three times by authorities to vacate a top floor of the North Tower but refused to stop doing business. While reading the titan's large obituary, a friend put it this way: "He lived like an asshole and he died like an asshole."

Jimmy Daley was beloved by everyone on the trading floor, and I can't think of many other people who fall into that category. A cheery and charming floor broker for Merrill Lynch, it was his name I was saddest to see on a list of missing colleagues circulating via email. Jimmy and I both had our fair share of wild Irish blood, and as a result we were both teetotalers. After work he liked sitting at Harry's Bar and drinking club soda. Whereas I didn't care for alcohol, quick-with-a-joke-Jimmy liked it quite a lot and still enjoyed a contact high, unspooling yarns and creating more than one "Irish Layover"— when you miss the last train or bus. The only good news came when it was discovered that Jimmy Daley's phone had been out of order and he was indeed alive and conversing.

Still, the losses kept coming and were too difficult to bear. The tiny threads that held a tapestry of eight million people together had been torn apart. A woman at my church wrote this poem.

"Nine-Eleven" by Charlotte Parsons

You passed me on the street
I rode the subway with you
You lived down the hall from me
I admired your dog in the park one morning
We waited in line for a concert
I ate with you in the cafes
You stood next to me at the bar
We huddled under an awning during a downpour
We dashed across the street to beat the light
I bumped into you coming round the corner
You stepped on my foot
I held the door for you
You helped me up when I slipped on the ice
I grabbed the last Sunday Times
You stole my cab
We waited forever at the bus stop

A Theory of Everything Else

We sweated in steamy August
We hunched our shoulders against the sleet
We laughed at the movies
We groaned after the election
We sang in church
Tonight I lit a candle for you
All of you

After 9/11 I went to seminary and became an interfaith minister with plans to sign on as an army chaplain. However, my husband was diagnosed with prostate cancer, and then my stepmother crossed the Rainbow Bridge, leaving Dad alone and at loose ends, so that had to be put on hold. My husband made a good recovery, and I aged out of military service. Nevertheless, most of my friends had left the religions of their youth, so I was in demand for family funerals and a number of pet departures. Hands down, cat people have the best stories for eulogies and really know how to throw a memorial service. Otherwise, I'm relieved not to be languishing in a Manhattan jail, since burying pets in Central Park is illegal, and I've presided over a number of "going home" ceremonies at dusk featuring twigs tied into crosses and garlands of black-eyed Susans, to which mourners brought their own garden spades. Thank goodness for Emily Dickinson's "Hope is the thing with feathers," because you'd be surprised how slight the funerary canon is for avian burials, and I happen to be neighbors with a woman who has experienced a string of bad luck when it comes to parrotlets. Dickenson's verse is also mercifully short in case park police show up, and the funeral-goers are required to make a run for it. There's no dress code, but sneakers are recommended.

Art is the lie that enables us to realize the truth.

—Pablo Picasso

Chapter 33

Is Art Necessary?

A liberal arts education has become rather a punch line of late. In the early 1980s, I paid $10,000 a year to attend New York University. It now costs over $50,000 a year, which, by the way, Midwesterners think is insane for a school without a football team. There's a valid argument that a good living cannot be fashioned from a humanities degree, and worst case, won't even allow the recipient to pay off student loans. On the bright side, William Shakespeare had, at best, a high school education.

Otherwise, many people wonder how in the throes of a national political crisis anyone can sit and read a book of fiction or watch a frothy musical. If you must enjoy yourself, shouldn't it be done by engaging with art that has morality and meaning, that expounds upon the experiences of marginalized groups, the perils of lawlessness, and dangers of prejudice, or at the very least acknowledges suffering? Must art be necessary to be valid? Is all art pointless? Does escape count as a justification? Can we just have art for art's sake?

A Theory of Everything Else

I spent a number of years on Wall Street valuing things—determining what a share of XYZ is worth right this minute. To make such calculations, we employed formulas involving everything from interest rates and volatility to weather forecasts and elections. So is the value of art what someone will pay at a gallery, studio, auction, or street fair? Or does it depend upon the way it makes us feel—and how do you put a price on that?

In 1930s Vienna, the husband and wife owners of the Café Hawelka took pity on their starving artist patrons and exchanged paintings for food and drink. A piece of abstract expressionism would be hung on the wall to pay for a plate of *spatzle* and *schnitzel mit strudel* and schnapps. By the 1980s, this collection was worth millions, enough to buy the café many times over. In the meantime, strudel prices had risen only slightly.

Growing up in the Rust Belt, like most people at the time, my family didn't have much disposable income, because it all went for heat, Hamburger Helper, and galoshes. Also, we weren't particularly sophisticated, though we knew enough to have gold shag carpeting, a sand sculpture, spider plants in macramé hangers, and a bottle of Blue Nun on hand for company. However, on the modest salaries of a court reporter and a nurse, we had access to an amazing amount of culture: concerts, plays, dance, exhibitions, museums, galleries, craft fairs, poetry readings, festivals—from highbrow to pierced brow. At the height of the Blizzard of '77, locals didn't yell and curse—they went on television singing "Send in the Plows" to the city's head of transportation.

Watching *Peter Pan* at the Studio Arena Theatre when I was seven, during a recession so entrenched that Christmas was very much in doubt, made me think I could fly. It transpired that I couldn't, and the attempt ended badly, but you never know until you try. Art makes one dream. It can turn our thoughts from

232

necessity to possibility. And turn a youngster toward good books rather than hard drugs.

I saw Andrés Segovia play classical guitar one particularly stormy night when I was eleven and had a heck of a case of bronchitis. As other people live with cancer or Parkinson's, the children of Western New York lived with upper respiratory distress. If we stayed home for every case of pneumonia, pleurisy, or bronchitis, we'd have been shut-ins the first eighteen years of our existence. Still, I was terrified of coughing or sneezing during the great Segovia's concert, and so right before the curtain rose, I hacked and honked and blew my nose until I was certain my entire head was empty. The dowager to my left turned, lowered her opera glasses, and inquired, "Do you plan on doing that all throughout the performance?" I said, "No, ma'am, I am getting it all out now."

And then a man almost ninety years old walked onto that enormous stage at Shea's, a theater where we'd seen knights on horseback in <i>Camelot</i> and an entire Thai village in the <i>King and I</i>. One small man on a low wooden stool, who didn't speak to us in English, yet filled that large stage and enormous theater for over two hours with soaring melodies, transporting us from a seemingly endless winter, to a place warm and romantic where Valencia red roses bloomed.

My parents took me to see numerous shows in a hollowed out and dodgy downtown Buffalo. We'd walk across Main Street, past people in dada attire prophesying end times in loud voices, talking to themselves, and even arguing with themselves. My mom, a psychiatric nurse, explained they had problems and most likely thought they were talking to other people. As an only child, I could certainly understand the value of having an imaginary friend, but I remember thinking, wouldn't you choose someone you got along with?

Nowadays, one walks down Main Street in a completely revitalized city with people all yammering into their cell phones so absolutely everyone looks crazy. Maybe you'd call it installation art, performance art, or art-of-the-moment. My mother the nurse calls it people not watching where they're going who will end up in the head injury ward at the hospital, and don't call her when it happens because she told you so.

My Sweet Home Junior High School class went to see a matinee of *A Christmas Carol* at the Studio Arena Theatre, and kids in the row in front of us threw pennies onto the stage. Even worse, it was the seventies, and so the actors picked them up. As a result of this close proximity to the penny pitchers, our teachers scolded us during intermission, but the change-tossing dumbbells had worn their school jackets, so when we all shouted the name at once they believed us. I won't name names other than to say that the school is also a city in Northwest Spain that is the capital of the Province of Salamanca. Our teachers were 99 percent Christian, in favor of forgiveness, and guardedly optimistic about our futures. They were trying to help and guide us "before it was too late."

On another class trip, the world-renowned ballet dancer Mikhail Baryshnikov was performing in Balanchine's *Jewels* when he fell and improvised a somersault off the stage, and I realized that no matter how famous you are and how much you practice, things can still go wrong. However, the real show was on the way home when the big yellow school bus chugged down West Chippewa at eleven thirty on a Saturday night. It was 1978 and the street was an entrepreneur's paradise. You want to talk about art? This was a mixed media presentation if I ever saw one. That you could dress a fur coat up or down, I guess I was aware of that. But fur hot pants? No, those were definitely something new. And hot pants with platform shearling boots? Can anyone say Eskiho?

The majority of people have only been literate a fraction of our time on Earth. In 1820, just 12 percent of the world's population could read and write. Religions were explained mostly through plays, paintings, pageants, and especially stained-glass windows. New York City's notoriously corrupt Tammany Hall boss William Tweed was finally brought down in 1877 as a result of cartoons. Ninety percent of Tweed's constituents were illiterate, or at least they didn't read English and couldn't grasp the scathing articles in the newspapers. But they were perfectly capable of understanding Thomas Nast's incriminating cartoons. As Roman soldier, senator, and lyric poet Horace said, a picture is a poem without words. In an attempt to "stop them damn pictures," Tweed offered Nast the equivalent of two million in today's dollars to go study art in Europe. Failing to bribe Nast, Tweed proceeded to threaten him. But Nast continued to generate public outrage, and the rank and file eventually responded by voting Tammany candidates out of office. Following the 1871 election, charges were brought against the boss, and a corrupt regime was toppled. Many, including Tweed, were sentenced to prison. Ironically, Tweed landed in the Ludlow Street jail, one he'd originally helped open, and that was where he died.

Which brings us to dueling German philosophers. Immanuel Kant (1724–1804) said that beauty can't be objectively determined. Insisting that it's a matter of subjective taste, Kant denied the intelligibility of creativity. On the opposing side we have German poet and philosopher Friedrich Schiller (1759–1805) who, during the French Revolution, suggested that art, with its ability to expand the mind, could be a route to meaningful freedom. As an example, he used the Parable of the Good Samaritan—a traveler who abandons his belongings to carry a wounded man to safety acts freely and beautifully of his own accord, a result of his inner nature and not any external compulsion. Schiller said the ultimate end of art is to represent an individual's "moral freedom" or "free principle," and to stop death from transgressing his autonomy by dedicating him or herself to a higher purpose, one which is immortal. Of course, the traveler had to consider whether the distressed man was in reality a key actor in a plot to rob him.

In July of 1937, leaders of the Nazi Party mounted two art exhibitions in Munich. The Great German Art Exhibition showed works that Chancellor Adolf Hitler considered acceptable and representative of an ideal Aryan society, featuring blondes in heroic poses and idyllic landscapes elevating the German countryside. The second exhibit featured 650 works confiscated from German Museums that Hitler and his followers viewed as "degenerate art" for being modern or abstract and "insulting German feeling" or "confusing natural form." These were produced by artists the Nazis disavowed because they were suspected of being Jewish, communist, and/or homosexual and who had naturally "sick brains." Going forward, the Third Reich would strictly control how artists lived and worked in Nazi Germany because they fully comprehended that art could play a major role in the rise or fall of their dictatorship.

It's no surprise that many US administrations have proposed cutting the National Endowment for the Arts budget, astonishingly slim as it is to begin with, and the Trump administration has been no exception. As Hitler well knew, writers, painters, musicians, and performers serve an important role in society, especially when it comes to challenging authoritarianism and exposing discrimination. Art is a conduit for solidarity among like-minded voters and coalition builders. In fact, the message is no different from that of a good religion, that lives other than our own have value. The Good Samaritan parable came in answer to the question, who is my neighbor? The artist can challenge power structures in ways that otherwise might be dangerous or even impossible.

Hitler was far from the first tyrant to understand this. Pianist and composer Dmitri Shostakovich wrote in his memoir that the Stalinist government executed all the Soviet Union's Ukrainian folk poets. Similarly, when General Augusto Pinochet became the dictator of Chile in 1973, he persecuted leftists, socialists, and political critics in addition to having muralists arrested, tortured, and killed, or exiled. After the Chilean teacher, theater director, and singer-songwriter Victor Jara was shot gangland style, his body was displayed publicly as a warning to others. In 2010, Chinese artist Ai Weiwei was placed under house arrest and had his studio demolished by the government, not angry villagers with torches. In Cuba, graffiti artist Danilo Maldonado Machado was arrested and jailed in 2014 after criticizing the Castro regime.

This may all be considered extreme to Americans until we recall our own President's public denouncement of the *Hamilton* cast after they requested the administration work on behalf of everyone at the end of a show attended by Vice President Mike Pence. Pence is the man who flew to a football game in Indiana for the sole purpose of walking out after some team members knelt during the national anthem to protest racial injustice, and whose wife works at a school that bans LGBTQ teachers and students.

Last year the National Endowment for the Arts gave $10,000 to a music festival in Oregon for a dance performance by people in wheelchairs. A cultural center in California was granted

$10,000 for workshops led by Muslim filmmakers, a comedian, and a hip-hop artist. A Minnesota chorus received $10,000 for a concert highlighting the experiences of LGBTQ youth to be performed in public schools. Each grant championed the voices of people the current administration has mocked, marginalized, or actually harmed through legislation. Youth, immigrants, minorities, and alternative lifestyle communities have long used the arts as a way of dismantling powerful institutions trying to silence and even kill them. Controlling or suppressing the arts is, at its heart, about creating a society where propaganda reigns supreme and dissent is silenced. Because it's harder to denounce art as "fake news."

When New Orleans mayor Mitch Landrieu was considering how to celebrate the city's three hundredth anniversary, his friend, the musician Wynton Marsalis, said he should think about taking down the confederate monuments that were city landmarks. Landrieu's initial response was, "You're crazy." Yet Marsalis, the first person to win the Pulitzer Prize for Music for a jazz composition, *Blood on the Fields*, had dared to imagine a discussion about the art of the possible. Three years later, Landrieu presided over the removal with a speech on race and monuments that became so famous it would embolden other Southern leaders to reconsider disturbing symbols of racism.

As a teenager I attended numerous shows with a friend despite both of our ailments—me with cough drops and packs of tissues for colds and allergies and him chain-chewing Imodium tablets, always sitting on the aisle in case it was necessary to exit in a hurry. If art is personal and about the human condition, then clearly we were that human condition. Performances often suggested how to look, or where to look, and then left us, as Virgil left Dante, to go beyond where a guide can take us.

Is Art Necessary?

My elementary school teachers were fond of saying: That which does not kill you makes you stronger. Specifically, they were referencing the blinding snowstorms we often walked home in, but I think more broadly it means that inspiration comes from all places. If you'd told me that writing about waiting for the bus with snot frozen to my face would later become my art, I wouldn't have believed it, but as usual, those teachers were right.

When we experience art, we can never know what will come of the encounter. People insist their lives were changed by the novel *All Quiet on the Western Front*, Picasso's "Guernica," or the movie *Apocalypse Now*. Bagpipes blaring and drums beating led many a soldier into battle, while protestors of the Vietnam War queued up a banjo and guitar-charged antiwar soundtrack to accompany their marching and speeches.

There's a woman who's seen *The Sound of Music* over a thousand times. Maybe she misunderstood the line, "With songs they have sung for a thousand years," or maybe that musical is the art that speaks to her. As a fifteen-year-old, at a garage sale I purchased a sketch of Mr. Peanut melting in the sun because it was weird and I liked it. An art teacher friend discovered that it was a misshapen clock by surrealist painter Salvador Dali and worth considerably more than the five dollars I'd paid.

When I tutored in East Harlem, the students needed extra help in so many areas that we had to constantly prioritize between math and reading and college prep. But the activities that always took precedence involved exposure to art—dance, theater, music, sculpture, gardens, architecture. We dropped everything if we could get tickets and transportation to a show, concert, or exhibit.

Although we don't know the exact value of art, whether a work sells for a dollar or millions, if it's at your local street fair

239

or in the Museum of Modern Art, we intrinsically know when it's powerful, and most important, transformative. Because art is a form of communication, and communication is how we try to understand one another; it has the capacity to instill values, change opinions, and translate experiences across space and time. Most important, it helps us understand who we are as individuals and a society, and following that, who we wish to be as individuals and as a society. Because when we're evocative, it transpires that we're capable of being quite provocative.

Here is one final statistic with regard to performance art. In 1975 there were forty-eight professional Elvis impersonators. Now there are 7,328, and that doesn't include the flying Elvises, or would that be Elvii? If this growth rate continues, by the year 2025, one in four people will be an Elvis impersonator. So next time you're out, look to your left, look to your right, and at the person across from you, and if you don't believe they possess the goods, then it may just be you.

The universe is made of stories, not of atoms.

—Muriel Rukeyser

Chapter 34

What's Your Story?

" For Sale: baby shoes, never worn." This is often described as a six-word novel, and sometimes attributed to Ernest Hemingway (who was nothing if not terse), though its provenance is unsubstantiated. A good short-short story, with its power to surprise and amaze, almost counts as a magic trick. Here are two more short-short stories I like:

"Headed For Trouble" by Dick Skeen

The scantily clad hitchhiker knew she was in trouble the moment she stepped into the car.

The driver gazed disapprovingly at her costume. "Looking for some fun?"

"No . . . I'm just going to the beach."

"Think so? Well, I've got other plans for you, sweetie, and they don't include beaches."

"Guess I'm grounded, huh Mom?"

"The Caretaker" by Steven MacLeod

"Don't walk on the grass!" shouted the little man.

"Don't be stupid," the large man replied. "It doesn't feel anything."

"You must care for it," retorted the little man. "It gives us beauty, but it's fragile."

"Whatever." The large man walked away.

Years later, each had moved on. Indifferently, the cemetery grass grew over both.

Cave drawings suggest that stories have been with us since humans first walked together on Earth. A powerful story can do many things, such as help us make sense of our world or shed light on a dire situation that couldn't otherwise gain attention. At its best, a story can reduce suffering in the world. At its worst, a story can overwhelm the facts at hand. Every narrative has a message; it's just a question of whether the message is in line with the status quo. For better or worse, stories have a unique capacity to unite and divide us.

My mother went back to school for nursing when I was in junior high. As I said, times were tough back then and the nursing students' "lab rats" were basically family members, so she made liberal use of my body when doing homework. One night I woke up with a cold hand around my neck in the dark. It was the heyday of serial killers like the Boston Strangler, Son of Sam, and the Zodiac Killer, and also the film genre best described as "animals gone wild" featuring *Frogs, Jaws, Cujo, Piranha, Alligator, Empire of the Ants,* and *Kingdom of the Spiders.*

Screaming, I leapt out of bed, assuming that Mother Nature had run amok again, and logically expected I'd have to fight off a swarm of African killer bees in the midst of a frigid Buffalo winter. It transpired that mom was taking my pulse using my carotid artery. "You scared the hell out of me," I shouted. "I didn't want to wake you," she matter-of-factly replied. "The main thing is that your pulse is normal." At least it was until I'd woken up.

There was an Ethan Allen furniture store on our corner, and my mother would regularly remind me that Allen was a famous Unitarian. He landed in a heap of trouble after inoculating himself against smallpox one Sunday in front of a church at a time when vaccinations required approval by the town selectman, because one was supposed to trust in God and not look to man or medicine for help in such matters. Allen was fined and fifteen years later, during the Revolutionary War, while being held prisoner by the British in New York City, his son died of smallpox.

It was quite a story. However, I always thought it would have made more sense to name a hospital after Allen, or at the very least a chain of pharmacies, rather than a furniture store. Somehow a vaccination crusader doesn't bring to mind a new five-piece dinette set. Anyway, this was an anecdote of minor significance that I was told over forty years ago, yet because of it, whenever I'm in a furniture store I wonder if I'm up to date on my vaccinations, and whenever I'm getting a flu shot I consider buying a new credenza.

As a child in kindergarten, the best part of the day was after lunch when the teacher would gather us in a circle and regale us with the doings of clever Charlotte and her billboard of a web or that poor Ugly Duckling. Story time came to an end once we learned to read for ourselves the following year (most of us . . . I was put in a reading group called the dinosaurs, which I tried not to read too much into), but that didn't quench our love of being told tales.

Even in Manhattan I'm continuously amazed at the number of people, from housekeepers and bus drivers, to thoracic surgeons and those dressed in giant hotdog suits, who go home after a hard day's work and want to read a story or watch one on TV or play a video game with a narrative. We use stories to put children to sleep, and also ourselves. Even after we fall asleep, the mind stays busy telling itself stories. On top of that, studies show we have two thousand daydreams every day. More if it's a particularly long winter or you're on the church budget committee.

We all have our preferences for storylines that are sad, funny, true, or scary. In our free time we read them in books, magazines, comics, blogs, and newspapers, and see them played out in movies or performed onstage as plays, musicals, and operas. In school, stories were used to help us synthesize enormous historical events such as *Johnny Tremain* for the American Revolution and *Uncle Tom's Cabin* for the Civil War. To learn about World War I we were assigned *Johnny Got His Gun* and *All Quiet on the Western Front* by teachers who were clearly opposed to the Vietnam War. *Anne Frank* was the bellwether teaching tool for World War II because it featured a person our age, and *Trinity* to grasp the Irish struggle for Independence. Putting on Lorraine Hansberry's stage play *A Raisin in the Sun* opened a window into a single family's fight again racism in 1950s Chicago.

Perhaps the most famous collection of stories is the Bible. At least I hope they're stories and not the actual word of God, or else for starters you have the right to kill anyone who trespasses on your property and it's okay to bring back slavery and polygamy. In my church, people tend to say "the historical Jesus" to differentiate from the "walking on water Jesus." Unless they spill their coffee, in which case "Jesus!" or "Jesus Christ!" is still the norm.

But religions, tribes, and other types of communities regularly employ stories to convey social norms and regulate behavior.

People don't normally empathize with facts, statistics, or equations, and that's why most big news stories start with an individual. "Fred Murray takes his fishing boat out every morning in the Gulf of Mexico, but since the oil spill he's worried about his livelihood." Show a picture of the boat on land. Now we can get into the specifics of how much oil, how far it's spread, and all the devastating effects. "The death of one person is a tragedy whereas the death of a million people is a statistic," to quote none other than Joseph Stalin. The minute that spill was reported you knew it was only a matter of time before the oil-covered pelican showed up.

A picture on its own can also tell a story. After decades of famines in Africa where millions died and which people around the world routinely read about in the newspaper—"another one"—a haunting photograph shocked the world in 1993. It showed a vulture eyeing a single starving Sudanese child. Hundreds of people came forward wanting to rescue and even adopt this single child. In the wake of Hurricane Katrina, a dog was shown stranded on a rooftop while floodwaters encroached. I was well aware that many humans were in similar circumstances and other animals too, so I was embarrassed by how much I wanted to save that one particular dog along with thousands of other people who did as well.

War, famine, and natural disaster are often confusing and overwhelming until we can focus on a single being and say, "That could be me, or my parents or my child or my dog." It reminds us that *one million* is not incomprehensible but actually one plus one plus one and so forth. I know I can't save an entire country or city but I am capable of helping one person or one animal. Similarly, when an average Joe breaks out on a TV talent show and the video goes viral, it's so much more interesting than if they'd trained and practiced for years, paid their dues, and worked their way up the ladder. It's a great story and one can't help thinking, "Hey, that could be me! My special talent might be discovered."

During my childhood a shocking story unfolded just a few miles away. The ironically named Love Canal was a working-class neighborhood built on a toxic waste dump that caused residents to develop a multitude of cancers, and their children were born with horrendous birth defects. This is a case where corporate counsel and many local officials had an incentive to tell the story in a way that wouldn't lead to expensive lawsuits and bad publicity. Love Canal residents weren't doctors, lawyers, professors and journalists; they were factory workers and lunch ladies. It was before the Internet. The recession was bearing down hard, and residents were forced to move, quietly taking their problems with them.

However, an area housewife named Lois Gibbs persisted in telling the individual stories of her neighbors—how they were denied healthcare and stonewalled and not compensated for having to move. Local activists took two Environmental Protection Agency workers hostage. *That* certainly made national news. Had it not been for Lois Gibbs insisting that this version of the story be heard, Love Canal would not have become the first government Superfund cleanup site in 1978. This enabled residents to be properly bought out of their homes and file medical claims. It was the first time in American history that federal funds were used for a situation other than a natural disaster. The fact that Buffalo has Roswell Park Cancer Care and some of the best cancer treatment facilities in the country is rather a medical catch-22, sort of like eating enough pork products to cause heart blockage that will require the installation of a pig valve.

"Stories have to be told or they die, and when they die we can't remember who we are or why we're here," said author Sue Monk Kidd. Stories help us make sense out of life—by trading subjective experiences we connect and identify with others. This transforms a biological existence of eating, sleeping, and procreating into a human one. Unfortunately, stories can create division as easily as unification. Each side in a conflict has its own version of events that can become a justification for killing. Terrorists are called Freedom Fighters at home. Churches are built over pagan worship sites and then mosques on top of those, thereby replacing one story with another. Meantime, humans conjure gods and spirits to fill explanatory voids, and often to find courage. Irish-American Frank McCourt wrote in his memoir *Angela's Ashes* how the shame of dire poverty was lifted by his father's superb storytelling, especially when it came to great Irish heroes such as the fearless Cú Chulainn.

You almost can't have a religion without a creation myth and narratives such as those in the Bible, Book of Mormon, or Koran. I've always said there'd be a lot more UUs if we had a good creation myth—maybe a giant monster with a thousand heads, eyes, and feet whose body parts became the world. Oops, the Hindus took that one. Can a billion people be wrong? Some Native Americans adopted the Earth riding on the back of a giant turtle. Then there's the guy in the sky going on a six-day work bender. Heaven and Earth hanging together in an egg-shaped cloud? The Chinese got there first. Scientology has Xenu, an intergalactic ruler about to be overthrown, who brings billions of people to Earth in a spaceship. They're destroyed in a volcano, but the vibrations produce a new population. This is very filmable. How about something with vampires for Unitarian Universalists? They're really in vogue right now. Maybe environmentally-friendly vampires who roam around seeking alternative fuels instead of drinking human blood, which is probably high in cholesterol anyway.

As we all know, religious groups can do plenty of good work. On the flip side, more wars have been fought over faith than any other subject, aside from gay marriage and what public restroom you can use in North Carolina. It's the old, My God is better than Your God. The Crusades involved Christians going off to kill Muslims, and killing Jews along the way, because God was on their side. The Spanish Inquisition featured Christians killing, expelling, and converting Jews and Muslims. Fighting over the divinity of Jesus has even led to Christians killing other Christians.

As a kid I firmly believed that I was Wonder Woman's super-secret sidekick, Galaxy Girl, and would repeatedly leap off the couch wearing a green-and-white crocheted poncho with matching macramé bracelets. Fortunately, since it was Buffalo in the 1970s, our windows were covered with heavy-gauge plastic and no one could see inside. More recently, my students devoured the Harry Potter stories. A disconnected youth finds out he's actually a wizard, which not only makes him special but gives him confidence along with a rich social life. Readers discover the joys of inclusivity, standing up for what's right, and working toward the greater good, without sitting through a boring school assembly, church sermon, or parental lecture. This bit of advice, for example, is best received coming from Hogwarts Headmaster Dumbledore: It takes a great deal of bravery to stand up to our enemies, but just as much to stand up to our friends.

What's Your Story?

As kids, most of us want to be superheroes, adventurers, spies, or explorers. As adults, many of us still wish to be those things, and watching an Indiana Jones movie can, just for a second, make us consider running away from of our responsibilities. Fortunately, there are books, movies, and plays like *The Bridges of Madison County*, *It's A Wonderful Life,* and *Minding Frankie* to remind us of the quiet brand of heroism that lies in staying the course, and that everyone's life is better when individuals, communities, and governments work together to care for those of us in trouble. Or as that master storyteller Charles Dickens suggested in his most autobiographical novel, *David Copperfield,* to discover whether we shall be the heroes of our own lives.

So let's embrace any guilty pleasure that involves reality TV, even if you have a PhD. Let's relish the dozen new versions of Bram Stoker's *Dracula* and Jane Austen's English countryside overrun by flesh-eating zombies. Enjoy young adult fiction if you're fifty, *Lifetime* "television for women" if you're a man, YouTube videos of lions befriending humans, and dogs who somehow manage to survive and thrive on two legs. In stories we search for reasons, causes, ideals, and missions. They help us fight an uncomfortable randomness by locating plots and patterns and purpose, thereby forcing a narrative structure on chaos. Stories can provide us with unlimited potential for learning and compassion and help us discover what it really means to be human.

Life is a spell so exquisite that everything conspires to break it.
—Emily Dickinson

Chapter 35

The Good Life

While the news often makes it sound as if everyone is wanting to come to America, the United Nation's "World Happiness Report" ranked us eighteenth, trailing behind Finland (#1), Canada (#7) and Costa Rica (#13). Yet we're the ones cranking out thousands of self-help books every year, on everything from relationships and personal finance, to seaweed diets and the ten-minute work week. But what if you successfully diet, compost, declutter, lighten up, decompress, sleep better, win friends, improve your memory, find your passion, flush the toxins, think positive, grow rich, and don't sweat the small stuff, but still don't feel satisfied?

Everyone who has ever attempted retirement planning discovers that there's one enormous variable—knowing how long our lives will be. This makes budgeting more challenging, along with deciding whether to spring for a Costco membership and buy in bulk. A friend's father was recently given a diagnosis of cancer with only a few weeks to live. He was in his eighties and had been feeling poorly, so it wasn't a complete shock. The doctor asked his adult children if he should tell the father or if they'd rather do it. His children said everyone would gather together but the doctor should deliver the bad news. Upon hearing his fate, their father appeared crestfallen. After a few moments the doctor asked if he had any specific concerns about his situation. The father finally said he was very upset because he'd just purchased a 500-tablet bottle of aspirin.

Indeed, most of us consider surviving into our ninth decade a long life, but what is meant by a good life? In general terms it suggests a meaningful, satisfying, pleasant existence. But how can we set about building one among the unavoidable practicalities that real lives involve—the challenges, setbacks, accidents, good luck, bad luck, demands made by others, and our own limitations? Compounding that is the fact we tend to live five or ten times as long as our beloved pets, which makes one wonder why tortoises, chimps, and parrots aren't more popular.

This chapter is called The Good Life because I assumed readers would skip one called The Bad Life or The Hard Life. Either way, the concept is a very large one indeed. About 2,400 years ago, Socrates wrestled with the question, "How should one live?" And 240 years ago Thomas Jefferson edited British philosopher John Locke's "life, liberty, and property" to read "life, liberty, and the pursuit of happiness" for our Declaration of Independence.

The Good Life seems to be at the heart of the matter, no matter how we approach life. Why do we go to the doctor? To be in good health. Why be in good health? If I'm not, then I can't do my work. Why do we work? To make money. Why do we want money? To pay the bills. The point isn't to go in an infinite regress, but if we did, we'd most likely end up with the word "happiness." Thus, how to achieve that flourishing existence is the goal of our actions. A life for which we're the only candidates—not animals, not slaves, not cult members, not even children. We have choices and the ability to make a rational plan for life. The main reason religion has survived and thrived is because it offers to do this for people, as do cults and other lifestyle dominating organizations.

Yet, we can't adopt and adhere to someone else's idea of a good life, but must decide for ourselves based on what we know of human experience in the real world. Our ethics should be informed by what human beings are actually like and what will help them thrive in this world, rather than the next. It's our individual responsibility to make our own moral judgments, rather than receive them from a political or religious leader or movie star or SoulCycle instructor. Because when individuals submit to systems, they're handing over the right to do their thinking and choosing for them. Philosopher Bertrand Russell joked that "Most people would rather die than think, and most people do." Surely it's easier to grab a one-size-fits all model from a pile of subway literature or the Center for Eternal Everything in Times Square. However, this is an abdication of responsibility, which at the same time means a loss of opportunity. We need to be able to explain and justify our moral choices, as should others if they come under scrutiny, to ensure they're not having a harmful impact elsewhere.

One ancient school of thought on how to live was founded by Epicurus, who advised the pursuit of pleasure and the avoidance of pain. His view was that conventional happiness associated with food, drink, and love contain the seeds of pain within them, and are therefore to be avoided for the true pleasures of learning, discussing, and moderation in our appetites. Epicureanism has since come to mean the exact opposite, indulgence. Much like "hook up" has apparently changed its meaning from the days when we phoned a handyman to hook up the dryer.

Aristotle, who famously proclaimed, "Happiness depends on ourselves," also pointed out that saying the happy life is one that's desirable and lived well is not saying very much at all. Everyone wants to be happy, and everyone agrees that being happy is related to an individual's well-being. Aristotle's ingredients for a happy life were pleasure, political activity, and philosophy, with the key being balance. However, his virtues tended to be more self-serving than social, and that's where it's possible to take a slight turn.

By a good life, I think we mean one that's fruitful, flourishing, worth living, and has a positive impact on others. More than one intro to philosophy student has incorrectly quoted Socrates on his midterm exam: "The unlived life is not worth examining." Characteristics of such a lived life tend to be that it feels meaningful and purposeful to the individual doing the living. Everyone will have a different definition for his or her own Good Life, but at the core will be intimacy—love and/or friendship with others; activity—doing and making; learning—reevaluating as new information arrives; and freedom—the freedom to not be enslaved by having to live an inauthentic life.

Being true to ourselves also carries over to career choice, whether to marry, and whether to have children. There should be a sense of integration with a community, and hopefully society as a whole. Humanists believe we live in a world where we have certain duties to other beings, as they hopefully do to us. And I'd be lax if I didn't add my mother's secret to The Good Life: Upon entering a building, immediately locate your fire exits.

The Good Life manifests autonomy, but with an acceptance of responsibility for the choices we make. Only what tough choices they are! Whenever we decide to do something, it's time not spent doing something else. My Manhattan UU Church is a great example. There are six hundred members but seven hundred committees you can join. One has to make tough choices, such as whether to get out the vote or get out the coffee.

Maybe you've heard about the management consultant vacationing in a quaint Costa Rican village. One morning a fisherman rowing a small boat came ashore with a basket full of fish. The consultant was impressed and asked, "How long does it take you to catch that many fish?"

The fisherman replied, "Oh, just a few hours."

"Then why don't you stay out longer and catch even more?"

"This is enough to feed my whole family," said the fisherman.

"So, what do you do for the rest of the day?" asked the consultant.

"I go home, play with my kids. In the afternoon, I take a nap with my wife, and in the evening, I join my friends in the village square for a drink, where we play music and dance."

The consultant offered a proposal: "I could help you become more successful. Going forward you should spend more time at sea and try to catch as many fish as possible. Then you can buy a bigger boat and catch even more fish. Soon you'll be able to afford several boats, hire people, have your own production plant and a headquarters in Rio de Janeiro."

The fisherman asked, "And after that?"

"After that, you can go public and you'll be rich."

The fisherman asked, "And after that?"

"Then you can retire, move to a village, catch a few fish, play with the kids, spend time with your wife, and relax in the square."

The fisherman was puzzled, "Isn't that what I'm doing right now?"

In New York City we say that all may make sense, but aren't there any tricks or shortcuts to The Good Life? We're in a hurry. Television has become really good the past few years and aqua cycling takes up time. If we're in a twelve-step program, we like to try and get it down to seven or eight.

Albert Camus makes a surprising suggestion in his essay "The Myth of Sisyphus"—ask yourself the most important philosophical question, "Do I or do I not wish to go on living?" If you say "Yes, I do," and I hope that's what we'd all say, it's because we have reasons for living, or at the very least, hope that we can find such reasons. The next question is "What are the reasons I have for saying 'yes' to that question?" The answer contains the meaning of our life.

The Stoics also had some good ideas about The Good Life. My father was a Stoic. I don't believe he read anything about it and adopted the lifestyle so much as he just naturally was one. Dad got rid of a house full of stuff and required nothing but the 4Cs—coffee, Corona, cashews, and cigarettes—and you never met a happier man. When the government demanded that all seniors have their social security checks directly deposited, I had to go to the bank and organize it while he smoked out front. The banker leaned over and said, "You're very lucky, some of the old people in town have problems. Your father gets the biggest pension check but will never be robbed because he looks like a homeless person." Thank you for sharing. That's good to know. And she was right. I'd just been in the supermarket while he was having a cig out front and someone handed him a buck. *He* thought they mistook him for a grocery bag guy, while I thought, "No, it's *much* worse."

Stoicism has similarities to Zen Buddhism, where there's a fear of the "satisfaction treadmill"—an unfulfilled desire leads to unhappiness, hard work to satisfy it, but upon satisfaction there's unhappiness in finding it didn't make us happier. To avoid this trap we can recount things we previously desired that *have* given us happiness—perhaps a spouse, a home, our friends, pets, or a job—and recreate the desire for the things we already enjoy. Going a step further, the Greek sage Epictetus, who was incidentally born a slave, advocated "negative visualization"—imagine these being taken away and how we'd feel.

The Stoics always liked to push the envelope and said to consider if you lost all your possessions, and then consider if you lost your freedom. Now aren't you feeling happy? This may have come naturally to my father because he was Danish, and I always think there's a reason that *Hamlet* was set in Denmark.

Vice Admiral James Stockdale was an American Navy pilot shot down over Vietnam in 1965 and held as a prisoner of war until 1973—seven and a half long years. During that time, he experienced poor health, primitive living conditions, and brutality by his jailers. How did he survive? He said in large part through Stoicism. "I never lost faith in the end of the story, I never doubted not only that I would get out, but also that I would prevail in the end and turn the experience into the defining event of my life, which, in retrospect, I would not trade." When asked who didn't make it out of Vietnam, Stockdale had an interesting reply: "Oh, that's easy, the optimists. They were the ones who said, 'We're going to be out by Christmas.' And Christmas would come, and Christmas would go. Then they'd say, 'We're going to be out by Easter.' Easter would come, and Easter would go. And then Thanksgiving, and then it would be Christmas again. And they died of a broken heart." Stockdale added, "This is a very important lesson. You must never confuse faith that you will prevail in the end . . . with the discipline to confront the most brutal facts of your current reality, whatever they might be."

This philosophy of duality was described by business writer James Collins as the Stockdale Paradox. Where I grew up in the Snowbelt we just said, "Well, it could be worse." The rainstorm could be a hailstorm. The snowstorm could be a blizzard. The barn fire could have killed the livestock, but fortunately the animals were out to pasture. Instead of a well-meaning friend signing you up for the Fruit-of-the-Month club, they could have enrolled you in the Cat-of-the-Month club. Yup. It definitely could have been worse.

Normally we consider an optimist to be someone who looks at a glass as being half full rather than half empty. A Stoic would go on to express his appreciation at having a glass at all. It could have been broken, lost, or stolen. And then perhaps marvel at how astonishing glass vessels are—cheap and durable, they add no flavor to what's placed in them, and allow us to see what's contained inside. Glasses are incredible! Then there's the New York City couple summoned to their teenage daughter's school because of her bad grades. On the way home the wife said, "Well, at least we know she's not cheating."

German financier Nathan Rothschild was the richest man in the world when he died in 1836. Adjusted for inflation, Rothschild would be way ahead of Microsoft's Bill Gates. But was he richer than we are? Rothschild died of septicemia in 1836, despite buying the best medical attention available, from an illness that could today be cured for, depending on your healthcare plan, anywhere from a few dollars to a few hundred.

What if we were to consider every day to be our last, not in the hedonistic sense that we should fly first class to Bali, but to focus on how wonderful it is to be alive and able to fill this day with activities of our choosing? Consider saying grace before a meal—some do it out of habit and some because they fear God will punish them if they don't. But grace or any prayer of thanks is also a form of negative visualization. When saying grace before a meal we pause to reflect that this food might not have been available to us, in which case we'd go hungry. Or we might not be able to share it with the people at our table, and experience loneliness. Said with these thoughts in mind, grace turns an ordinary meal into a celebration.

A good friend growing up was Baptist, and her mother regularly warned us kids not to pray for anything that we needed to work toward, such as doing well on a test or winning a soccer game. Still, it's natural to want things. Only what if it turns out we wanted the "wrong" things, and these don't make us happy, or perhaps make us unhappy?

The Stoics would view this as a problem with our life philosophy or our failure to have such a philosophy. They believed in a connection between external circumstances and satisfaction, understood that governments could wrong their citizens, and were in agreement that we need to fight against social injustices. But they felt this was most successfully accomplished by individuals who had already embraced a *personal philosophy* that was affording them a good life in order to be able to create the same for others.

Life doesn't have any meaning until we give it meaning through the choices we make. If you don't stand for something, you may fall for anything. And not choosing is a dangerous form of choosing. I'm sure we can all think of examples, personal or political, large and small. In 1998 US President Bill Clinton apologized to Rwandans for Western inaction during the 1994 genocide where approximately 800,000 Rwandans were killed. Currently there's a horrific refugee crisis. I imagine the government may end up apologizing once again for all the lives lost due to its failure to act.

Viktor Frankl's remarkable book *Man's Search for Meaning* chronicles his experiences as an inmate at Auschwitz and other concentration camps. He considered why some inmates survived the starvation and inconceivable physical cruelty while others succumbed and died. Frankl said: "We who lived in concentration camps can remember the men who walked through the huts comforting others, giving away their last piece of bread. They may have been few in number, but they offered sufficient proof that everything can be taken from a man but one thing: the last of the human freedoms—to choose one's attitude to any given set of circumstances, to choose one's own way . . . Between stimulus and response, there is a space. In that space is our power to choose our response. In our response lies our growth and freedom."

Irish philosopher Francis Hutcheson spoke of the senses that make us human, in particular our public sense, defined as a determination to be pleased with the happiness of others and to be uneasy at their misery, and is possibly best remembered for his quote: "That action is best which procures the greatest happiness for the greatest numbers." Collective bumper sticker wisdom tells us that outwardly directed activities are the foundation of a Good Life, and personal experience tells us that the best way to be happy is to work at making other people happy.

I once had a babysitter who liked to fight on the phone with her boyfriend. And because she had six siblings, there wasn't much chance to do this at her house. It was before cell phones, back in the day when Spam arrived in a tin can. Only for this phone conversation to work, Lizzy had to keep me occupied. I liked puzzles, so she'd cleverly remove a picture from a magazine, cut it in pieces, and hand it to me as a puzzle. Once, she and the boyfriend were having a major blowout, so she took a *National Geographic* and cut a map of the entire world into very small pieces. Much to her frustration, I returned in five minutes with the map assembled. Lizzy was stunned. "How'd you finish that so fast?" she wanted to know. "Easy," I said. "There was a person on the back, and when I put the person together the world came together."

As any experienced airline gate agent will tell us, for the most part we can only control our own behavior in this life, but if we try and do that in as thoughtful a manner as possible, we often find that the whole world comes together.

Humanity is like an enormous spider web,
so that if you touch it anywhere,
you set the whole thing trembling.
−Frederick Buechner

Chapter 36

If Truth Be Told

"Liar, liar pants on fire, nose as long as a telephone wire" was a common chant on the playground growing up (and more recently in the United States Congress). But what if our pants actually did catch fire every time we lied? Or our noses grew like that of the wooden marionette Pinocchio? What if there was some other technology to expose a falsehood? We already have polygraph tests—I see no reason they can't be used on a cell phone app. Or have the face of your Apple watch turn red. We could tell whenever we were being lied to by a salesperson, Ponzi schemer, teenager, or a politician fibbing about . . . where to begin? And . . . they could tell if we were lying. Would we want everybody to wear one?

Lying is always wrong, according to German philosopher Immanuel Kant. If a murderer is at your door looking for someone inside, you can't say he just ran out to get some more limes.

Kant believed that honesty is a mark of rationality and that rationality is the foundation of human dignity. However, my Aunt Sue says white lies are okay when they spare someone's feelings. Blaming a broken vase on the cat when I was a kid certainly spared my sorrow over being grounded for a week. Our attitude toward truthfulness impacts all our relationships and shapes our expectations for behavior by others. On a larger scale, when our faith in the honesty of our leaders breaks down, society is at risk. As institutions decay and social norms fray, democracies are prone to apathy, demagoguery, and disintegration. I can't find a single American who wishes to return to a time before driver's licenses could be renewed online.

What if everyone wore lie detector devices and children could tell if we were fibbing about Santa Claus or the Easter Bunny or the Tooth Fairy? Or that old Shep didn't go to a farm and live out his days breathing fresh air and chasing rabbits? What if a five-year-old asks where her chicken McNuggets come from? Or what if she has terminal cancer and wants to know if she's going to die? Well, those are of course children. So maybe that's an exception.

What if we want to get someone we love into rehab? "Come on over! We're having a party." On the subject of parties, is a surprise party a lie? Or when writers pen fake memoirs, are they hurting us? Is Beyoncé lip-synching a song harming our children who admire Beyoncé or want to be Beyoncé? What about a doping athlete who accepts corporate sponsorship, headlines a charity, and is a hero to many?

The biggest recipient of lies might be ourselves. *I'm going to go to the gym more. I'm going to attend church more. I can put my money to better use than the IRS.* Will Rogers said the income tax has made more liars out of the American people than golf. Or how about, *I'm not going to lie anymore?*

Almost all of us, aside from Immanuel Kant, recognize that a bit of dishonesty provides valuable social cushioning and lots of excuses to have dessert—why, it would be impolite not to! Without such social niceties, our relationships might fray rather quickly, and this is the main reason we have such a complex relationship with the truth. There are two things you can say for sure about human beings: our opposable thumbs make us great at using tools, and we're all big, fat liars. By age four, 90 percent of children have grasped the concept of lying. According to a study by the University of Massachusetts, 60 percent of adults cannot have a ten-minute conversation without lying at least once. But even that number makes things sound better than they really are; those who did lie actually told an average of three lies during their brief chats. Which shines a whole new light on cocktail parties and church coffee hours.

Is lying biological? Are we hardwired that way? Is it in our DNA? Animals lie. In one instance, a gorilla named Koko, who knew a large number of hand signs, was asked who tore a sink off the wall, and she pointed to one of her handlers and laughed. Deceptive body language, such as feints that mislead as to the intended direction of attack or flight, is observed in many species, including wolves. A mother bird deceives when she pretends to have a broken wing to divert the attention of a perceived predator—including humans—from the eggs in her nest to herself.

Presidents lie. Trump lies to the American people an average of fifty times per week. Barack Obama's thoughts on gay marriage were supposedly evolving until he was reelected. Bill Clinton's lie about his relationship with an intern led to an impeachment trial that cost millions of taxpayer dollars. Richard Nixon's lies about the Watergate burglary almost collapsed our democracy. Assertions made to justify a war in Iraq were reminiscent of claims that US ships were attacked in the Gulf of Tonkin in order to launch a full-scale assault on North Vietnam. Now researchers are concluding that the Bush White House misled the public about Iraq's having weapons of mass destruction, as well as Saddam Hussein's link to Al Qaeda. Four major results of this government deception: 1) Over 4,000 military casualties and 32,000 injuries, the death of hundreds of thousands of Iraqi civilians; we don't even know exact numbers. 2) A broken country and the rise of extremism. 3) A hesitancy on the part of Americans when it comes to intervention in the Middle East. 4) Skepticism. Skepticism about whether our government is telling the truth. Not just about intelligence, but everything.

What else might be going on—monitoring our phone calls, killing children in drone strikes? And we can't have a conspiracy list without including probes by space aliens. Just ask my dad's neighbor Clark in New Mexico. He'll show you all the UFO photos you want—silver disks, fireballs, egg-shaped spacecraft, he's got the whole collection. I laugh, but that's another problem. Every conspiracy theorist out there starts looking right about every whackadoodle idea they've ever come up with: the moon landing was a sham, the government carried out 9/11, global warming is a hoax, and let's not forget reptilian humanoids controlling us all. Because if the government lied about A, B, and C then they must be lying about X, Y, and Z.

In this way a government lie compromises the entire social fabric. Police and politicians in Chicago tried to cover up a fatal shooting by an officer in 2014. There have been enormous repercussions and mistrust, understandably so. Our attitude toward truthfulness impacts all our relationships, but on a larger scale, when our faith in the honesty of our leaders breaks down, our democracy is at risk.

Shortly before the Chicago cover-up, the US government blew up a working hospital in Afghanistan. Credit to them, they came out with the truth. An investigation done in a timely manner revealed multiple human errors. It gave us a lot to think about with regard to what our elected leaders are doing over there, but at least we're working with tangible information, however awful. For this reason, I'm wary about voting for politicians who have a problem admitting they were wrong about something at one time or another.

Occasionally, we get public and private collusion against the truth, such as the existence of institutionalized racism. I'm old enough to remember redlining–the practice of denying minorities loans and access to white neighborhoods. Former FOX news anchor Bill O'Reilly liked to claim that he'd *never* benefited from "white privilege" and that his success was solely a result of his own hard work. For starters, O'Reilly is from Levittown on Long Island, which was a whites only segregated community when he was growing up there.

At other times we get religious and political collusion against the truth. Scripture was employed to justify slavery in this country. It's currently being used in the Middle East to reject modernity and send people back to a time when entire segments of the population were disrespected or disregarded. A sad parallel is that there are politicians and constituents in this country who want to take us back to an era when many groups were marginalized and suffered officially sanctioned discrimination.

The entire vocabulary that's sprung up around dishonesty is rather fascinating in and of itself, and perhaps the best exhibit of a difficult relationship. There are lies of omission and commission. Bald-faced lies, honest lies, noble lies, and contextual lies where you state part of the truth but without the framework. We have white lies, black lies and gray areas. Minimization, misdirection, misinformation, denial, deflection, exaggeration, fabrication, prevarication, propaganda, fibs, half-truths, self-deception, revisionism, and of course fake news. You can speak with a forked tongue, use weasel words, and my favorite—employ the fudge factor. Winston Churchill liked to say that "A lie gets halfway around the world before the truth has a chance to get its pants on."

I lied to my parents about having a hernia operation. Every morning I email my mom because if I don't, she calls to see what I'm up to. I forgot and went to the hospital early. It was raining so the doctors weren't in a hurry to play golf and therefore running late. I didn't get into the recovery room until 5 PM. The surgeon came by to see how I was and I told him, "You look twelve years old. You look like Robin the Boy Wonder from *Batman & Robin*." That should have been a red flag. My cell phone rang. It was Mom. I figured I could pull it off, even though her biography will be called *Too Nosy to Die*. She said I sounded strange. I said I have allergies and took medication. She wanted to know what it was. I tried to remember the name of an allergy medicine but couldn't. Instead of Sudafed I said I took sulfuric acid. It was all too confusing. I told her I'd call back. She phoned my husband, who was in Chicago on a business trip, and reported that I'd ingested poison. He told her I was in the hospital. Now it was the time of evening I always called my dad. He couldn't locate me and phoned my mom, who said I was in the hospital after attempting suicide. My friend Julie brought me home. I took the pain medication, climbed into bed, handed Julie my cell phone, which was lit up like a Christmas tree, and said, "Good luck."

What I learned was that silence can also be a lie, and I deprived my parents of the opportunity to worry about me, to care about their only child, and as parents they have a right to do that. However, some cases are trickier. In 1991 a gay rights group held a press conference to announce a senior Defense Department official was a homosexual. *The Advocate*, a gay magazine, did a story on the official and justified its action by pointing to the Pentagon's own policy of outing gays in uniform and discharging them. Around the same time, the group Out-Post covered NYC with posters featuring the faces of movie stars who were allegedly closeted homosexuals. Most papers refused to name the "outed" celebrities. Individuals have a right, they maintained, to keep information about their private lives private. The gay community split between the right to privacy and closeted gays contributing to oppression.

But clearly if a group is hiding their identity to avoid harassment, or lower pay, less opportunity for work, and fewer civil rights, there are inherent problems with the system, and perhaps that's where our gaze should land. Does anyone think that if actress Jodie Foster had come out as a lesbian in 1983 rather than thirty years later in 2013 she would have been allowed to play so many romantic leads or produce and direct big budget films? It's wonderful to say that since 1991 much progress has been made toward equality, especially with regard to gays in the military and same-sex marriage, though there is still a long way to go. However, if we exclude a group of people from this country based on creed, we're forcing them to be dishonest about their faith and perhaps worship in secret, like Jews and Muslims during the Spanish Inquisition.

Recently the Library of Congress wanted to replace the subject heading of "illegal aliens" with "noncitizens." Most Republicans insisted on keeping the term "illegal aliens." They also don't like "undocumented workers" because that doesn't sound sinister enough. Why? Because it's not. It's like if some-one sneaks into the garage and washes my car. I might be a little confused, but I'm not calling the police. In fact, I may just leave out the Dustbuster and a jar of Turtle wax. Representative Joa-quin Castro from Texas responded by saying, "These folks may not be American citizens, but they are not people from outer space. They are human beings. When ugly, belittling terms are used to describe groups of people, those terms can make dis-crimination seem okay." I'll add that an intolerant society creates self-loathing people who may act out inappropriately.

A code of silence in many police departments has prevented good cops from being honest. Secrecy is the handmaiden to deception and is not uncommonly used to oppress and exclude. It's necessary for human survival and yet can enhance every sort of abuse. By removing discrimination and penalties for truth-tell-ing, we remove the need for a great deal of subterfuge.

When politicians, or even presidents, sow racism through divisiveness, I'm reminded of something another president said. John F. Kennedy, our first Catholic to sit in the Oval Office, and no stranger to having his patriotism questioned because of his religion, observed, "The great enemy of truth is very often not the lie—deliberate, contrived, and dishonest—but the myth—per-sistent, persuasive, and unrealistic. Too often we hold fast to the clichés of our forebears and thereby enjoy the comfort of opinion without the discomfort of thought."

More often than not, a lie is merely about getting out of activities or delaying deadlines. A professor of biology at East-ern Connecticut State University produced a study showing that students' grandmothers are ten times more likely to die before a midterm exam, and nineteen times more likely to expire before a final exam. Moreover, the grandmothers of students who aren't

doing well in class are at an even higher risk—students who are failing are fifty times more likely to lose a grandmother compared with students who are passing. The real lesson here is that if you're the grandmother of a struggling student, you may want to stay inside during finals week, and spring for some tutoring.

Are there any tools available to tackle this complex relationship with the truth? It's been shown that most often we begin courting trouble when our emotional and physical resources are depleted. We can try not to make any promises when tired and overextended, which is not dissimilar from the Weight Watchers decree not to go food shopping when hungry. Or my rule not to visit an animal shelter when I'm feeling sad.

Studies also show we're less likely to be dishonest when regularly reminded of our morals and principles. Maybe those books of daily meditations with rainbows on the covers are onto something. Studies show that "resetting rituals," which even include New Year's resolutions, can effectively work against what social scientists call the "Oh, what-the-hell effect." New Year's resolutions are rather like campaign promises we make to ourselves.

The old saying goes: Lead me not into temptation, I can find the way myself. We can also avoid temptation. For instance, by not telling friends we'll help them move if we're just setting ourselves up for failure. And then a grandmother has to suddenly die on the day of the big move. Along the same lines, the easiest way to live more honestly is to manage our time as well as possible so we don't have to be "stuck in traffic" as much. Finally, we can imagine if the roles were reversed and being on the receiving end of that lie. Or, as this was called back in kindergarten, The Golden Rule.

Still, I don't entirely agree with Mr. Never Tell a Lie Immanuel Kant. The main reason is because he was never married and therefore never asked by his wife, "Do I look fat in this?" Likewise, he didn't have children, and was never asked "Daddy, who is your favorite?" So we're talking about balance, with some good judgment thrown in.

"What is truth?" Pontius Pilate famously asked Jesus during his trial. Unfortunately, St. John's gospel doesn't record how J.C. responded. When it comes to our expectations for the truth, we have to decide whether we want a life of transactions or a life of relationships. Because dishonesty damages trust, hurts people, and is stressful to the teller of the lie. Likewise, creating or tolerating an environment that contains judgments about lifestyle, income, skin color, or religion that push people into lying is equally detrimental. Democracies are not immortal and have swiftly evolved into autocracies, as far back as two millennia ago in ancient Rome and as recently as China.

Truth and *trust*—there's only one letter that's different in those two words, and maybe that's because one leads to the other. By striving for honesty, we strengthen ties with the individuals about whom we care most, our larger communities, and our elected officials to build a democratic society of equal rights and equal obligations. And it's been proven that lying is extremely dangerous when it comes to the health and well-being of grandmothers everywhere.

To live fully, we must learn to use things and love people,
and not love things and use people.

–John Powell

Chapter 37

Enough Is Enough

A s a kid I was jealous of anyone who had the large box of sixty-four crayons with a built-in sharpener, and when drawing the sky had their pick between blue-gray, midnight blue, navy blue, blue-green, green-blue, cadet blue, blue-violet, lavender, periwinkle, turquoise, violet, and the overly obvious sky blue. Surely Van Gogh had been given more choices than just "blue" to color his first starry night! On the bright side, my modest eight-pack dodged the moral dilemmas of a crayon called "flesh" in a pale peach hue, and also "Indian red."

Nowadays, Americans are presented with more options than ever before in just about every endeavor we undertake. Not only is having a choice considered a fundamental part of our democracy, but it is also thought to enhance our lives. However, while some choice is better than none, more can also become less.

It's not just people who've exploded into categories of mixed nationality, ethnicity, and sexuality, but also products. When my parents were growing up in the 1930s, they had milk and they had cream. There was chocolate milk, but it was too expensive, so they mixed chocolate syrup into their milk. There was skim milk—it was a byproduct of cream, poured into waterways, used as hog slop or in the making of adhesives. It wasn't until after World War II that marketers decided to sell this as a health product. When I was a kid in the 1970s, supermarket shelves contained whole milk, skim milk, 1 percent, and 2 percent. In addition to chocolate milk, Nestlé came up with strawberry milk. When I was a teenager, lactose-free milk arrived on the scene.

Recently I walked down the milk aisle of the grocery store, where I haven't been in a long time because I no longer drink milk and don't have children at home, and I was confused. No, I was paralyzed. There was a wall of milk. In addition to whole milk, skim milk, 1 percent, 2 percent, and Lactaid, we now have organic milk, almond milk, soy milk, vanilla soy milk, cashew milk, coconut milk, and those are just the ones I remember. I think there may have been cage-free milk from peripatetic cows.

It isn't just milk. Pick any food sector and the choices of organic, semi-organic, free-range, sodium free, gluten free, seasoned, or stuffed pile up fast. Don't even get me started on the bread aisle. Although maybe someone can explain why bread crumbs are more expensive then bread. I was similarly incapacitated while shopping for a pair of blue jeans with options such as straight, skinny, boot cut, baggy, boyfriend, stone-washed, acid-washed, zipper, or button fly. Amazon sells 283 varieties of toilet cleanser. If you're like me, you probably receive dozens of catalogues a week in addition to what's available online, which is essentially everything.

Purchasing milk or jeans should be a trivial matter in the greater scheme of our lives. But it's become a complex transaction demanding an enormous amount of time and energy, often accompanied by self-doubt and anxiety. It's true that when people have *no* choices, life can be unbearable, or at the very least much less enjoyable. But as the number of choices continues expanding, negative aspects begin to arise until a barrage of options leads to overload, at which point choice no longer liberates but debilitates, and may even be said to traumatize and tyrannize.

Assessments of well-being by social scientists reveal that increased choice and increased prosperity have been accompanied by decreased happiness and declining longevity in the US and most affluent societies. As gross domestic product more than doubled in the past thirty years, the segment of the population describing itself as "very happy" declined by 5 percent, about 16 million people, and more individuals than ever before were diagnosed as clinically depressed.

No one believes a single factor explains decreased well-being, but a number of findings indicate that the explosion of choice plays a substantial role. It seems that as society grows wealthier and people become freer to do whatever they want, they're less happy. Yet marketers and advertisers have made products and experiences impossible to ignore. It can be addictive to look at one more store, catalogue, or website before making a decision.

The tsunami of choice has swept into all areas of life, including education, career, friendship, romance, parenting, housing, travel, and religious observance, to name a few. Again, choice is essential to autonomy, which in turn is fundamental to well-being. Healthy people want and need to direct their own lives. However, the options for retirement plans alone are mindboggling. Medical choices abound. Health care has shifted from what I experienced growing up with the all-knowing paternalistic doctor telling the patient what must be done, or sometimes just doing it. Doctors often withheld crucial information, like the fact that you were going to die. Patients could be forbidden from examining their own medical records. We suffered for it, either because doctors were arrogant or careless, or they were making a life choice that depended on our own philosophy and psyche. The patient revolution which started in the 1980s has no doubt greatly improved medical care, but has also gone too far.

My husband had prostate cancer, and the doctors said he could watch and wait, do a radical prostatectomy, or implant radiation seeds. We asked which option was best for his age and stage. They said, "You decide." Seriously, they had sixty years of medical practice between the three of them, while he's a business professor and I'm a writer. We voted on prostate removal and he's fine. It was the size of a grapefruit, by the way. For all our advanced scientific knowledge, health care is still mostly about fruits and vegetables—lumps the size of blueberries and limes and avocados. How's the new baby? Already as big as a watermelon! I'm fine with hailstones being the size of "golf balls" and "baseballs" and "softballs" but when it comes to my tumors, it would be nice to move from the ballpark to the imperial system which is at least based on the size of people's feet. With the revolution in traditional care came an array of herbs, vitamins, diets, acupuncture, aromatherapies, copper bracelets, chakra stones, crystal clusters, and alternative practitioners. More recently we have widespread advertising for corrective surgeries and prescription drugs.

I don't recall any drug commercials in the 1970s except for a school bus driver who understandably needed Excedrin. There were plenty of liquor and cigarette ads—cigarettes were touted as being good for you. It was ridiculously easy for kids to buy cigarettes, since there were vending machines inside most restaurants and outside every gas station. Put in forty cents and out they popped like a pack of gum. Grownups regularly gave kids a couple quarters and had them run to the store for smokes. "Get Grammy a pack of Winstons and some candy cigarettes for yourself."

Now TV and radio present a barrage of ads for drugs to make us feel better, live better, look better, pee better, and date better. What's the point of advertising prescription drugs on TV? We can't go to the pharmacy and just buy them. Why are pharmaceutical companies investing vast fortunes to reach us, the consumer, directly? Ask your doctor if taking medical advice from TV commercials is right for you. Obviously, they hope and expect we'll notice their products and ask for prescriptions. I can't watch the news without seeing commercials for sleep aids featuring butterflies floating around the room. We didn't have those when I was growing up. We also didn't have Starbucks selling Frappuccinos in pitchers on every corner. Does anyone else see a connection here?

Have you glanced at a college catalogue recently? There can be over 350 courses to satisfy the basic requirements, out of which students will choose a dozen at most. This is nothing compared to the television revolution—a thousand times as many shows on networks, cable, and video streaming, available any-time we want.

In the 1970s if we missed an episode of *All in the Family,* we had to try and catch it in reruns. If we were lucky enough to find an old movie to watch late at night, we did not have a sense that we were missing anything. And commercials were good for con-versation, letting the dog out, snack runs, and bathroom breaks. There was no cell phone to check.

The conundrum is that just because some choice is good

doesn't necessarily mean that even more choice is better. There is a cost to having an overload of options. As a culture, we're enamored of freedom, which is synonymous with patriotism and Americanism. We prize and value self-determination and are reluctant to give up any of our choices. But clinging to all the possibilities available contributes to bad decisions, anxiety, stress, dissatisfaction, and even depression. Demands for perfection increase and we suffer from regret, missed opportunity, and feelings of inadequacy. This is often most keenly felt when we come home and put on the jeans we spent hours or maybe days weighing up.

Political philosopher Isaiah Berlin made an important distinction between "negative liberty" and "positive liberty." Negative liberty is "freedom from"–freedom from constraint and freedom from being told what to do by others. "Positive liberty" is "freedom to"–freedom to be the architect of our own lives, and thereby make them meaningful and significant. Often these two kinds of liberty go well together. When I was young, AT&T had a monopoly on phone service and treated its customers shabbily with high rates and poor customer service. Yet we were prisoners with no alternatives. Older people may remember Lily Tomlin as Ernestine, the snorting, power-drunk AT&T operator. "The phone company handles 84 billion calls a year, everything from kings, queens, and presidents to the scum of the earth. We're the phone company. We don't care; we don't have to." We'd take the day off from work to wait to have our phone installed but no one showed up, time and again, and there was no way to phone them. Long distance rates were exorbitant–if a long-distance call came in, you dashed off shouting "long distance" dementedly through the house, yard, and basement, until someone zoomed toward the phone. We all had the fee schedule memorized.

On weekdays the rates dropped after eleven at night, so if you received a long-distance call before then, someone was very sick. If the person was dead, the relatives would wait until eleven, because what were you going to do anyway?

So yes, it's good that this monopoly was broken up. Of course there's a dark side to freedom, just like there's a downside to giving children cake for dinner. Suddenly we had Sprint calling in the middle of dinner to talk about our phone service and MCI calling during dessert with their best offer. I used to play them off against each other by saying that Sprint was already there sanding my floors, what could MCI do for me . . . the gutters needed cleaning.

Perhaps the real seismic shift in choice has come in the areas of relationships and having children. Most social norms about who you should or could marry have fallen away, thank goodness. Meantime, the Internet has made dating into a shopping exercise where you can click on a partner and drop it into your shopping cart. Science has opened a whole world of reproductive options. When I was growing up, you could either have children or you couldn't. Gender reveal parties happened in the maternity ward a few minutes after crowning and just before the umbilical cord was cut. I think my friend Lynn was the last person in the US to give birth to a baby boy and start climbing off the table, only to hear, "Hold on, there's another one." Partnering and procreating are two more enormous choices to occupy our attention and fuel our anxieties.

What to do about all this? Well, we'd be better off if we embraced certain voluntary constraints on our freedom of choice. For instance, buying Fair Trade coffee, tea, and chocolate—not as much to consider and ethical—a win/win. During a recession, oil crisis, and double-digit inflation, shopping was simple. Which was the cheapest? Or as my grandfather said when asked if he wanted to be cremated or buried, "Surprise me."

Instead of "the best," we're better off seeking "good enough." When I was a kid there weren't any waterproof boots. Now there are many. If your boots are waterproof that's good enough. And as my mother liked to say regarding just about anything, "If someone is your friend because of your boots, then that doesn't say much about either of you." Pick some boots and embrace and appreciate those boots. There are people who don't have any boots.

We can remind ourselves not to be second-guessers. That's why people renew their wedding vows. There have been a lot of choices since the day you first said "I do." And there's a reason it's called a Wedding March rather than a Wedding Romp.

I had an argument with a writer over a book called *The Bridges of Madison County*. My friend mercilessly ridiculed the bestselling love story for its sappy plot and purple prose, like many other critics. It elevated to a spiritual level the fantasy in which an exotic stranger materializes in the kitchen of a lonely housewife and takes her into his arms. One passage read: "With her face buried in his neck and her skin against his, she could smell rivers and wood smoke, could hear steaming trains chuffing out of winter stations in long-ago nighttimes, could see travelers in black robes moving steadily along frozen rivers and through summer meadows, beating their way toward the end of things." Should she stay or should she go? Spoiler alert: she stays, he goes. But at least see the movie. The reason the novel sold fifty million copies worldwide and became one of the bestselling books of the twentieth century is because it was about a choice, the kind of choice we've all made where we don't ever get to see The Road Not Taken. No spirit appears, like in Charles Dickens's *A Christmas*

Carol or Frank Capra's *It's a Wonderful Life,* to reassure us that when faced with a difficult decision we've done the right thing, or whether we've chosen the perfect person to be our partner.

We tend to define "perfection" as flawless or unsurpassable. The Latin origin suggests "per" means "complete" and "facere" is "to make." Perfection can therefore mean to make something complete. I prefer this definition as it demonstrates how it's possible to pass contentment right by in search of something perceived to be better, when the pursuit of happiness often means to decide on happiness.

Similarly, we're better off when we lower our expectations about the results of our decisions. And always include a gift receipt. This was summed up in kindergarten—it's the thought that counts. We'd be better off if many of the decisions we made were nonreversible, such as working with the children we have rather than scanning the playground for different ones. If raising children were meant to be easy, it certainly wouldn't start with a process called "labor."

We might pay less attention to what others around us are doing or buying. Back to that cadre of elementary school teachers who said, "Just worry about yourself." Conventional wisdom attempts to convince us that the more choices people have, the better off they are, the best way to get great results is to have very high standards, and it's always good to have a way to back out of a decision. But unless you're extremely dissatisfied, make it a point to stick with things, at least the more mundane ones. Shopping around too much can be like drinking too much—it can leave us with a pile of poor decisions and a bad hangover.

To best manage the problem of choice overload, we must decide which choices in our lives really matter and focus our time and energy there, letting other opportunities pass us by. We of course want the best surgeon and the best cancer care, and the best politicians, so be sure to vote. By focusing on the important decisions, we'll choose better and feel better. *When Breath Becomes Air* is a memoir by the neurosurgeon Dr. Paul Kalinithi, who attempts to answer the question, What Makes a Life Worth Living? He wrote it while battling Stage IV lung cancer. Here is his final quote in the book, which is directed at his infant daughter, and what he desires most to communicate to her, knowing that he'll probably die before she has the ability to remember him.

"When you come to one of the many moments in life when you must give an account of yourself, provide a ledger of what you have been, and done, and meant to the world, do not, I pray, discount that you filled a dying man's days with a sated joy, a joy unknown to me in all my prior years, a joy that does not hunger for more and more, but rests, satisfied. In this time, right now, that is an enormous thing."

Dr. Kalinithi died in March of 2015 at age thirty-seven when his daughter was just seven months old. The words "sated joy" resonate with me. Sated joy, not sacred joy, whatever that is and as nice as it may sound. The conscious decision that a desire has been fulfilled and you've been blessed with enough.

The current culture of abundance can so easily rob of us satisfaction. English poet, painter, and printmaker William Blake said, "You never know what is enough unless you know what is more than enough." When it comes to each choice, we need to ask ourselves whether it nourishes us or deprives us, whether it makes us mobile or constrains us, whether it enhances self-respect or diminishes it, and whether it enables us to participate in our communities or precludes us from doing so. Freedom is essential to dignity, public participation, mobility, and nourishment, but not all choice enhances freedom. In particular, increased options among goods and services may contribute little or nothing to the kind of freedom that counts. Indeed, it may impair freedom by taking time and energy we'd be better off devoting to other matters, because the most important things in life aren't things. Singer-songwriter and peace activist John Lennon said, "If everyone demanded peace instead of another television set then there'd be peace." Unfortunately, the man who sang "imagine no possessions . . . and the world will be as one" was assassinated by a mentally ill man with a gun. I find it interesting that we have locks on phones but not guns.

The writer Kurt Vonnegut once told a story about his close friend and fellow novelist Joseph Heller. Both were attending a party in Heller's honor hosted by an enormously wealthy hedge fund owner at his home in the Hamptons. Vonnegut called his friend aside and asked, "Joe, does it bother you that our host probably made more money today than you've made in your entire career as a writer?" Heller replied, "No, not really." Vonnegut asked, "Why not?" Heller said, "Because I have something this man will never have." His friend asked, "And what is that?" Heller replied, "Enough."

Choices, like so many things, can be a blessing and a burden, so in tackling them, instead of wishing each other the very best, we can perhaps wish each other good enough. Or sated joy.

I think God, in creating man,
somewhat overestimated his ability.

−Oscar Wilde

Chapter 38

Is God Watching?

Despite attending public learning institutions from kindergarten through high school, I always had the sense that someone was watching, and I don't mean the principal. My teachers were fond of saying, "You'll have to answer for that." And if you complained about the heat someone was quick to reply, "But we know a hotter place, *don't we?*"

Before soccer games we gathered in a prayer circle. There were a total of two spectators on the sidelines, out in the middle of nowhere, or Where Jesus Lost his Sandals, as my mom liked to say, and as the only UU kid I couldn't help wondering, *is* God watching, and if so, does he decide girls' athletic events? Because not even the school cared that much, evidenced by the fact we were given the boys' old uniforms to wear.

Are there advantages to thinking that God is watching? Of course. During the French Revolution, three insurrectionists were sent to the guillotine. The first one, a Christian, said his prayers and bowed his head, but the blade malfunctioned. If it didn't work, you were allowed to go free, so he was spared. He looked up and said, "Thank you, God, for your benevolence." The Jewish man was next, the guillotine malfunctioned again, he looked up and said, "Blessed is the Lord, I have set him before me always." Then it was the Unitarian's turn. The blade malfunctioned. He looked up and pointed and said, "I think I see the problem."

The simple but powerful idea of an all-knowing God has long served to deter self-interest and achieve remarkable levels of cooperation. Indeed, as most societies have discovered, supernatural beliefs are so good at promoting collaboration that they may have been favored by natural selection. Members of religious groups describe themselves as treating each other as fictive kin, so it makes sense that many churchgoers employ terms such as "brother" and "sister."

So if God is watching, does everything happen for a reason? Like meeting your soul mate on the C train when you almost always take the A train. When you went to the animal shelter and that one dog grabbed your pant cuff? What about an earthquake that kills thousands of people? A man emerged unscathed after the 2017 Las Vegas Massacre where fifty-eight people died and almost five hundred were wounded and said he'd become a believer in God because his life had been spared. Growing up, how many times did I hear the phrase, "There but for the grace of God go I"?

Any disaster, manmade or natural, causes us to wonder why this house was destroyed and this one spared, why this life was saved and this one taken. After 9/11 I asked myself that same question when many dear friends were lost. Some people find it reassuring to think that there are no accidents and what happens to us—good and bad—reflects an unfolding plan. I called this chapter "Is God Watching?" but after reading the news this past year, I almost called it "Is God Punishing Us?"

Most of us are familiar with the biblical story of Noah's Ark, which in its petrifying and dramatic simplicity embodies the notion of divine retribution. Though I do admire Noah's courage in bringing termites, beavers, and woodpeckers aboard a wooden boat. Early in life we're made to understand that individuals who commit crimes or diverge from religious and social mores will suffer punishment, while those who behave properly and follow the rules will be rewarded.

Today, with secularism at an all-time high, the willingness to believe in some kind of payback or karma remains nearly universal. Even atheists often feel they're monitored and judged, which may or may not be the result of dashboard cameras and being forced to work on everyone else's religious holidays. As a journalist I was trained to write atheist with a lowercase "a," while God was always capitalized.

We frequently find ourselves imagining what our parents, spouse, children, or boss would think of our actions, even if they're miles away and will never find out. We talk of eyes burning into the back of our heads, the walls listening, a sense that someone or something is out there, observing our every move, possibly aware of our thoughts and intentions.

The US, the world's most economically powerful and scientifically advanced society, also has the greatest number of religions, and is where two of the fastest growing—Mormonism and Pentecostalism—were founded. Over 75 percent of Americans believe in God, 72 percent believe in Heaven, 58 percent in Hell, and 40 percent believe in a literal interpretation of Genesis rather than evolution. Seventy-seven percent believe in angels, compared with 61 percent who believe in climate change. At least 14 percent believe that Joan of Arc was Noah's wife, 9 percent that Sodom and Gomorrah were married, and 4 percent that Noah had three sons: Shem, Ham, and Cheese.

Man has been around as long as God, or God has been around as long as Man, take your pick. The eighteenth-century French Enlightenment writer Voltaire said, "If there were no God it would be necessary to invent him." Going back in time, when we operated in small bands of hunter-gatherers, we tended to know everyone with whom we interacted. They were either kin, direct blood relatives, or kith, friends and allies we knew well along with their families. Gods back then also tended to be less versatile–they weren't omnipotent and didn't judge individual moral transgressions, mainly because communities were small, and therefore it was easy to keep track of people and punish them yourself.

About 12,000 years ago, when we began moving toward large-scale societies of anonymous strangers as a result of agriculture, God began watching and controlling our individual movements, which makes sense, because we didn't yet have cooperation in the form of institutions such as courts, police, and law firms to enforce contracts. This new societal arrangement fostered the birth of the individual out of a tribal system in which the strong ruled the weak.

It's commonly thought that religion is the antithesis of secularism, yet history and psychology reveal unexpected continuities. It transpires that an initial religious framework can assist us in building communities with the types of organizations, practices, and social conditions that help a cooperative society thrive, whether their members choose to be godless or god-fearing.

Do we behave differently if someone might be watching?

Drivers slow down when they see a police car. Cameras in stores reduce theft. With transparency in politics and corporations, there's less malfeasance. In the presence of others, there's more generosity, and also hand-washing. Thomas Jefferson said, "Whenever you do a thing, act as if all the world were watching."

Problems arise when society is affected by anonymity and can't check reputations, as is often the case with cyberbullying and fake news. The monotheistic God in the Hebrew Bible, New Testament, and Koran supposedly sees everything, especially when no one else is watching, much like my friend Mary's mom, a mother of nine who had eyes in the back of her head, even though we looked and couldn't find them. The Great Seal of the US on the one-dollar bill shows a watchful eye atop a pyramid. Buddhism has representations of eyes on flags and monuments believed to be looking in all four directions. In ancient Egypt, Horus the Sky God, also known as Horus Who Rules with Two Eyes, was often depicted as a falcon watching over towns and villages. Similar examples are found throughout Inca society and many native peoples.

If we examine the thousands of religions that have come and gone, most don't last, but the ones with the meanest gods do best. And they're the ones in which followers behaved the best. Think of your strictest teacher—the one nobody messed with. Nastier gods also made people better neighbors. Unitarian Universalists are a perfect example of being too lenient—we don't believe in damnation or maintain a strict set of rules; we respect your choices, don't judge your lifestyle or what you wore today, and we don't have a lot of people who want to join. Alcohol addiction—there's a meeting on Wednesday, we support you. A Starbucks opened nearby, and parishioners began showing up with seven-dollar coffees in hand while putting just three dollars in the collection plate, presumably their change. In the summer months church is officially on vacation and operated by a cadre of volunteers—a perfect storm of heat and heathens. Meantime, some religious countries jail citizens for drinking. We need to get tough about something—maybe more regulations about carrying NPR tote bags, a seating chart, or a dress code.

Supernatural monitoring is the outsourcing of social monitoring to watch when no one is watching, to care when no one can care, and to threaten when no one can threaten. In more modern terms, God helps stabilize cooperation levels among large groups. In 1904, on a long railroad trip through America, German sociologist Max Weber asked a traveling salesman about religion. The salesman's now famous reply was, "Sir, for my part everybody may believe or not believe as he pleases; but if I saw a farmer or a businessman not belonging to any church at all, I wouldn't trust him with fifty cents. Why pay *me* if he doesn't believe in anything?"

The interesting thing in this example is how the salesman doesn't care *what* his customers believe in, so long as it's something. The dilemma of the traveling salesman is the problem with all large anonymous societies where strangers interact with one other. And this is why religious groups have experienced a cultural evolutionary advantage until recently. Because mutual cooperation bestows phenomenal benefits with regard to individual and community success. But it doesn't come free and requires a considerable amount of ingenuity to foster the necessary trust.

In the post-World War II era, Americans flocked to church in record numbers, swelling the ranks of traditional denominations—Methodist, Baptist, Disciples of Christ, Lutheran, Catholic, and Presbyterian. Church building boomed, Bible sales skyrocketed, and communion wafers flew off the shelves. Amid the prosperity, the United States and the Soviet Union faced off in a Cold War, a spiritual struggle that pitted "Christian America" against "Godless Communism." The Soviets successfully tested their first nuclear bomb in 1949.

In 1952, President-elect Dwight Eisenhower famously said, "Our form of government has no sense unless it is founded in a deeply felt religious faith, and I don't care what it is." This statement suggests that the nonreligious, be they atheist or socialist, are fundamentally anti-American and unpatriotic. My parents said a different Pledge of Allegiance in the 1940s than I did in the 1970s. In 1954 the phrase "Under God" was added to the version that I was required to say every morning in a public school. "In God We Trust" was made our national motto in 1956, and rituals emerged like the National Day of Prayer and National Prayer Breakfast—which convinced many Americans, particularly future FOX News anchors, that their country has been, and always would be, a formally Christian nation.

So, is religion necessary for morality? Some extremist versions pose a threat. Others are considered oppressive to minorities, especially African-Americans, the LGBTQ community, and women. Many perform valuable local services, from providing counseling and shelter, to clothing drives and soup kitchens. The Scandinavian countries and Switzerland, the world's *least* religious societies, where the majority of people don't believe in God, top international rankings for being law-abiding, having high levels of cooperation and trust, having high rates of societal well-being, and having low rates of obesity (possibly a result of pickled herring on rye more than godlessness). Meantime, they don't have a distrust of atheists the way we do in the US, which is why you won't see an out-of-the-closet atheist running for high office here anytime soon. On the Supreme Court we have five Catholics, three Jews, and one Gorsuch, who is some type of Christian.

Secularism seems able to thrive where institutions operating the rule of law in the form of courts, contracts, and police without favoring any race, creed, or gender combine with societal benefits such as a good standard of living, health care, education, and tolerance of individualism. However, in much of the world, it's ties of blood, honor, and ethnic solidarity that are dominant, and so religion rules. Experiments show that words such as *police* and *judge* foster cooperation among strangers as much as God-related words. Monotheism may have inadvertently planted the seeds for atheism, because if so many other gods are false why not this one, but more importantly, monotheism served as the groundwork for secularism. By employing intermediaries in the form of priests and rabbis, monotheistic religious institutions made a personal god seem distant—he created the world but didn't actively manage day-to-day affairs.

Simply put, when government institutions are credible and successful, there's less religion. And when government is corrupt or lacking, there's more religion. Correspondingly, societies with greater income disparity tend to be more religious, while those with a more equitable distribution of wealth are less religious.

We tell children that Santa is watching to see if they've been naughty or nice. Similarly, in many households a God-like holiday Elf on the Shelf is installed to supposedly monitor behavior. This has also led to many an editorial questioning whether these supernatural creatures are 1) a harmless myth considered a threshold to adulthood, 2) leading us to a dystopian surveillance state, or 3) part and parcel of lodging false belief systems in young minds.

That brings us to Pascal's Wager, which supposes that believing in God is simply a safer bet against even the slimmest odds of eternal damnation. I guess Rudolph's Wager is professing belief in Santa as a good way of continuing to get presents. But it's based on a fatal premise: an omnipotent God would surely know you're merely covering all the bases.

Our core ethical instincts evolved long before religion spread through human groups. Early building blocks of morality predate religion and don't depend on it. Groups of animals regularly suppress self-interest for the collective good, and I assume they're not religious, although baboons and show poodles look like they might be part of a cult.

Secular institutions have weaknesses—understaffing, systemic racism, flawed evidence, being closed on Sunday. Religious societies believe God has no imperfections. And I will admit that God doesn't go out on strike the way teachers, bus drivers, and garbage collectors can. Likewise, it's hard to compare supernatural punishment with secular punishment.

To answer the question of whether we can motivate ourselves to behave without celestial supervision, there are two factors. Studies show that most people aren't helpful and generous because we fear the consequences of not acting so, but because we're happiest when demonstrating kindness to others, and this in turn releases the hormone oxytocin, which has positive health benefits. Like the line in the song "Santa Claus Is Coming to Town"—"So be good for goodness sake"—it transpires that being good is good for us.

Moreover, cooperation is vital to our society. It's how we wrote the Constitution, rocketed to the moon, split the atom, decoded our genome, mapped the brain, invented the Twinkie, and added caller ID to our phones. Cooperation is hard to achieve, hard to sustain, and hard to explain, yet vital to our existence. It's the root of our greatest triumphs and our bloodiest tragedies. It's what will make or break our future.

Meantime, the belief that everything happens for a reason can have some ugly consequences. It tilts us toward the view that the world is a fundamentally fair place, where goodness is rewarded and wickedness punished. It can lead us to blame those who suffer from disease or are victims of crimes, and it can motivate a reflexive bias in favor of the status quo—seeing poverty, inequality, and oppression as the workings of an all-encompassing plan.

Over time, history has favored religious groups, and that's why most of us are descendants of one faith or another. And why the joke about UUs is that we believe in, at most, one God. Another salient fact is that, at least for now, Christians, Hindus, Muslims, and Orthodox Jews reproduce faster than the nonaffiliated and spiritual-but-not-religious. It's no accident that religious conservatives' attitudes on sexual orientation, contraception, and reproductive rights are conducive to maintaining high fertility levels. In fact, the most secularized societies have the fewest children.

This dichotomy between a religious or secular way of life will continue to shape the century and leaves us asking, can we have a conscience without religion? Does the Golden Rule to treat others as we wish to be treated need a theological imprimatur to hold weight and value? We're still finding an answer to that.

Either way, whether it's because we're fearful of going to Hell or because we're flourishing on positive endorphins, we need to collaborate more and not less because there are epidemics, climate change, catastrophic weather events, a refugee crisis, racial strife, and enough nuclear weapons at large to blow up the world. And recently there was a lime shortage that proved devastating to margarita lovers everywhere. I've ruled out an alien invasion, even though we know for a fact there's intelligent life out there, mostly because it hasn't tried to contact us, to paraphrase cartoonist Bill Watterson.

Otherwise, prophets and professors work both sides of the aisle. *Heaven Is for Real* topped the nonfiction bestseller lists and became a movie. Richard Dawkins writes books debunking faith, and none other than Ron Reagan starred in a Super Bowl commercial asking you to support the Freedom from Religion Foundation, following which President Reagan's other son, the conservative commentator Michael Reagan, tweeted that their father was crying in Heaven.

Not long ago, in the town of Auburn, Illinois, a seventy-five-year-old man who couldn't walk was crossing the railroad tracks on a motorized scooter when the wheels became stuck. He began yelling and a train approaching at eighty-one-miles per hour blew its horn. Ashley Aldridge, a nineteen-year-old young mother making lunch for her two toddlers, looked out the kitchen window and, although she'd never seen this person before in her life, raced out of her home to try and help. Ashley attempted to lift the heavy scooter, but that didn't work. Despite her small size, she pulled the two-hundred-pound man to safety just as the train struck his scooter, which was completely destroyed. The rescued man, Earl Moorman, called the teenager his guardian angel. Ashley Aldridge said, "I would want someone to do that if my grandpa was stuck, so I just had to." The local martial arts school awarded Ashley an honorary black belt.

The bottom line, for now anyway, is that it's probably pointless trying to change one another's beliefs about God. Our time is better spent finding ways to communicate and cooperate with each other locally, nationally, and globally, or else . . . We can care for the least among us, as it says to do in the Bible, to please God or because it's the right thing to do. Just so long as we do it. Because bending toward a common purpose is more important than arising from a common place.

Life is just one damned thing after another.
—Elbert Hubbard

Chapter 39

We Will All Go Together

Isn't Google amazing? Does anyone else remember going around for weeks trying to think of the name of a song, humming a couple bars to whomever would listen and asking, "What is that?" Now you just punch in a few words and up pops the title, lyrics, different versions, and a way to hear the whole thing right there. Not only that, you can learn that the refrain doesn't actually say, "Sweet dreams are made of cheese" or "I can see clearly now Lorraine is gone."

The most popular Google search for "What is. . . ." is "What is love?" Awww. The most popular search for "Who is. . . ." is "Who is the Black Hood?" I had to Google that. You can also Google all kinds of diets. If you're like me, you can Google how old all the famous fitness cheerleaders were when they died. The results aren't encouraging. Clive McCay of the low-calorie diet died at age sixty-nine. Jim Fixx, who helped launch the fitness revolution with *The Complete Book of Running,* died at age fifty-two. Wild foods enthusiast Euell Gibbons was sixty-four.

Nathan Pritikin of low-fat diet-fame died at sixty-nine, while Dr. Robert Atkins, who promoted the exact opposite diet, expired at seventy-two.

Even if we do everything "right," we are victims of circumstances over which we have little, if any, control. We're fighting everything from bad genes and accidents, to pollution and pesticides. Did anyone else run or bicycle behind the DDT truck when they were kids, through a thick fog of what was called "the atom bomb of pesticide?" We shrieked and giggled while neighborhood dogs dashed alongside yapping. Did the fact that the guys spraying to kill wore hazmat suits not suggest a dance with death? On the bright side, we didn't get any mosquito bites that day.

So why am I taking the time to cheer you up like this? Because it's the decisions we make as a collective society that matter more than any individual choices we make. And if there's no common good, there can be no society. What is the common good? It includes schools, hospital emergency rooms, libraries, rebuilding war-torn Europe and Japan, guaranteeing the civil rights and voting rights of Americans, vaccinations, our national road system, meat inspectors, and laws that keep corporations from killing us. Pollution is the number one cause of shorter life spans. Pollution of our water, our food, and our air. There are no more Baltimore Orioles in Baltimore. It's the state bird of Maryland . . . that's awkward.

Starting in the 1970s, activists and politicians collaborated to outlaw leaded gasoline worldwide and reduce additional sources of lead exposure in the paint used on houses, furniture, and children's toys. It's one of the best choices we ever made—lead levels in our blood dropped more than 80 percent, thereby cutting down on heart disease, kidney ailments, anemia, brain damage to children, and dementia in adults. Sadly, we haven't taken the same action with regard to diesel engines, coal plants, and polluted water systems.

We ignore scientists' warnings at our own peril. In 1952 a "killer fog" of sulfurous coal smoke and diesel fumes poisoned London's air (as fans of *The Crown* TV series will recall). About four thousand people were killed in less than a week, and another eight thousand died in the months that followed. For years British scientists had been warning of exactly such a disaster, but no preventative measures were taken. It wasn't until four years after this calamity that the Clean Air Act was passed by Parliament.

Presently, we're seeing an increase in hurricanes, earthquakes, volcanoes, tornadoes, droughts, wildfires, mudslides, and floods, with devastating losses to life and property. Rather than enacting laws to lessen the damage, the government is doing the opposite and repealing regulatory measures. Our air and water are becoming more polluted and less safe by the day. Rollback of EPA regulations during the past few years is expected to kill more than 100,000 Americans over the next decade.

There are more pesticides on our fruits and vegetables, not fewer. There will be more outbreaks of infectious disease and widespread food poisoning, and that's a fact. Maybe the necessary incentive here is to inform celebrities that breathing polluted air leads to premature aging.

In the 1980s a crack epidemic resulted in mass incarceration, teenagers in juvenile detention, permanent records, no men to marry, and parentless children. Now we're seeing a repeat of that movie in the form of an opioid epidemic. These are public health crises just like a pandemic or AIDS that require a government response including research, medical help, treatment, support, counseling, and also compassion.

The difference between the crack and opioid epidemics is, of course, that instead of corner dealers, oftentimes minorities, the merchandise comes directly from corporate America, which uses highly-trained professionals in lab coats and carefully coiffed dealers in suits. You'd have to be blind not to see that the crack epidemic annihilated the black community while the opioid epidemic largely impacts whites. When a president suggests executing drug dealers, I don't think he means corporate CEOs and pharmaceutical reps.

If no one in my family is abusing opioids, or crack for that matter, what does the crisis have to do with me? Which brings us to the problem with Charles Darwin. Well, actually people have had many problems with Darwin. For one, he so aptly demonstrated that man wasn't created by God, but descended from apes. This threw a monkey wrench, if you will, into the idea that there's a natural hierarchy in the human race, and made problematic things like slavery, the divine right of kings, and the Hindu caste system.

Darwin proved that all living things are related. Full stop. And the evidence of their relation is in the very forms of their bodies—the wing of the bat is an alternately adapted version of the human hand. Look at a fish fin and then a bird wing and then your arm. Which brings us to the question: Is unforced cooperation possible in a world of egoists, superpowers, businesses, and individuals? It means wanting for others, complete strangers, what you want for yourself, for your own children and grandchildren. Darwinism can suggest a deep selfishness and indifference to the suffering of others; that our energy and resources are best devoted to our own success and then that of our families and friends at the expense of others, especially strangers, a.k.a. the survival of the fittest. In actuality, he demonstrates that whatever approaches create the best results are more likely to be employed in the future.

The disparity that occurs from tending just our own gardens is, in fact, harmful, and leads to social dysfunction. Examples are indentured servitude, sweatshop labor, subjugation of gays, and also women with no political or financial agency. Every time we moved away from inequality—by abolishing slavery, adopting labor laws, allowing same-sex marriage, outlawing discrimination, giving women property rights and the vote—this country became better and more prosperous.

Globally speaking, the countries where women have the fewest rights and opportunities are the poorest and most conflict-ridden— Yemen, Democratic Republic of Congo, and Honduras. Higher gender equality is commensurate with higher overall incomes. How do we define cooperation—by everyone having food and shelter, but just as important is opportunity, health care, education, and a tax system that doesn't benefit the wealthy while punishing everyone else.

In the US, almost 25 percent of the nation's income is drawn by just 1 percent of the population. Seventeen percent of Americans are poor by international standards. The life expectancy of our children born today is shorter than in Australia, Austria, Belgium, Britain, Canada, Chile, Denmark, Finland, France, Germany, Greece, Iceland, Ireland, Israel, Italy, Japan, Luxembourg, the Netherlands, New Zealand, Norway, Portugal, Slovenia, South Korea, Spain, Sweden, Switzerland, plus a few more. So much for American exceptionalism. And that's not a democracy, but an oligarchy or a plutocracy. The rich recently received a tax break. Bankers were just relieved of rules to protect the average consumer. Millions don't have, or else lost, health care. The idea of America being a place that gives everyone a "fair shake" is no more.

Twentieth-century British polymath Alfred North White-head started a movement known as process philosophy based on making our environment more satisfying. He defined God as the summation of human change, focusing on our interdependence. Meaning and value do not exist for the individual alone but only in the context of the universal community. Whitehead said, "No one who achieves success does so without acknowledging the help of others. The wise and confident acknowledge this help with gratitude." Which is similar to what politicians mean when they say you didn't build your business alone—you had help from the roads used, the post office, and the education your workers received growing up. And hopefully the clean air and water they enjoyed while their brains were developing. I automatically swim with my eyes closed because I learned in Lake Erie during the 1970s when all the fish were dead from industrial chemicals, and it was so toxic that rivers flowing into the lake actually caught fire. Who knows, maybe my eyes used to be brown before they turned green.

Alfred North Whitehead also said, "If a dog jumps into your lap, it is because he is fond of you; but if a cat does the same thing, it is because your lap is warmer." We can see he had a broad field of study.

All organic life is intricately interdependent, like the small community of George Eliot's *Middlemarch*, or a country visited by the plague, or my hometown of Buffalo during the Blizzard of '77. Currently, we have city slickers voting mostly Democrat and country cousins voting mostly Republican as our views on society are practically at war with one another, and yet we're completely dependent upon each other for survival. For instance, rural areas produce food, while the metropolis produces Apple stores, the Harry Potter play, and good divorce lawyers.

A Theory of Everything Else

Although change is constant, it is also gradual; even the most violent transformations, including earthquakes and tsunamis, develop from small, incremental origins that are ultimately comprehensible. We can't escape Darwin's continuity, connection, and causality. Through gradual change the past becomes the future. And we need to focus on what those changes will be.

Since 1900 the average lifespan in the US has increased by more than thirty years, and twenty-five of those are credited to advances in *collective public health*. The great leaps forward in well-being and longevity resulted *not* from your choice to avoid a Twinkie or do Pilates, but because of public sanitation, clean water, safety regulations, medical research, and control of infectious diseases. None other than Richard Nixon created the Environmental Protection Agency and passed the Clean Air Act, along with legislation that revived the Great Lakes.

In 2013, Australia tightened their gun laws and instituted a buyback of certain weapons. Since then, homicide rates have plummeted by almost half, and suicide rates by 74%. New Zealand made similar reforms following the Christchurch massacre in March of 2019, just nine days after the shooting.

My dream is to turn prisons into schools. On day one there are assessment tests and then placement, classes, study hall, music, art, homework, and exams. The parole board checks report cards and so can employment agencies. Is that expensive? Not compared to incarceration, recidivism, addiction rehab, and the resultant damage to families. Sound weird? Yes, well a decade ago, so did the idea that half the population would become amateur taxi drivers. The first thing anyone of my generation was taught is never to get in a car with a stranger!

Social reformer Jane Addams explained that her settlement house in a poor section of Chicago was *not* a charity. The purpose

300

of Hull House was to give others an equal opportunity, which was an essential aspect of the common good. In 1931 Addams was the first American woman to be awarded the Nobel Peace Prize.

Rather than pouring billions into a bigger and better system of mass criminalization, let's focus on the formation of safe, caring, thriving communities by investing in quality schools, job creation, housing, public transportation, law enforcement partnerships, drug treatment, and mental health care in the least advantaged communities. Fifty years ago, Rev. Martin Luther King Jr. warned that "when machines and computers, profit motives and property rights are considered more important than people, the giant triplets of racism, extreme materialism, and militarism are incapable of being conquered."

Cooperation leads to collective stability and, therefore, more cooperation. Diamond markets have always been famous for how their members exchange millions of dollars' worth of goods using verbal pledges and handshakes. A key factor is that they'll work with one another again. And again. Success results not from punishment or legal threats, but from the opportunity for mutually rewarding interactions in the future.

Put more simply, you go to dinner with seven others and plan to split the bill eight ways. Someone, no names mentioned, orders by far the most expensive dish and extra cocktails. In social biology this is known as "tragedy of the commons," or what my mom calls "a party spoiler." This is where our evolutionary cooperation genes come into play. First is individual restraint. Then there's holding a grudge. Next comes retribution or learning. The over-indulger is not invited the next time *or* everyone agrees to pay his or her own bill. And thereby we've evolved and honed a strategy for mutual cooperation. It actually helps that we're programmed either biologically or by our elementary school teachers to feel angry when cheated and guilty when we know we are the cheater. This sets the stage for correctives, or what my mom calls "tit for tat."

Most interestingly, friendship need not be involved for cooperation to occur and evolve. We've seen this with communal grazing land, informal truces during brutal trench warfare, and nuclear arms agreements between hostile nations. If reciprocity exists, there can be something just as good as friendship, which is durability. Once we expect others to reciprocate our transgressions just as quickly as our cooperation, it becomes wise not to start trouble, operate outside the norms, or cheat. Reciprocity becomes self-reinforcing and progressively more durable, which is why we haven't invaded Canada since 1812, except to buy Tylenol with codeine, Molson beer, and Hudson Bay blankets.

However, cooperation means exactly that. Did you hear about the two businesspeople bidding the price up wildly on the last crate of coconuts? It turned out that one needed the milk while the other needed the shells. Had they talked to each other, they would have found that out.

A current lack of cooperation between various branches of government and within political parties themselves is stressing the system and racking up millions in fees to taxpayers. Voters and parties are often in long-term relationships, and this gives parties incentives to select candidates who will not lose the trust of constituents. It also motivates voters to collectively punish a party for the behavior of its leaders, as happened to the Republicans in the wake of Watergate.

We need to fight for each other's health and well-being, not because we're friends, but because your decisions affect when I die and vice-versa. It's plain common sense. Unfortunately, as crossing guards everywhere know well, common sense is not so common. Consequently, it may be time for some new features to our diet and exercise regimens—calling our congresspeople, voting in every election, and supporting environmental justice. Because staying alive isn't a competitive sport we play against each other—we're all on the same team, and while Nature doesn't need us, we need Nature.

Whether you hail from Outer Mongolia or Lower Slaughter, from deep red Utah or bright blue Hawaii, our genetic makeup is strikingly similar; humans are 99.9 percent identical. It's safe to say that 99.9 percent of us, above all else, want a good life for ourselves, our children and grandchildren. Actions harmful to even 1 percent of the population hurt the greater good. Growing up, I regularly heard "God helps those who help themselves." I don't have any math on that. But it's been scientifically proven that when we help one other, we really do help ourselves. And nice guys, or rather nice people, finish first, not last, except maybe in dodgeball.

On January 27, 1838, a young country lawyer named Abraham Lincoln said, "America will never be destroyed from the outside. If we falter and lose our freedoms, it will be because we destroyed ourselves." The Civil War started twenty-three years later. Have we now entered a period of America changing from neighbors helping neighbors to some neighbors helping certain neighbors?

The Doomsday Clock, a symbol that represents the likelihood of a manmade global catastrophe, is currently at one hundred seconds before midnight, the direst setting since it was created in 1947. The United Nations announced we have only twelve years to rein in climate change if our species is to survive. Carbon is more dangerous than cancer. Suicide is ending more lives than war. Obesity is killing more people than starvation. Yes, sugar is now more dangerous than gunpowder. Is there hope?

When Airbnb tried to raise start-up funds, people laughed and derided the notion. Who would trust strangers to live in your home, either with you and your family and beloved pets, or while you're away, and leave all your possessions in their care? It's insane! After starting a decade ago by renting out three mattresses on a floor to conference goers, Airbnb has served over 300 million travelers, operates in 191 countries, and is valued in the tens of billions of dollars. In fact, when comparisons are made about people from Russia, Japan, France, Nigeria, Brazil, and the US, there is no national outlier with regard to trust and respect and honesty. Canadians are of course nicer. CEO Brian Chesky says, "Airbnb, without fundamental human goodness, would not work."

My father was a folk singer and attempted to stop the war in Vietnam by leading protest songs in a round. Dad especially enjoyed the Tom Lehrer song "We Will All Go Together When We Go." There was some patter leading into it which told of a philosopher friend who liked to advise people, "Life is like a sewer: what you get out of it depends on what you put into it," and that this song was in the tradition of the great old revival hymns, but it was a "survival hymn."

The final chorus went:

And we will all go together when we go.
Ev'ry Hottentot and ev'ry Eskimo.
When the air becomes uranious,
Oh we will all go simultaneous.
Yes we all will go together when we go.

Tom Lehrer, now ninety-two, taught political science and mathematics for forty years, and it just so happens his last class was on the subject of infinity. I think he'd agree that the key to succeeding in almost all aspects of life, from foreign relations to building a neighborhood playground, is not to dominate or overcome others but to elicit cooperation. If we understand that while selfishness might work or appear to work in the short run, mutually rewarding strategies succeed in the long run, and the faster we proceed down this path the faster we speed up the evolution of cooperation. Because we can't have civilization without civility.

On the bright side, there is indeed life after death. Just not ours.

About the Author

photo credit: Denise Winters

Laura Pedersen is a former *New York Times* columnist, the author of 4 plays and 16 books, including the award-winning *Life in New York: How I Learned to Love Squeegee Men, Token Suckers, Trash Twisters, and Subway Sharks*. She has appeared on national shows such as *Oprah, Good Morning America, CBS This Morning, Today, Primetime*, David Letterman and many others. Laura has performed standup at the Improv and writes for several well-known comedians. More information is available at www.LauraPedersenBooks.com and Facebook/Laura Pedersen Writer.

SELECTED TITLES FROM SHE WRITES PRESS

She Writes Press is an independent publishing company founded to serve women writers everywhere. Visit us at www.shewritespress.com.

Not a Perfect Fit: Stories from Jane's World by Jane A. Schmidt. $16.95, 978-1631522062. Jane Schmidt documents her challenges living off grid, moving from the city to the country, living with a variety of animals as her only companions, dating, family trips, outdoor adventures, and midlife in essays full of honesty and humor.

This is Mexico: Tales of Culture and Other Complications by Carol M. Merchasin. $16.95, 978-1-63152-962-7. Merchasin chronicles her attempts to understand Mexico, her adopted country, through improbable situations and small moments that keep the reader moving between laughter and tears.

Flip-Flops After Fifty: And Other Thoughts on Aging I Remembered to Write Down by Cindy Eastman. $16.95, 978-1-938314-68-1. A collection of frank and funny essays about turning fifty—and all the emotional ups and downs that come with it.

Notes from the Bottom of the World by Suzanne Adam. $16.95, 978-1-63152-415-8. In this heartfelt collection of sixty-three personal essays, Adam considers how her American past and move to Chile have shaped her life and enriched her worldview, and explores with insight questions on aging, women's roles, spiritual life, friendship, love, and writers who inspire.

Love Her, Love Her Not: The Hillary Paradox edited by Joanne Bamberger. $16.95, 978-1-63152-806-4. A collection of personal essays by noted women essayists and emerging women writers that explores the question of why Americans have a love/hate "relationship" with Hillary Clinton.

Her Name Is Kaur: Sikh American Women Write About Love, Courage, and Faith edited by Meeta Kaur. $17.95, 978-1-938314-70-4. An eye-opening, multifaceted collection of essays by Sikh American women exploring the concept of love in the context of the modern landscape and influences that shape their lives.